What Li'l Depressed Boy Means to Me
Or,
How I Spent My Summer Vacation

By: Amber Benson
(Grade 9)

I was sick with strep throat when I read the last four issues of LDB. I was supposed to be on my summer vacation in Seattle, but instead I was sick at home, lying in bed, my throat so sore it felt like I'd swallowed a hair shirt.

So here's the picture:

I am miserable and groggy (and in a foul mood from having to gargle children's Benadryl to numb the pain: both emotional and physical) when I pick up Issue #9 and start to read. I know what to expect from LDB. I know it will entertain me, make me forget about my sore throat for awhile, possibly make me laugh out loud a little bit.

What I don't expect is to be crying when I put down Issue #12.

Dang it, I'm sick and miserable already. Why you guys gotta make my heart hurt, too?

I guess the answer is: Because they can.

LDB is going through a lot of heavy stuff; real life stuff that any human being can relate to.

We've all been in love. We've all had everything crash and burn. We all know what it's like to meet someone new and hope the world is gonna open up again like a lotus flower, or some other over-romanticized, B.S. cliché.

Does it mend the broken heart?

No, but it makes it hurt a little less.

Get yourself a job. Take your mind off the sucky feelings swirling around your head like fetid molasses. Get yourself a crush. Take your mind off the hipster vixen that opened the door to a whole new world then left you hanging.

And so it goes.

Of course, it helps if said crush resembles a super-sexy, redheaded version of Tina Fey who is totally approachable and seems like she might be kind of crushing on you, too.

I can't pinpoint what it is, exactly, that makes me love LDB so much, but I can make an educated guess: He's the mopey guy inside all of us who just can't seem to get started without a little outside help. He chokes when he should fly, stays quiet when he should be screaming from the rooftops—and when he finally starts to get some self-confidence, the world cracks in two and he falls into the abyss again.

Would I want to spend another summer vacation at home in bed, feeling like crap? Yeah. Yeah, I would. If it meant I got to spend it with LDB.

-Amber Benson

"The girl with the most cake" and author of Among the Ghosts and Death's Daughter. Oh, she played a sexy, lesbian witch on Buffy the Vampire Slayer, too.

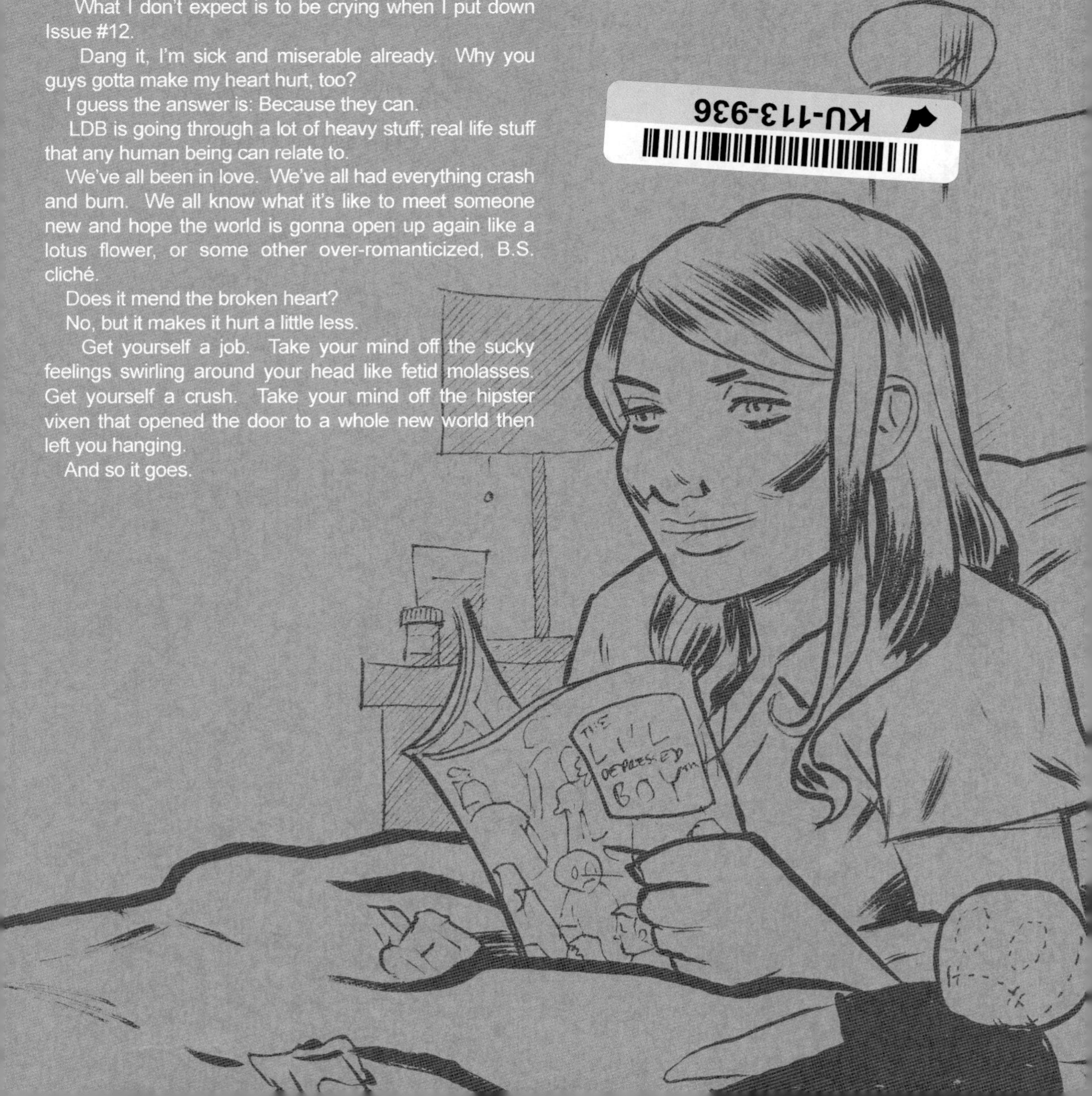
THE LI'L DEPRESSED BOY

To T.J. Lloyd, Raul Rodarte and Josh Frye -

Thanks for helping turn a moment of fiction into reality.

- SSS

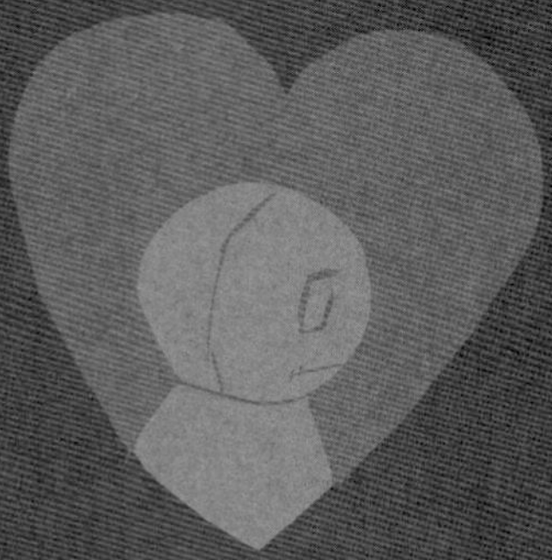

To Isabel Reyes and Daniel Freedman -

You dudes know how to set that crown on the ground.

- SG

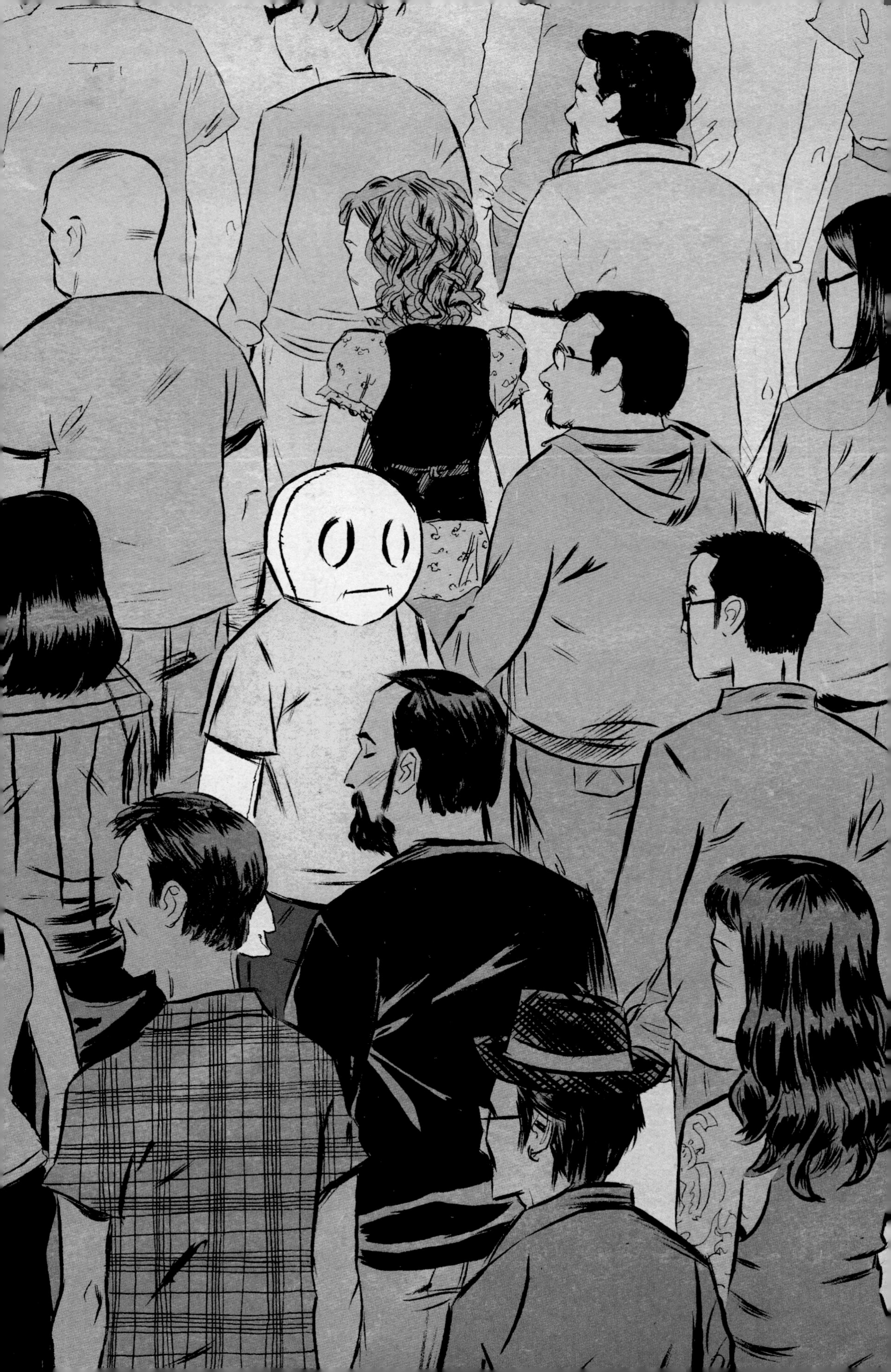

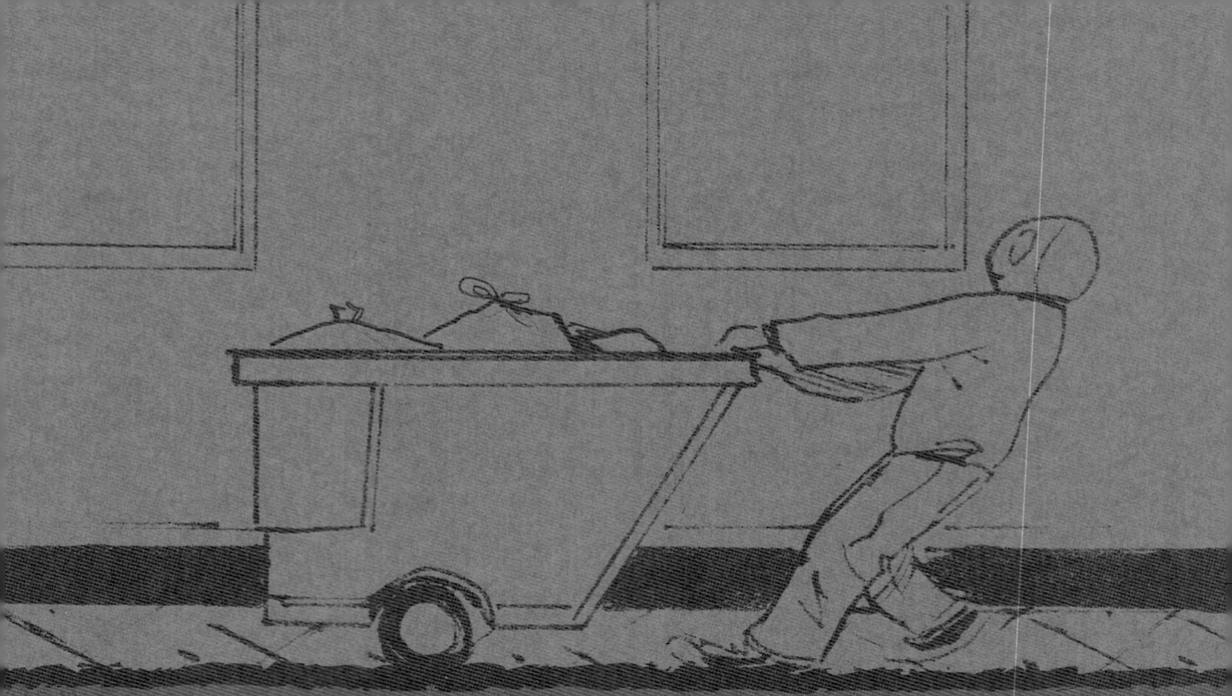

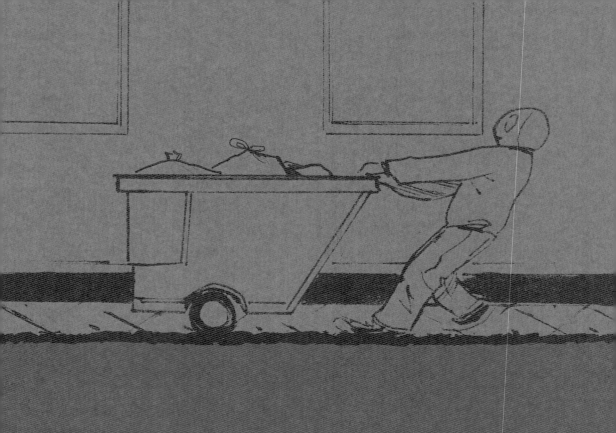

CHAPTER ONE:

"WELCOME TO THE WORKING WEEK"

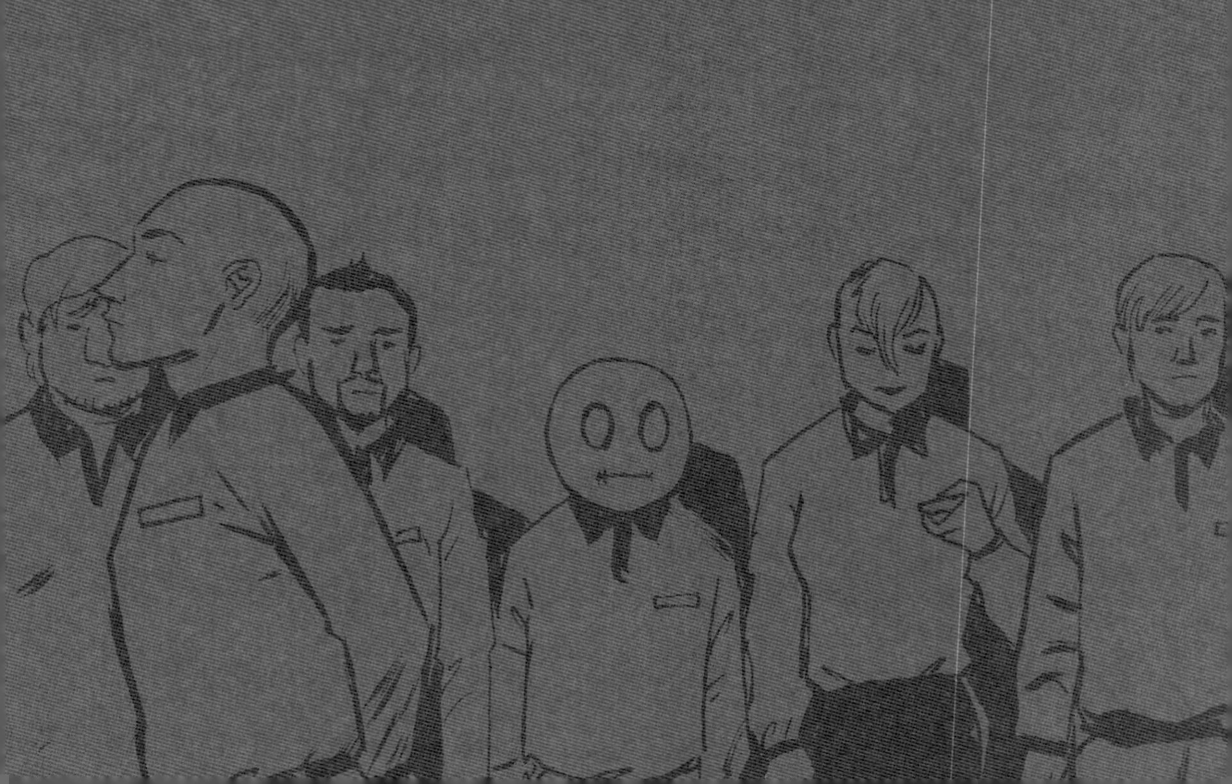

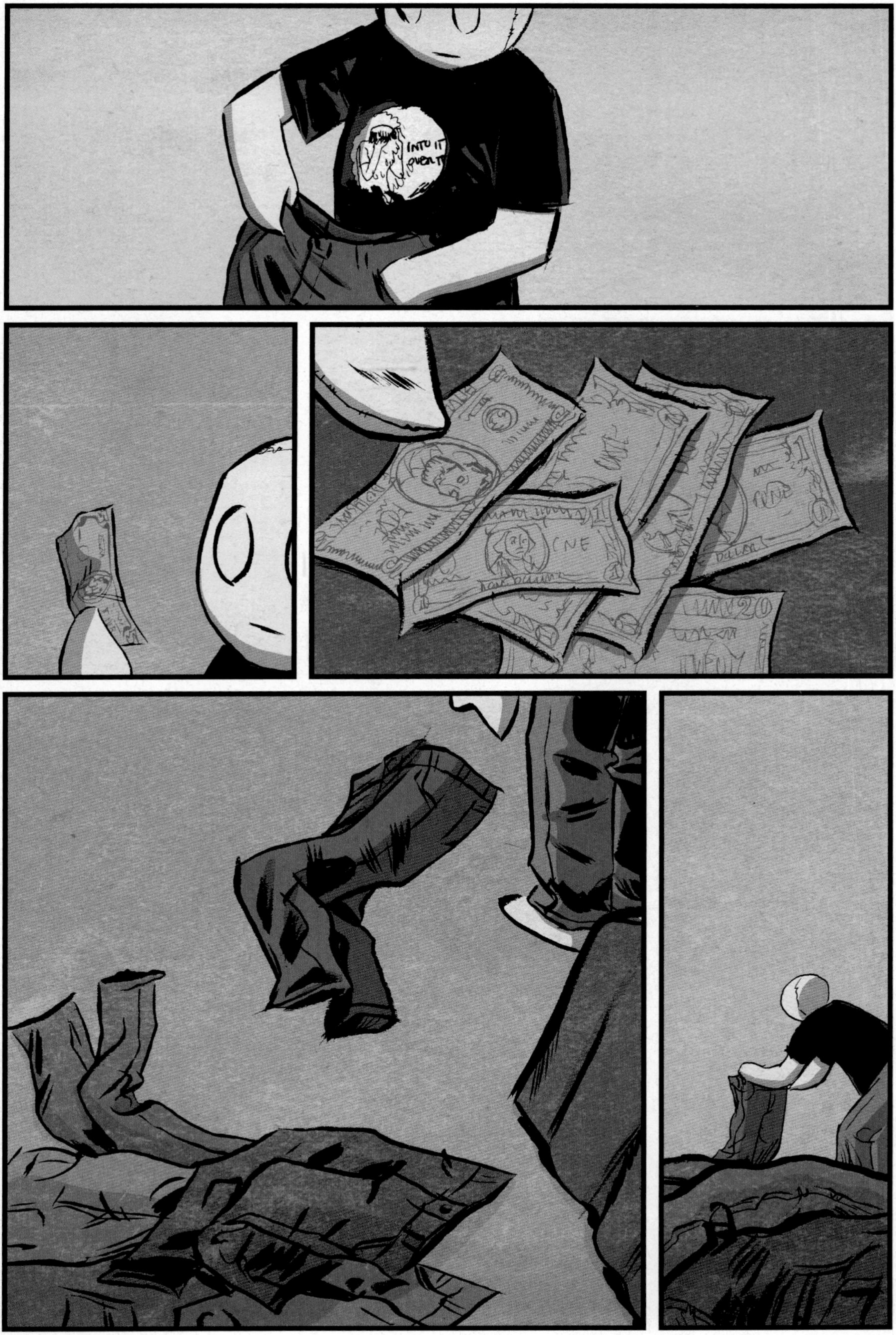

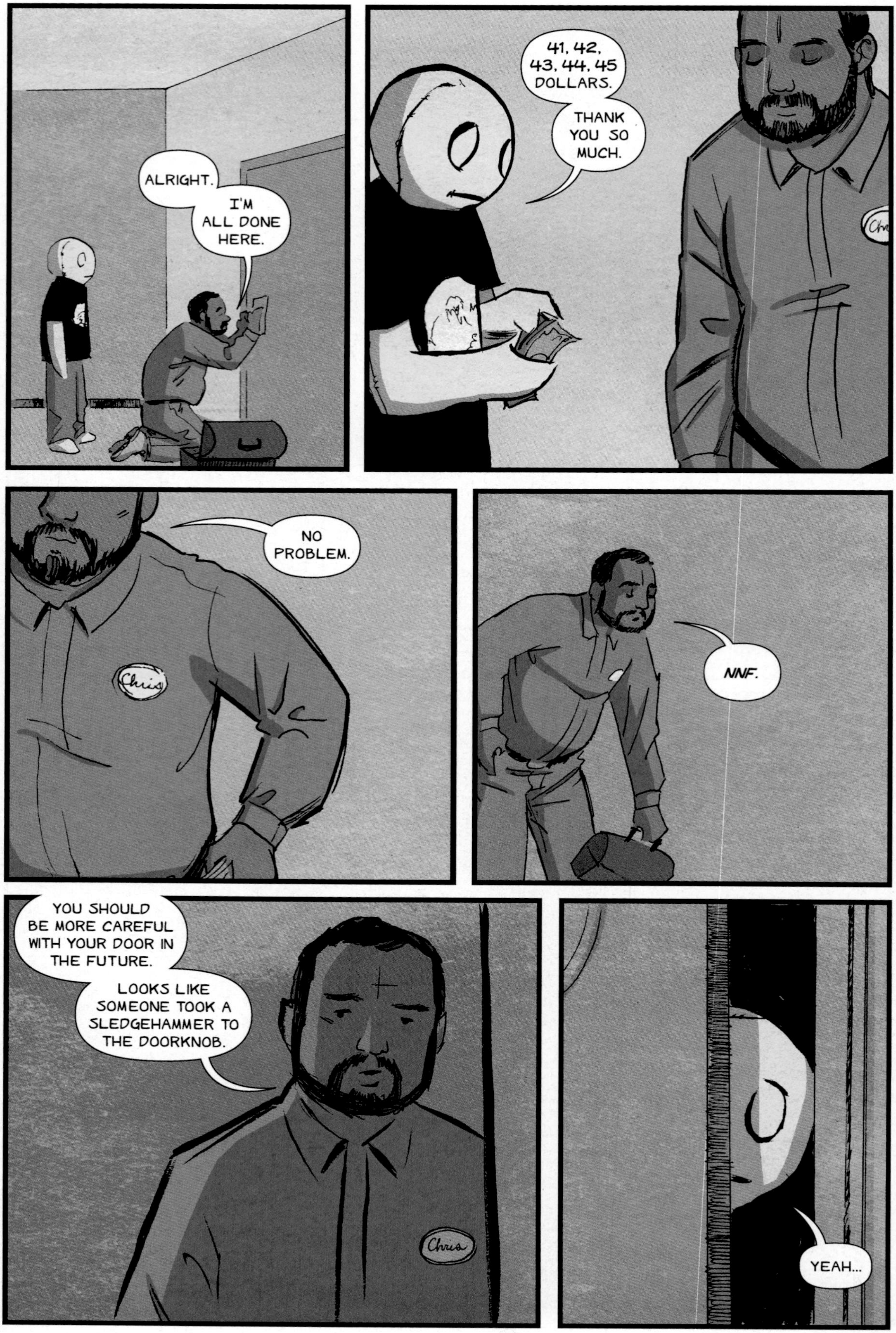
ALRIGHT.
I'M ALL DONE HERE.
41, 42, 43, 44, 45 DOLLARS.
THANK YOU SO MUCH.
NO PROBLEM.
Chris
NNF.
YOU SHOULD BE MORE CAREFUL WITH YOUR DOOR IN THE FUTURE.
LOOKS LIKE SOMEONE TOOK A SLEDGEHAMMER TO THE DOORKNOB.
Chris
YEAH...

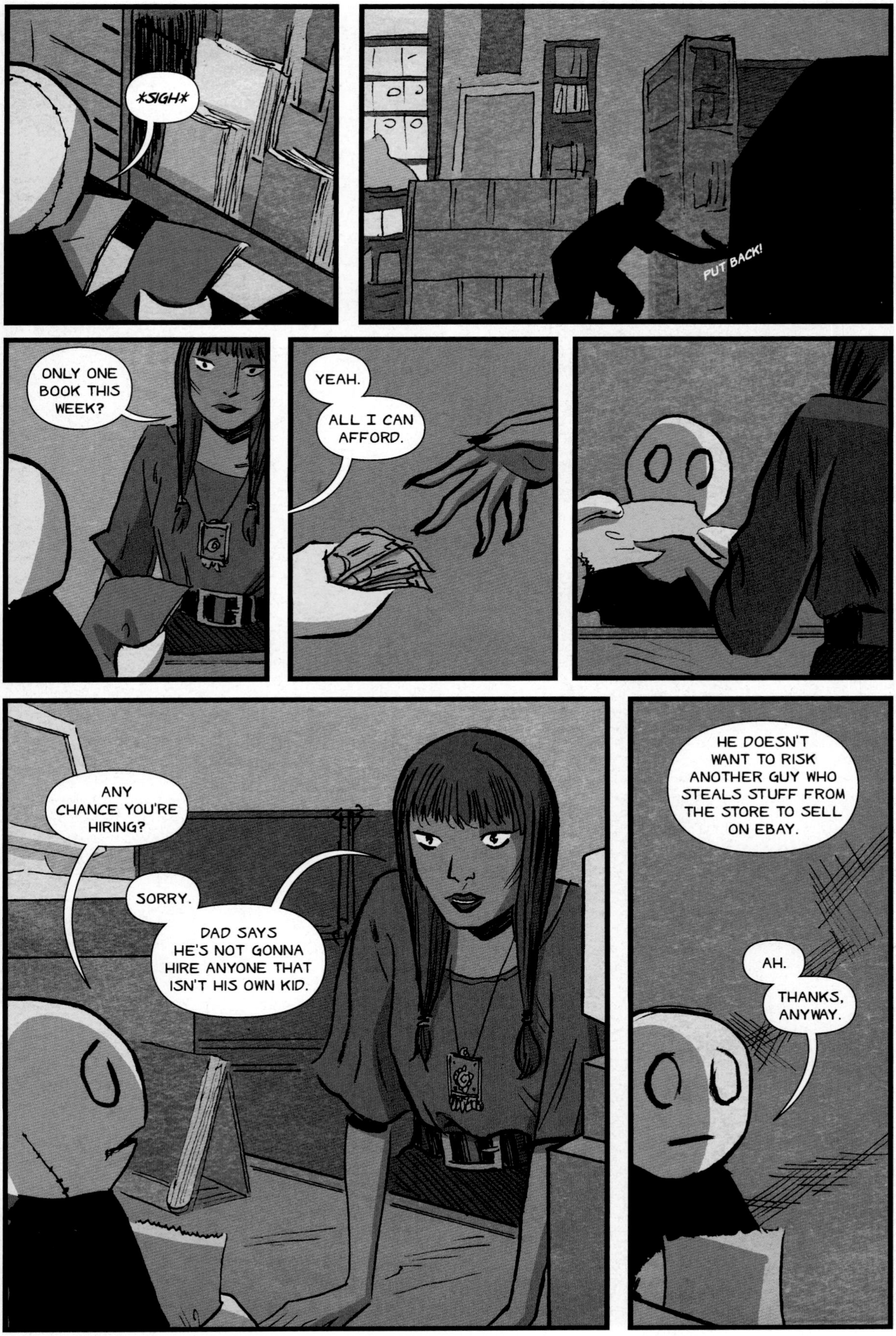
SIGH
PUT BACK!
ONLY ONE BOOK THIS WEEK?
YEAH.
ALL I CAN AFFORD.
ANY CHANCE YOU'RE HIRING?
SORRY.
DAD SAYS HE'S NOT GONNA HIRE ANYONE THAT ISN'T HIS OWN KID.
HE DOESN'T WANT TO RISK ANOTHER GUY WHO STEALS STUFF FROM THE STORE TO SELL ON EBAY.
AH.
THANKS, ANYWAY.

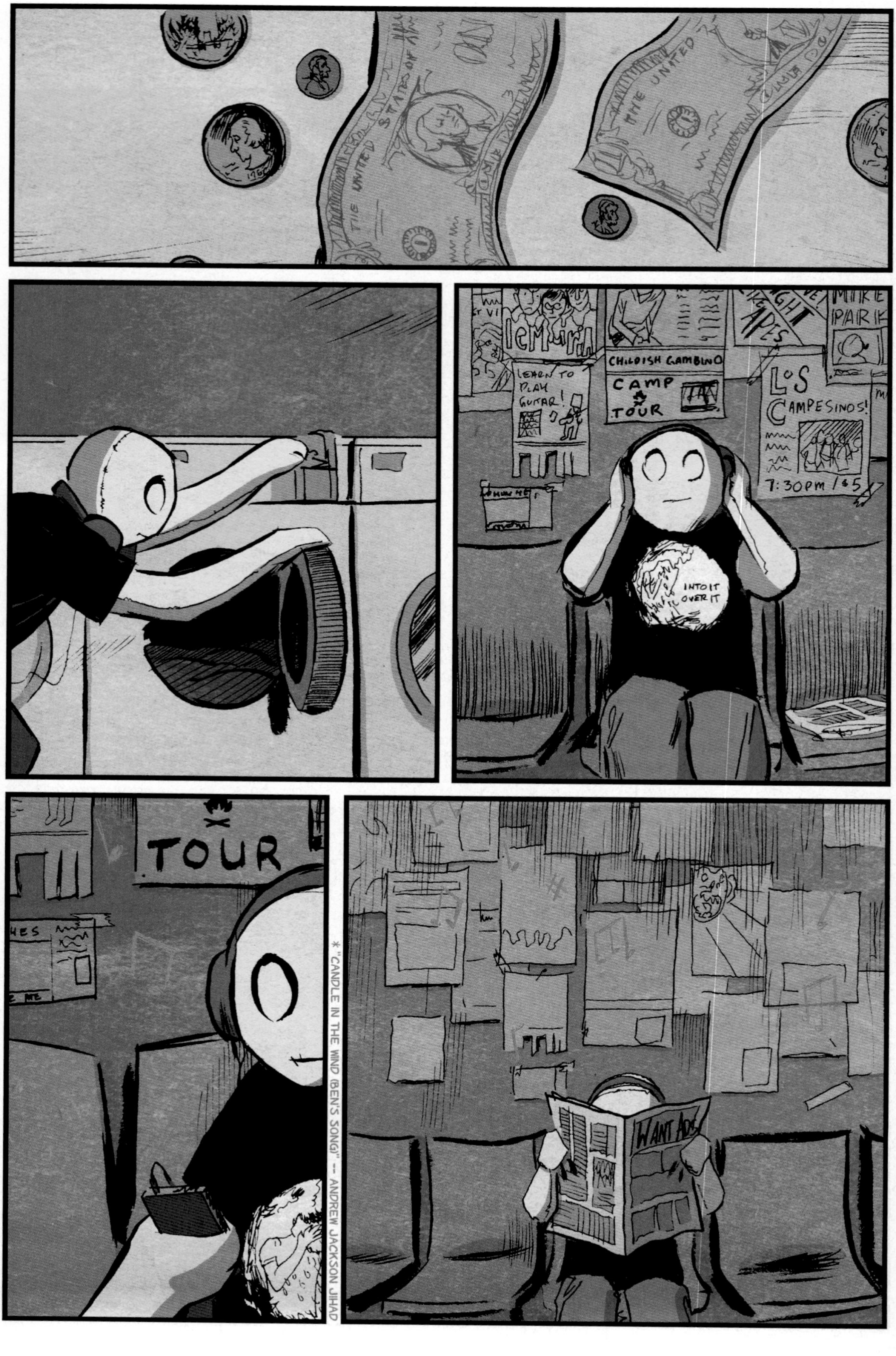
THE UNITED STATES OF
THE UNITED
LEARN TO PLAY GUITAR!
CHILDISH GAMBINO
CAMP TOUR
MIKE PARK
LOS CAMPESINOS!
7:30PM / $5
INTO IT OVER IT
TOUR
WANT ADS

* "CANDLE IN THE WIND (BEN'S SONG)" -- ANDREW JACKSON JIHAD

PART-TIME CLERK AT RECORD STORE
R.W.'s RECORDS
OPEN
RECORD STORE DAY IS APRIL 21st
ANYTHING I CAN HELP YOU WITH?
UH...
INTO IT OVER IT
NO.
JUST LOOKING.
LPs
BAGIN

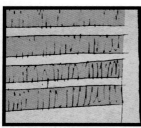

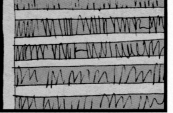

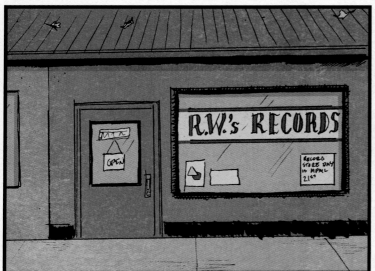

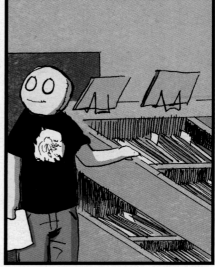

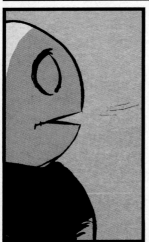

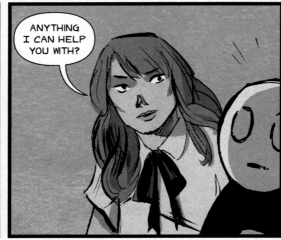

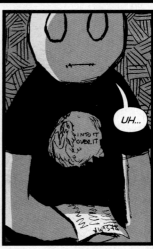

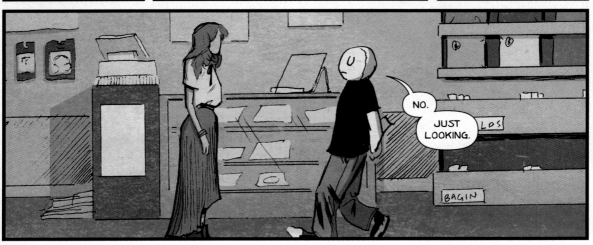

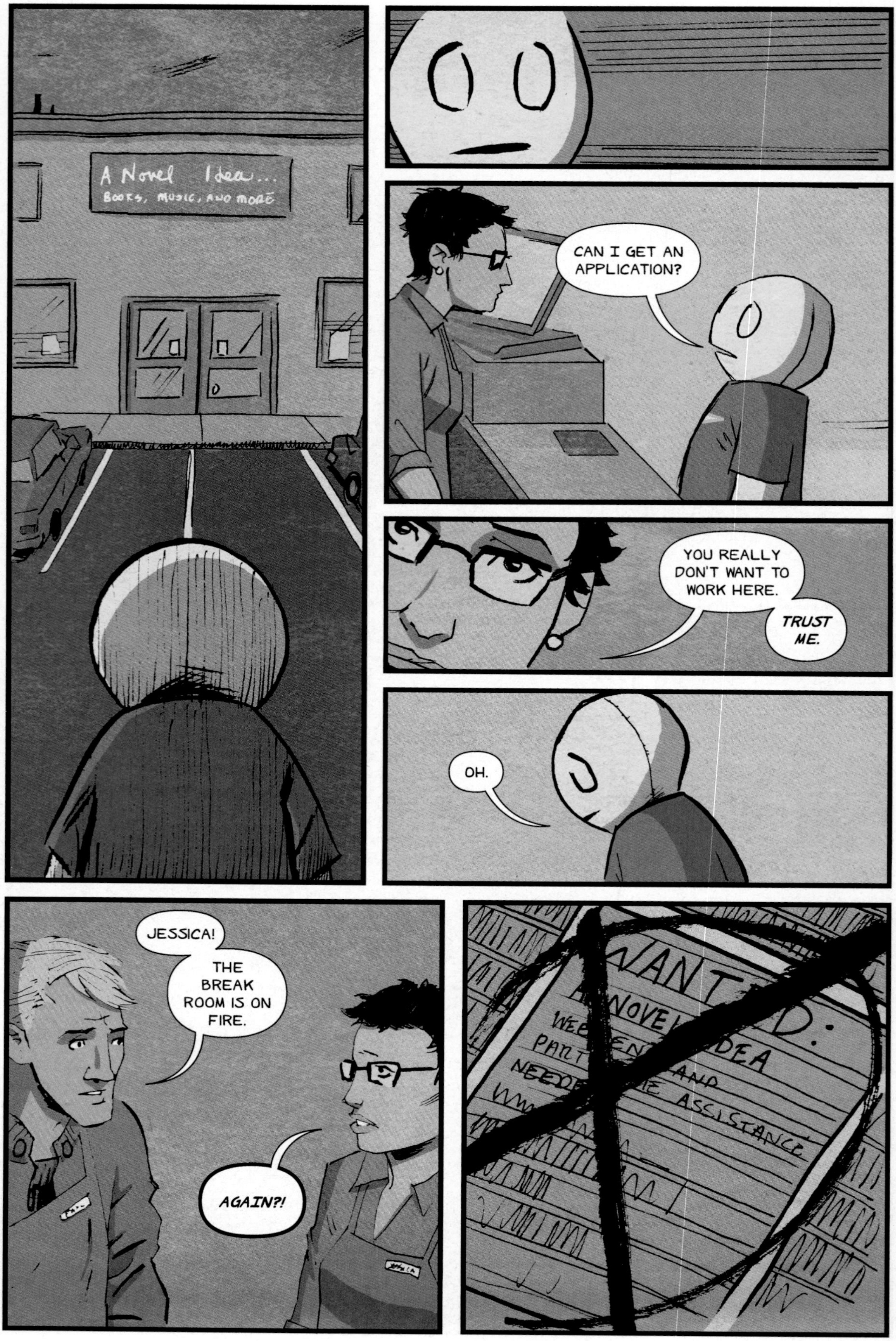
A Novel Idea...
BOOKS, MUSIC, AND MORE
CAN I GET AN APPLICATION?
YOU REALLY DON'T WANT TO WORK HERE.
TRUST ME.
OH.
JESSICA!
THE BREAK ROOM IS ON FIRE.
AGAIN?!

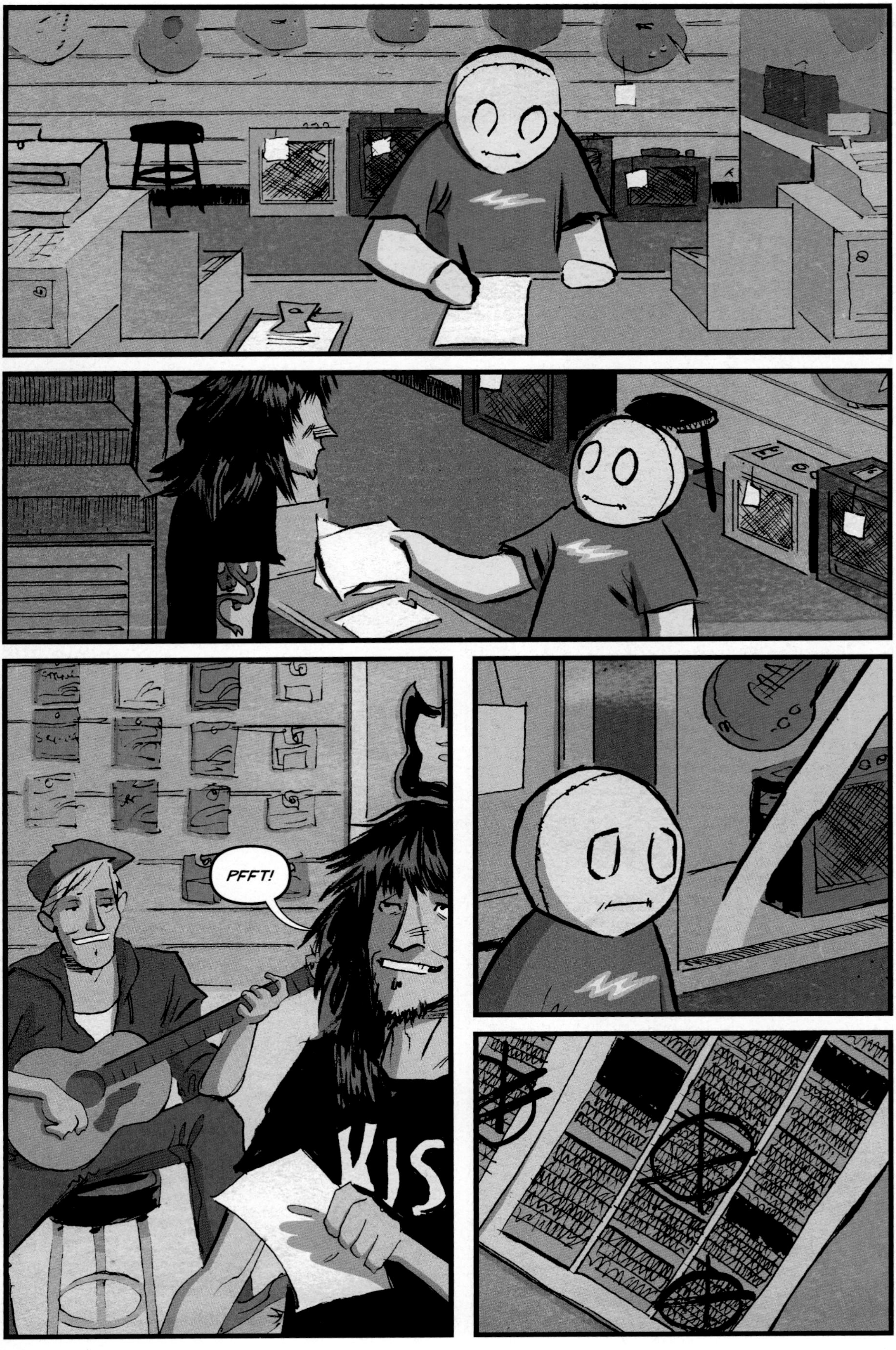

PFFT!

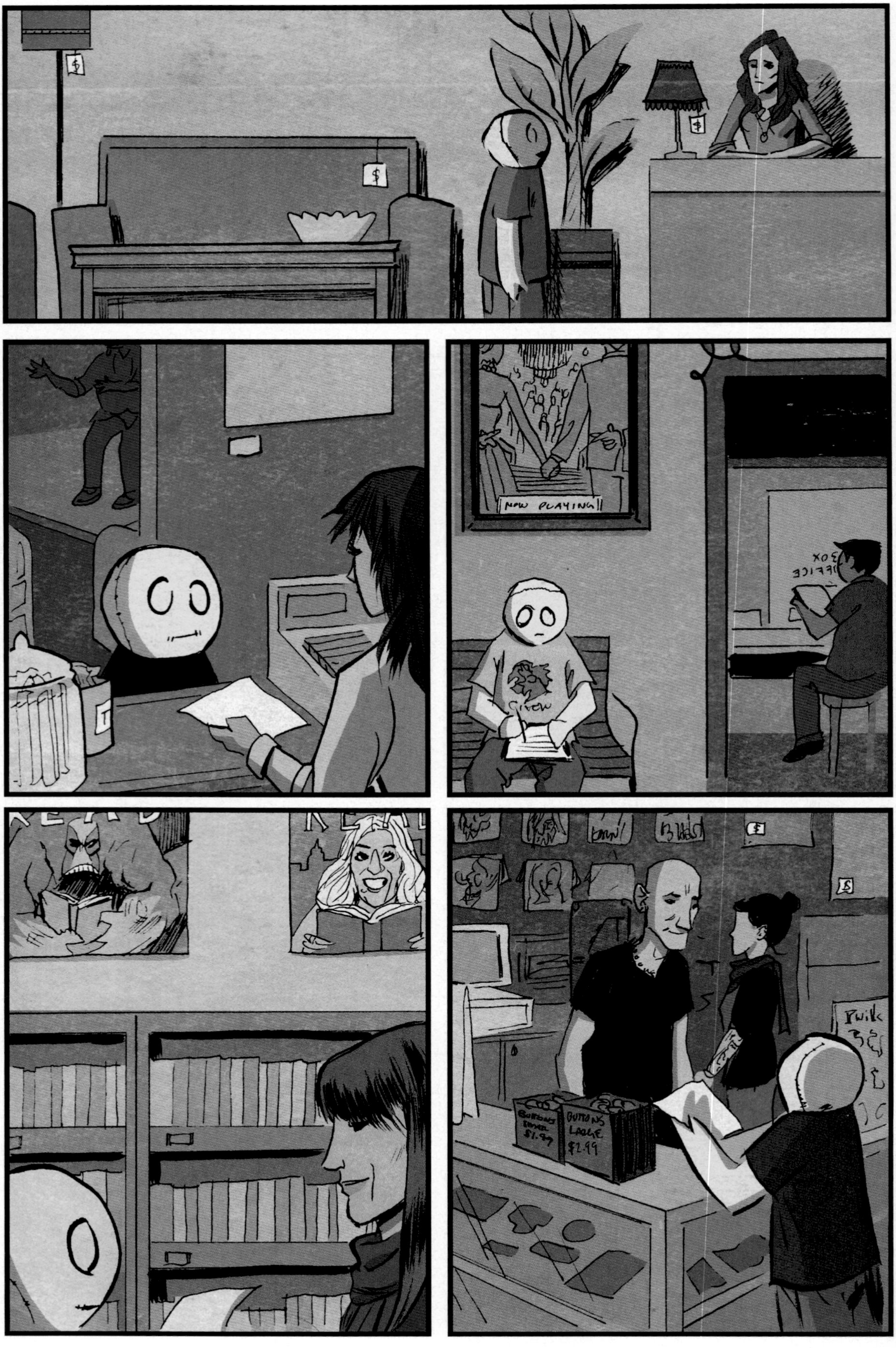
NOW PLAYING
BUTTONS SMALL $1.99
BUTTONS LARGE $2.99

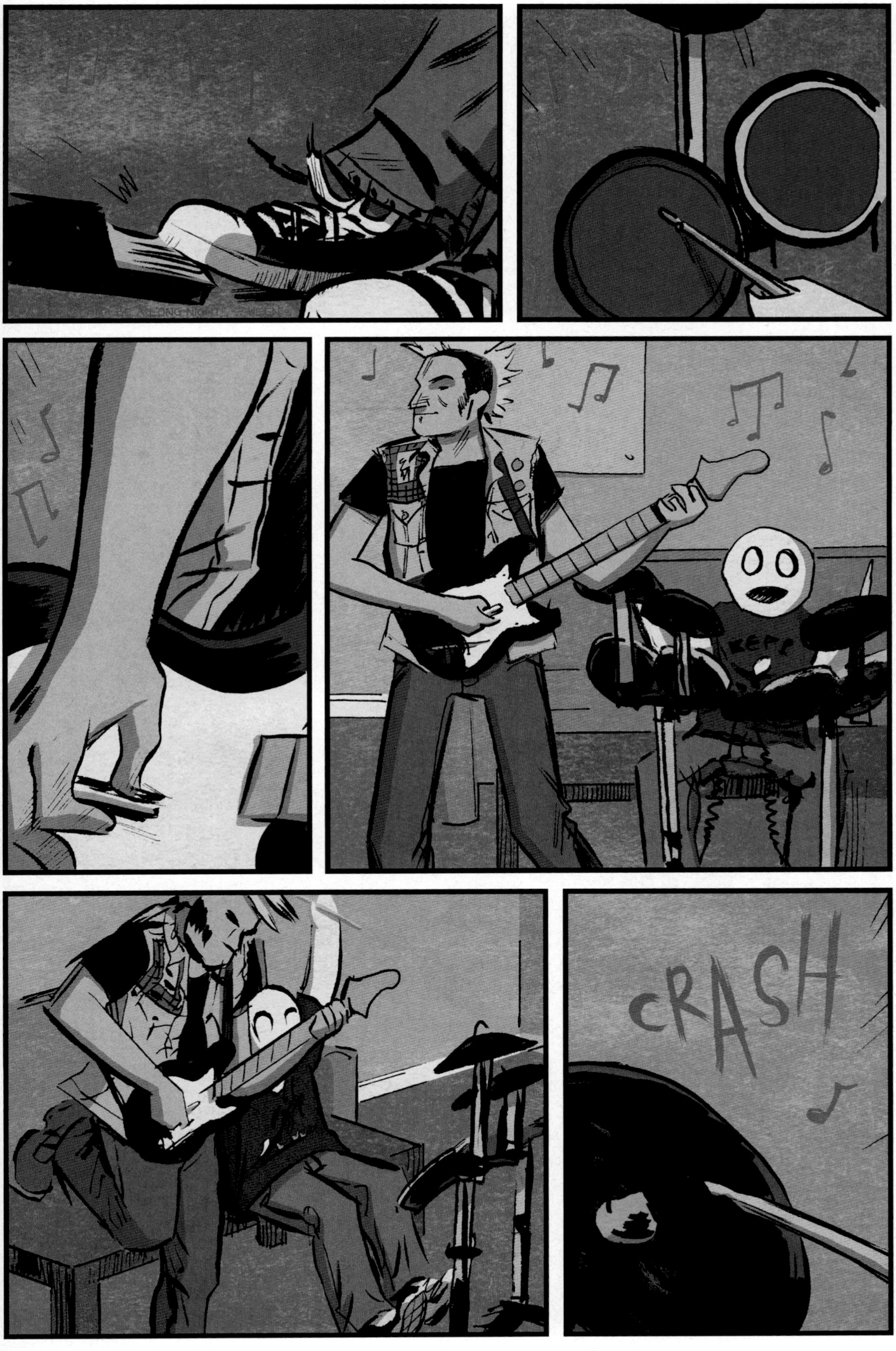
CRASH

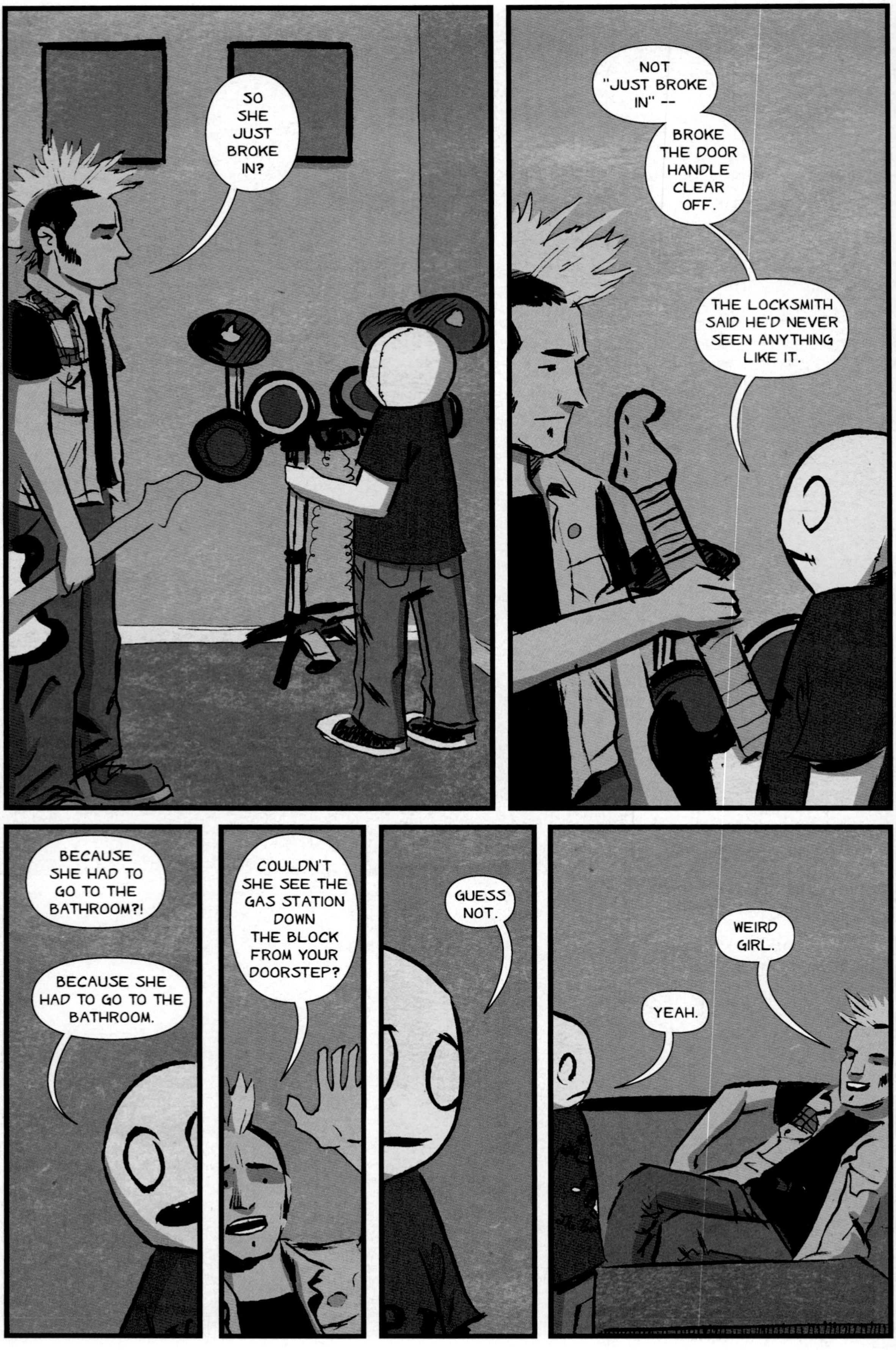
SO SHE JUST BROKE IN?
NOT "JUST BROKE IN" --
BROKE THE DOOR HANDLE CLEAR OFF.
THE LOCKSMITH SAID HE'D NEVER SEEN ANYTHING LIKE IT.
BECAUSE SHE HAD TO GO TO THE BATHROOM?!
BECAUSE SHE HAD TO GO TO THE BATHROOM.
COULDN'T SHE SEE THE GAS STATION DOWN THE BLOCK FROM YOUR DOORSTEP?
GUESS NOT.
WEIRD GIRL.
YEAH.

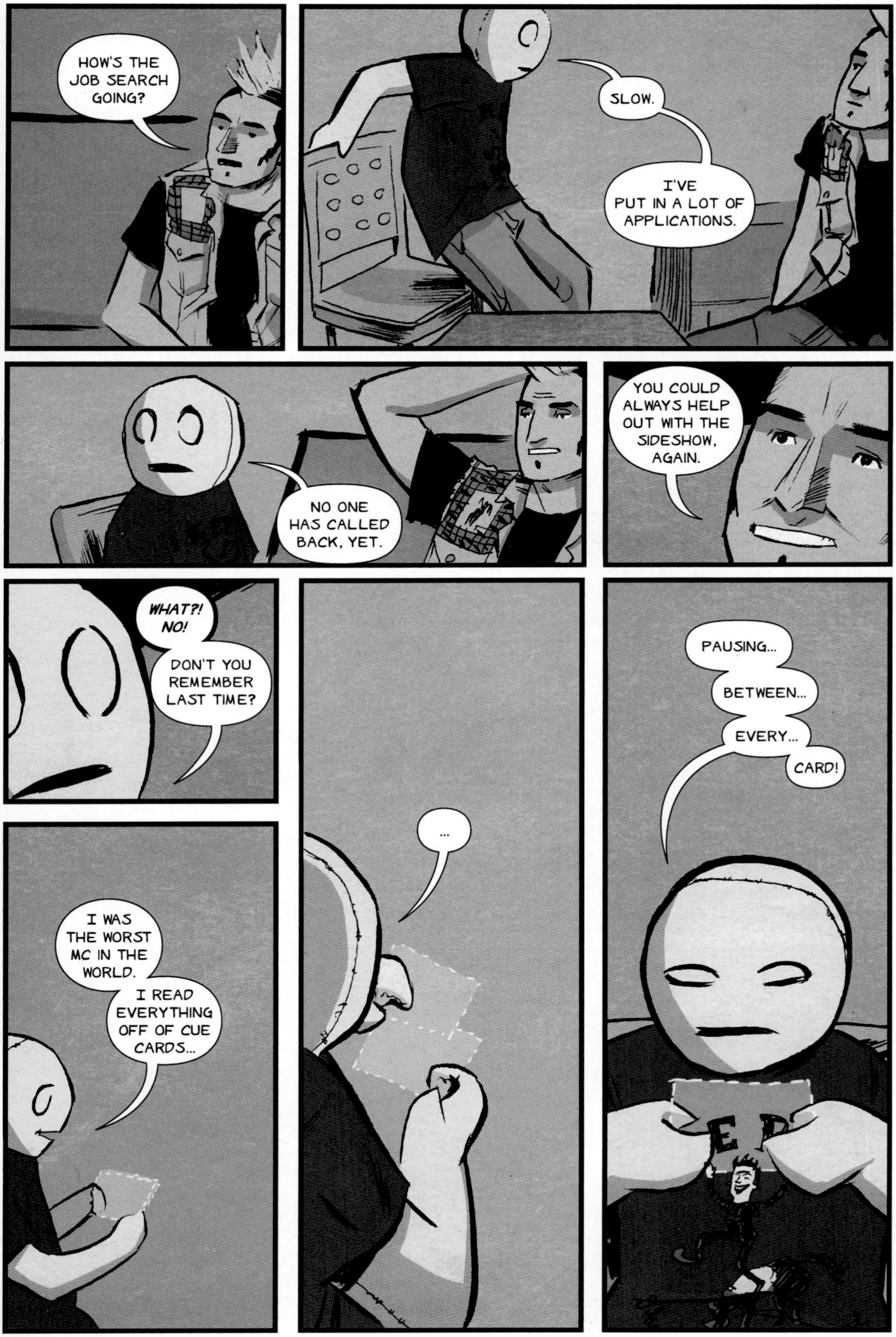
HOW'S THE JOB SEARCH GOING?
SLOW.
I'VE PUT IN A LOT OF APPLICATIONS.
NO ONE HAS CALLED BACK, YET.
YOU COULD ALWAYS HELP OUT WITH THE SIDESHOW, AGAIN.
WHAT?! NO!
DON'T YOU REMEMBER LAST TIME?
I WAS THE WORST MC IN THE WORLD.
I READ EVERYTHING OFF OF CUE CARDS...
...
PAUSING...
BETWEEN...
EVERY...
CARD!

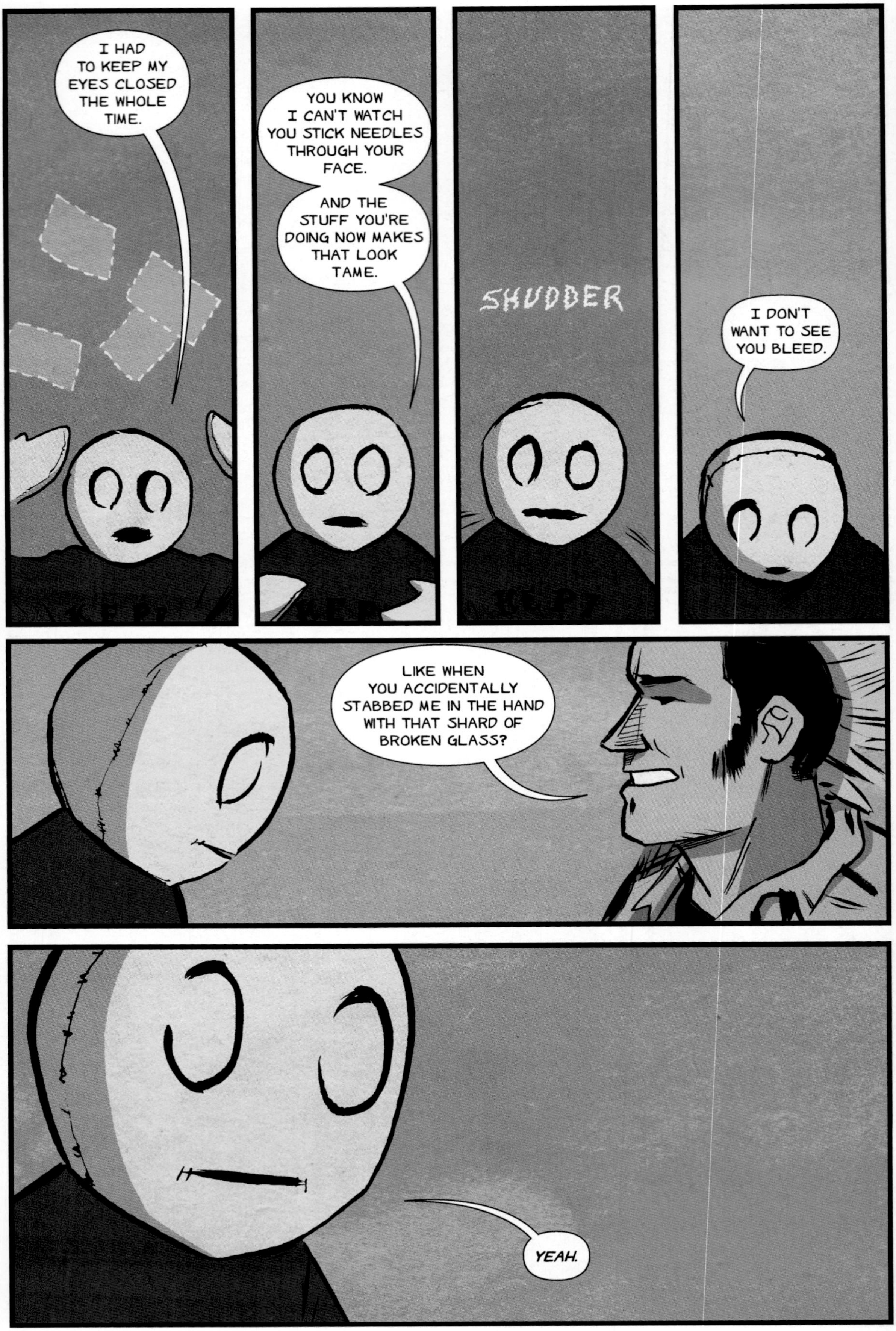
I HAD TO KEEP MY EYES CLOSED THE WHOLE TIME.
YOU KNOW I CAN'T WATCH YOU STICK NEEDLES THROUGH YOUR FACE.
AND THE STUFF YOU'RE DOING NOW MAKES THAT LOOK TAME.
SHUDDER
I DON'T WANT TO SEE YOU BLEED.
LIKE WHEN YOU ACCIDENTALLY STABBED ME IN THE HAND WITH THAT SHARD OF BROKEN GLASS?
YEAH.

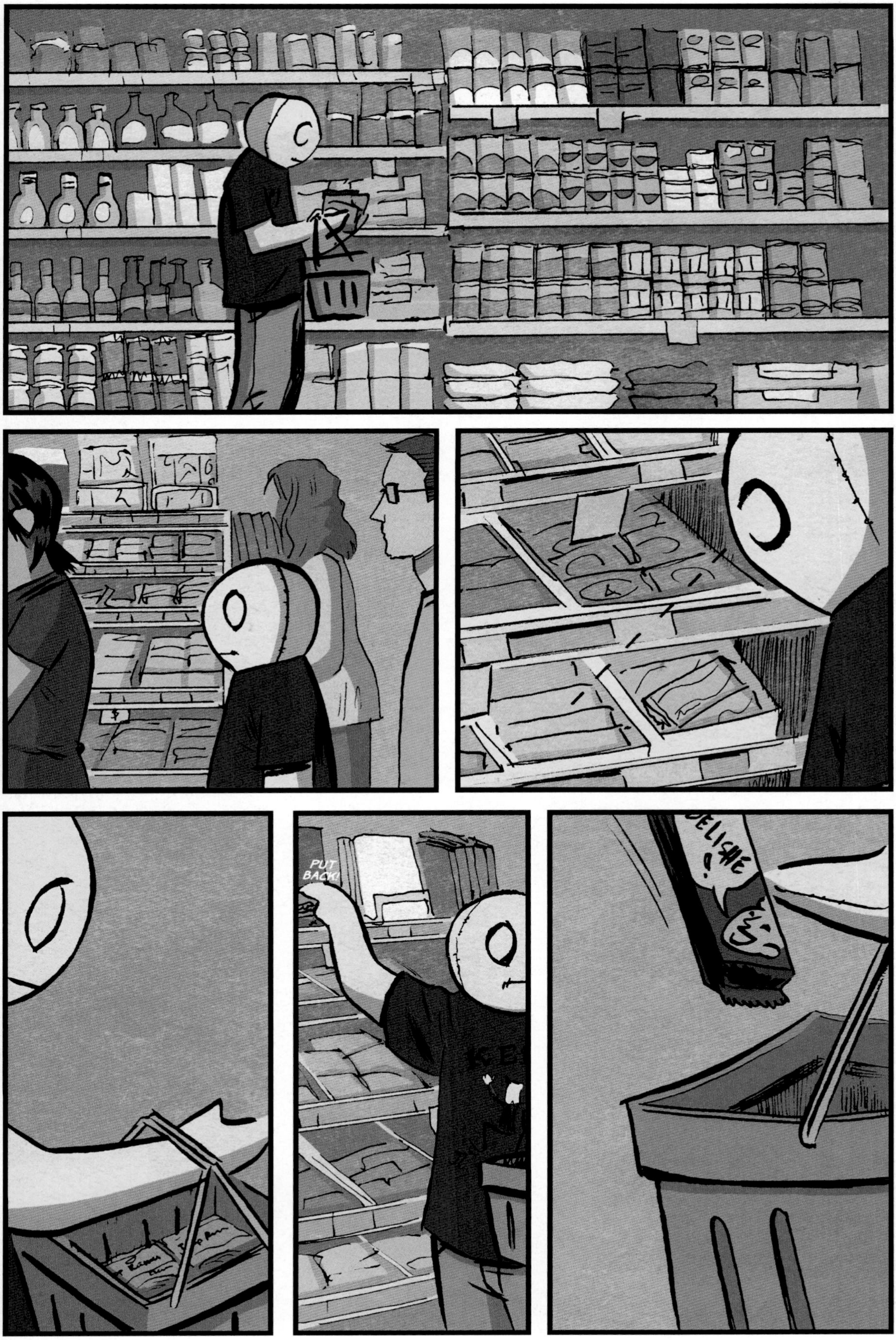
PUT BACK!

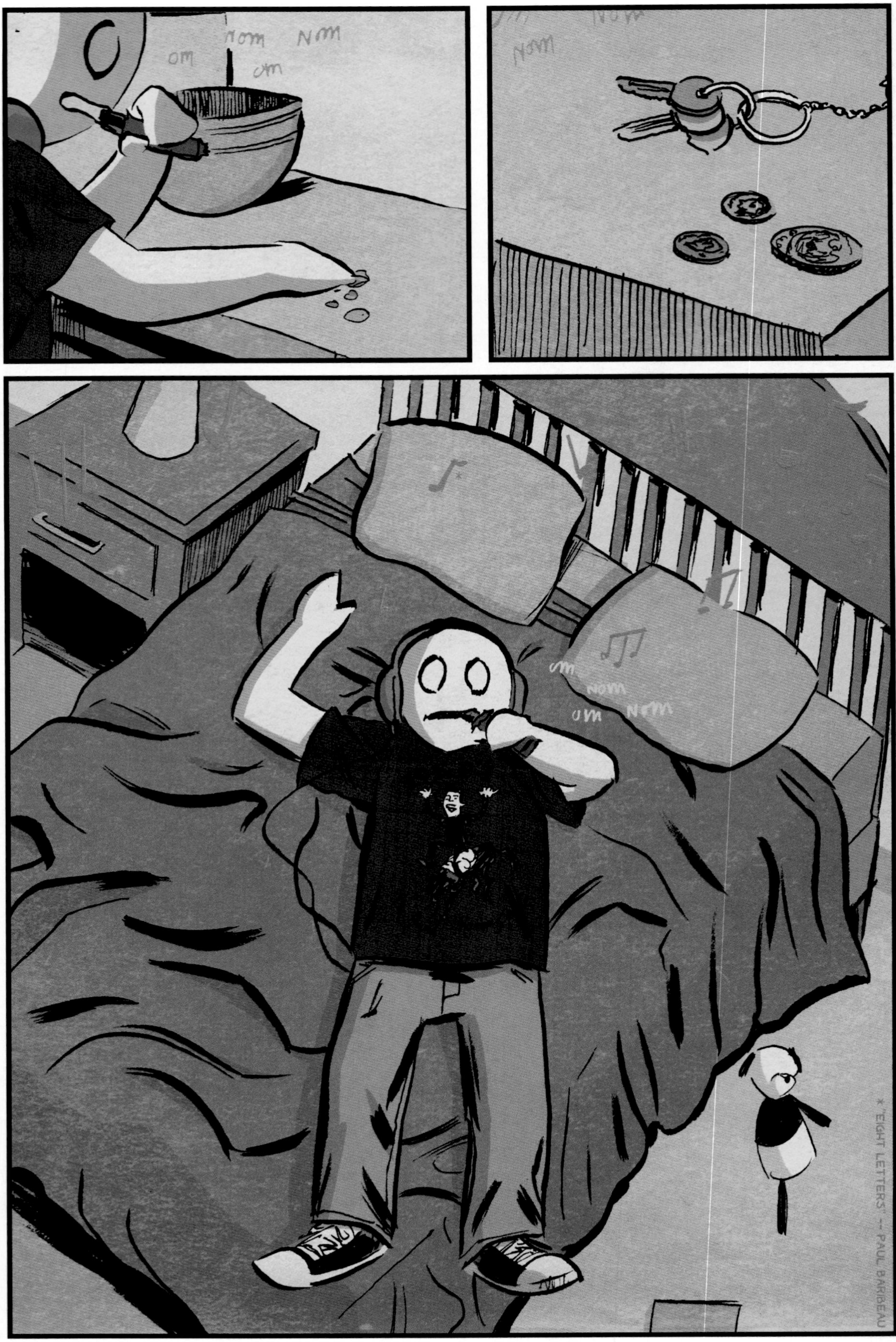

nom
Nom
om
om
Nom
Nom
om
Nom
om
Nom
* "EIGHT LETTERS" -- PAUL BARBEAU

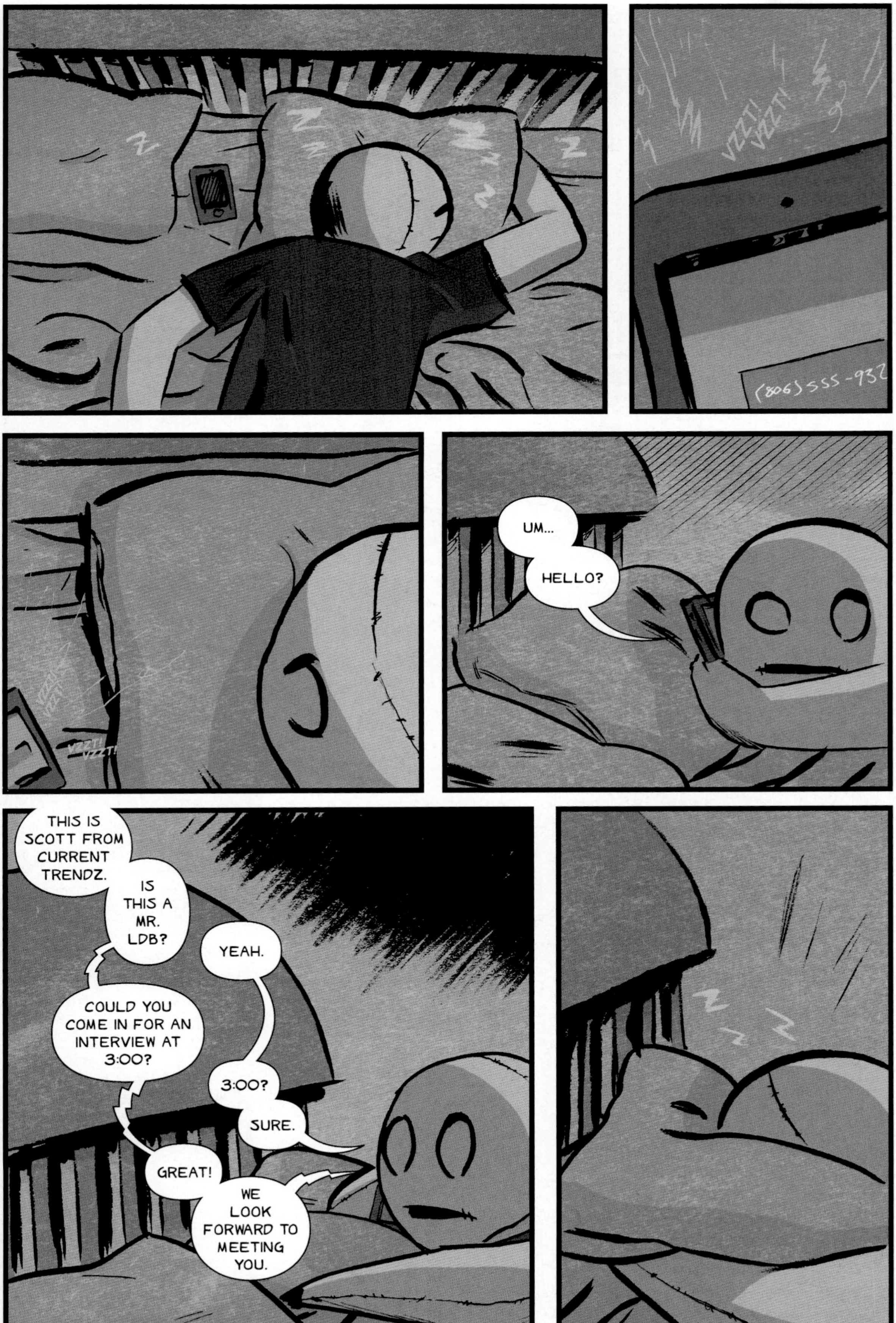
Z
Z
Z
Z
Z
VZZT! VZZT!
(806) 555-932
VZZT! VZZT!
VZZT! VZZT!
UM...
HELLO?
THIS IS SCOTT FROM CURRENT TRENDZ.
IS THIS A MR. LDB?
YEAH.
COULD YOU COME IN FOR AN INTERVIEW AT 3:00?
3:00?
SURE.
GREAT!
WE LOOK FORWARD TO MEETING YOU.
Z
Z
Z

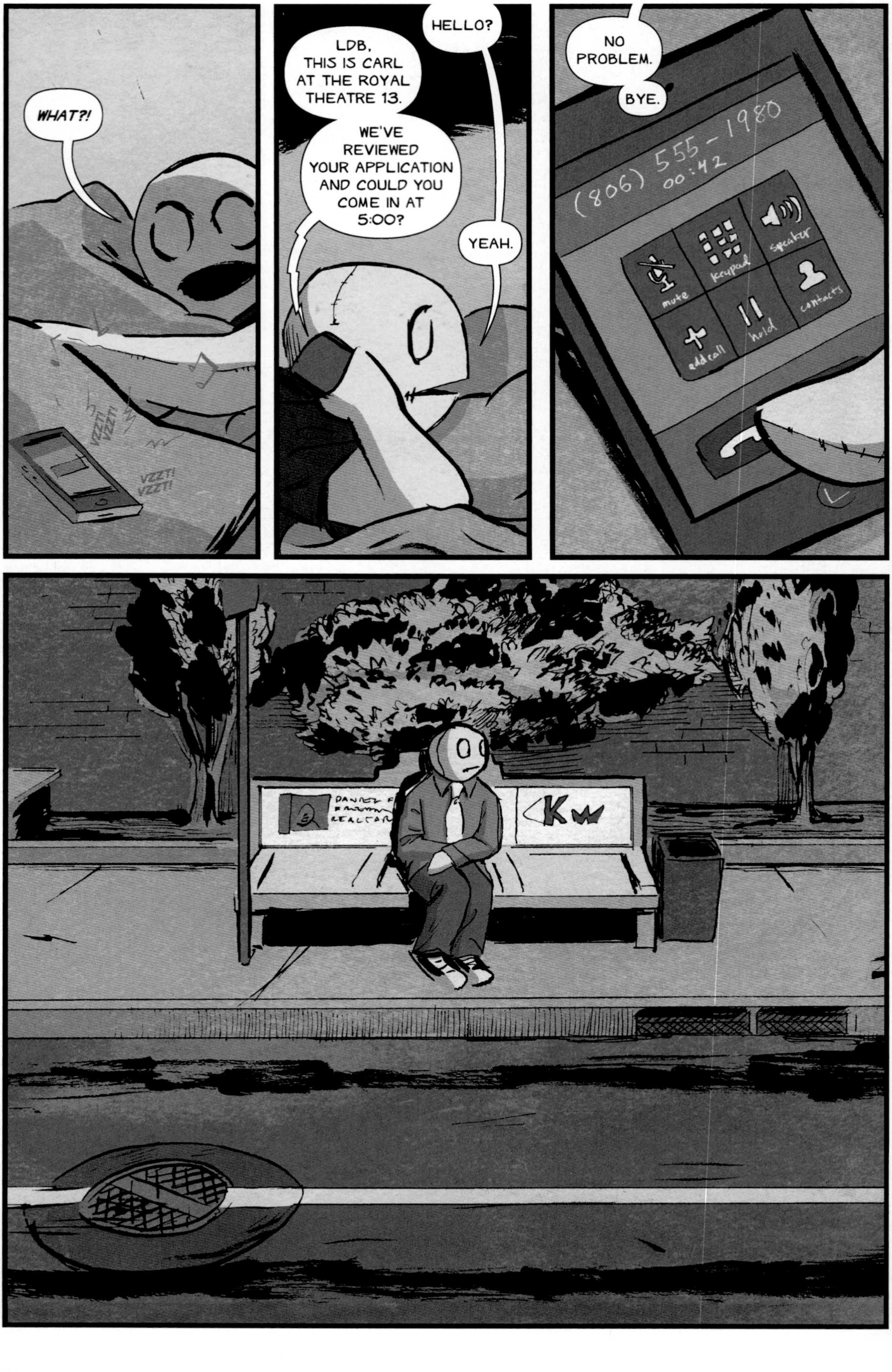
WHAT?!
VZZT! VZZT!
HELLO?
LDB, THIS IS CARL AT THE ROYAL THEATRE 13.
WE'VE REVIEWED YOUR APPLICATION AND COULD YOU COME IN AT 5:00?
YEAH.
NO PROBLEM.
BYE.
(806) 555-1980
00:42
mute
keypad
speaker
contacts
add call
hold

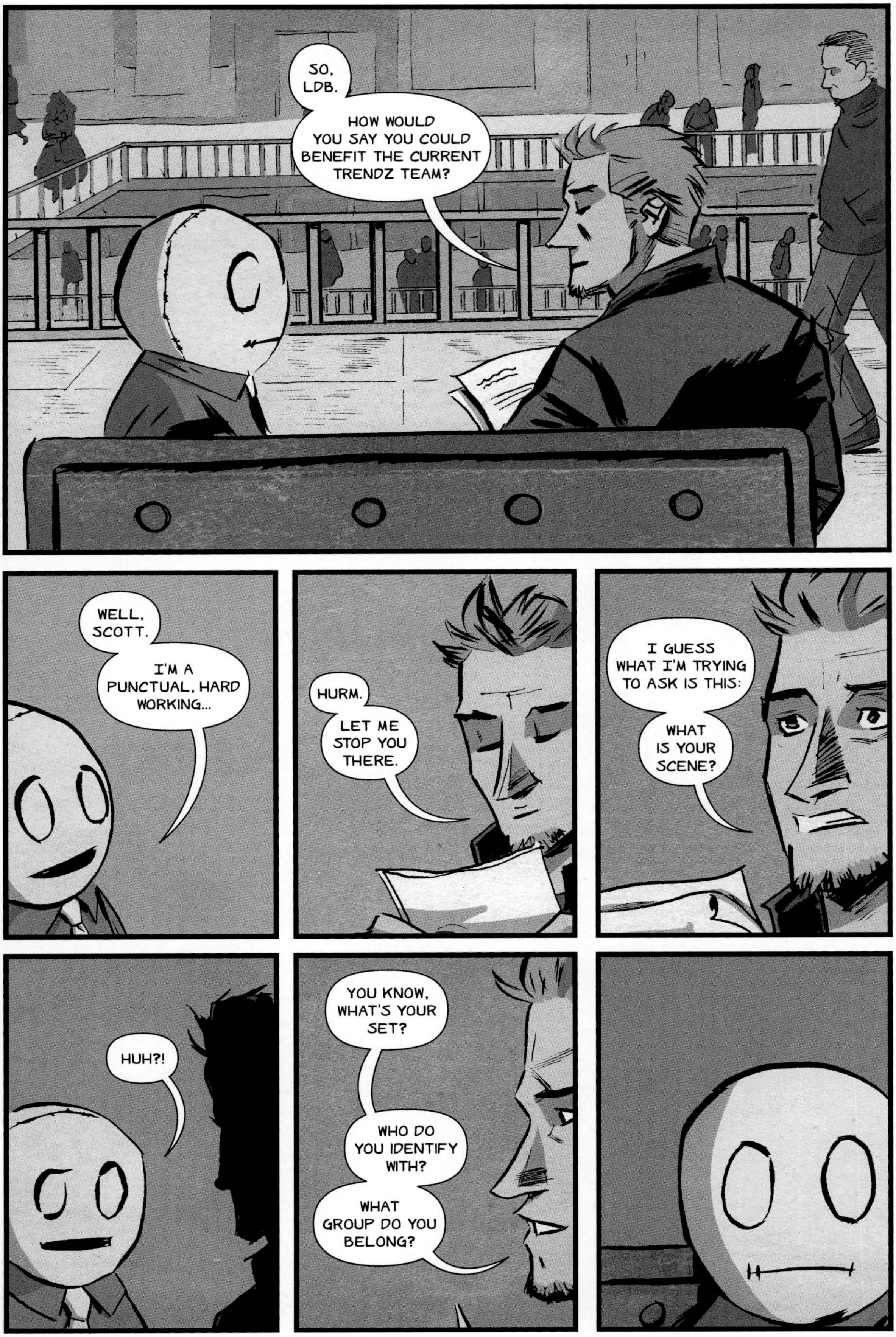
SO, LDB.
HOW WOULD YOU SAY YOU COULD BENEFIT THE CURRENT TRENDZ TEAM?
WELL, SCOTT.
I'M A PUNCTUAL, HARD WORKING...
HURM.
LET ME STOP YOU THERE.
I GUESS WHAT I'M TRYING TO ASK IS THIS:
WHAT IS YOUR SCENE?
HUH?!
YOU KNOW, WHAT'S YOUR SET?
WHO DO YOU IDENTIFY WITH?
WHAT GROUP DO YOU BELONG?

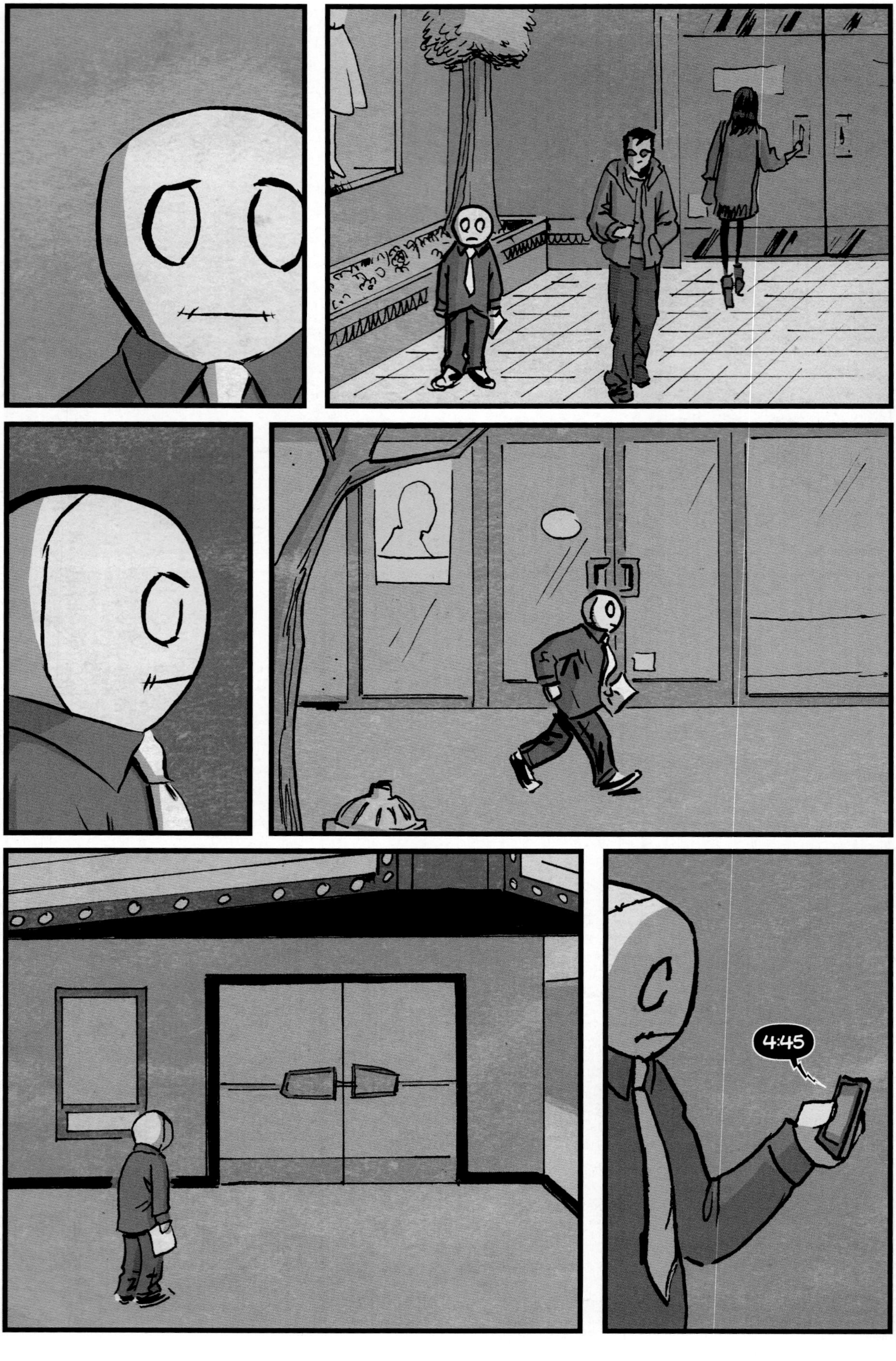
4:45

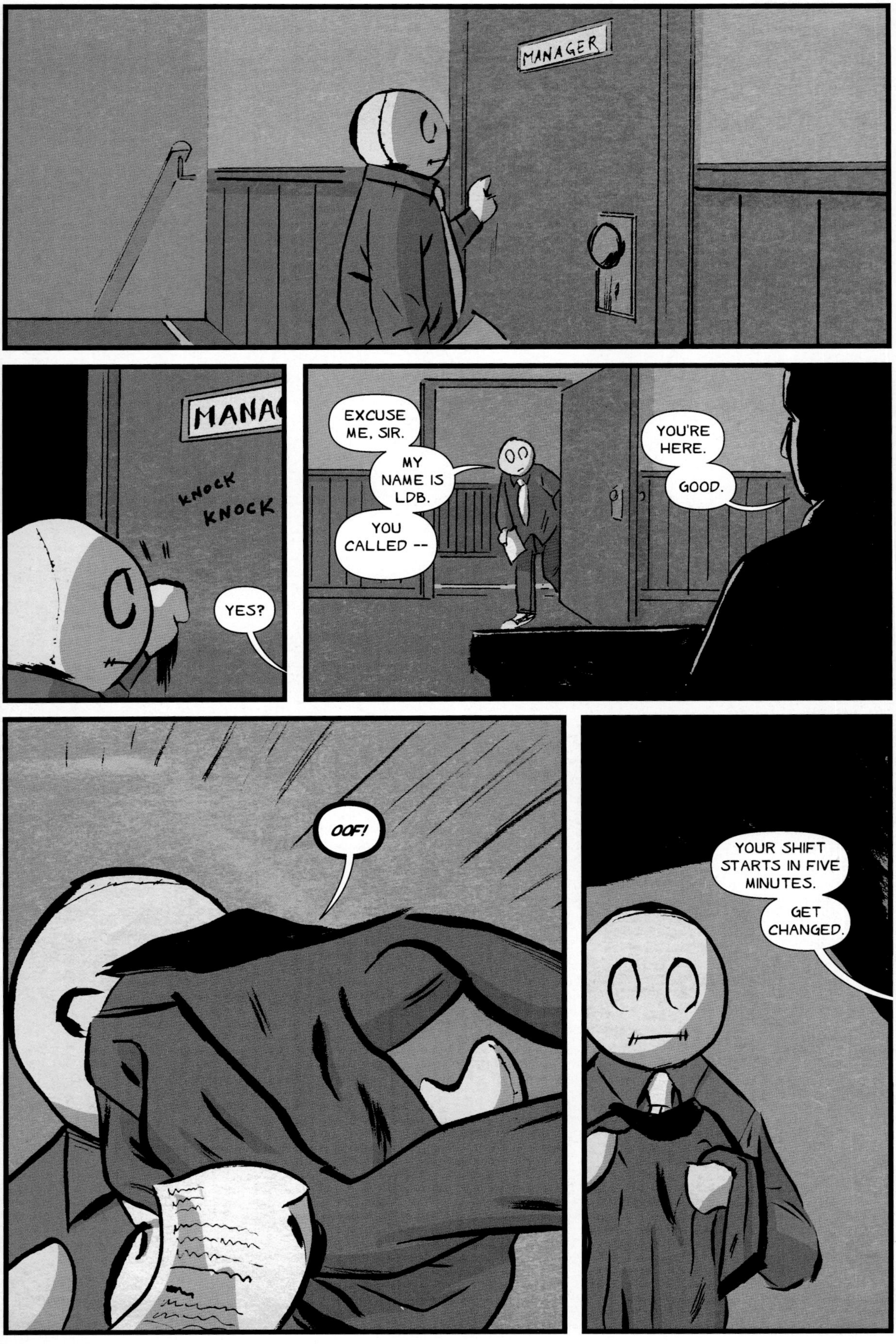
MANAGER
MANAG
KNOCK KNOCK
YES?
EXCUSE ME, SIR.
MY NAME IS LDB.
YOU CALLED --
YOU'RE HERE.
GOOD.
OOF!
YOUR SHIFT STARTS IN FIVE MINUTES.
GET CHANGED.

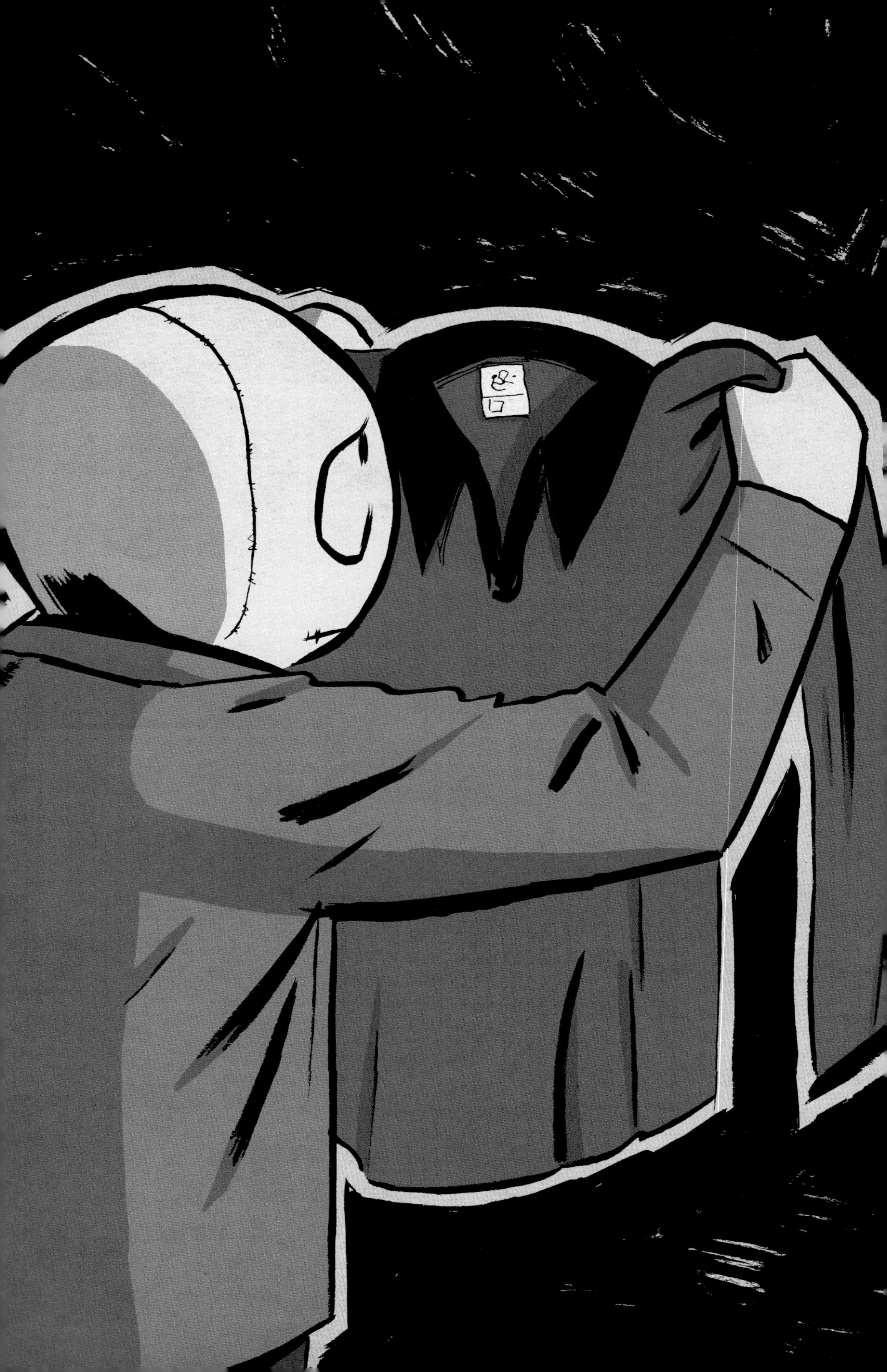

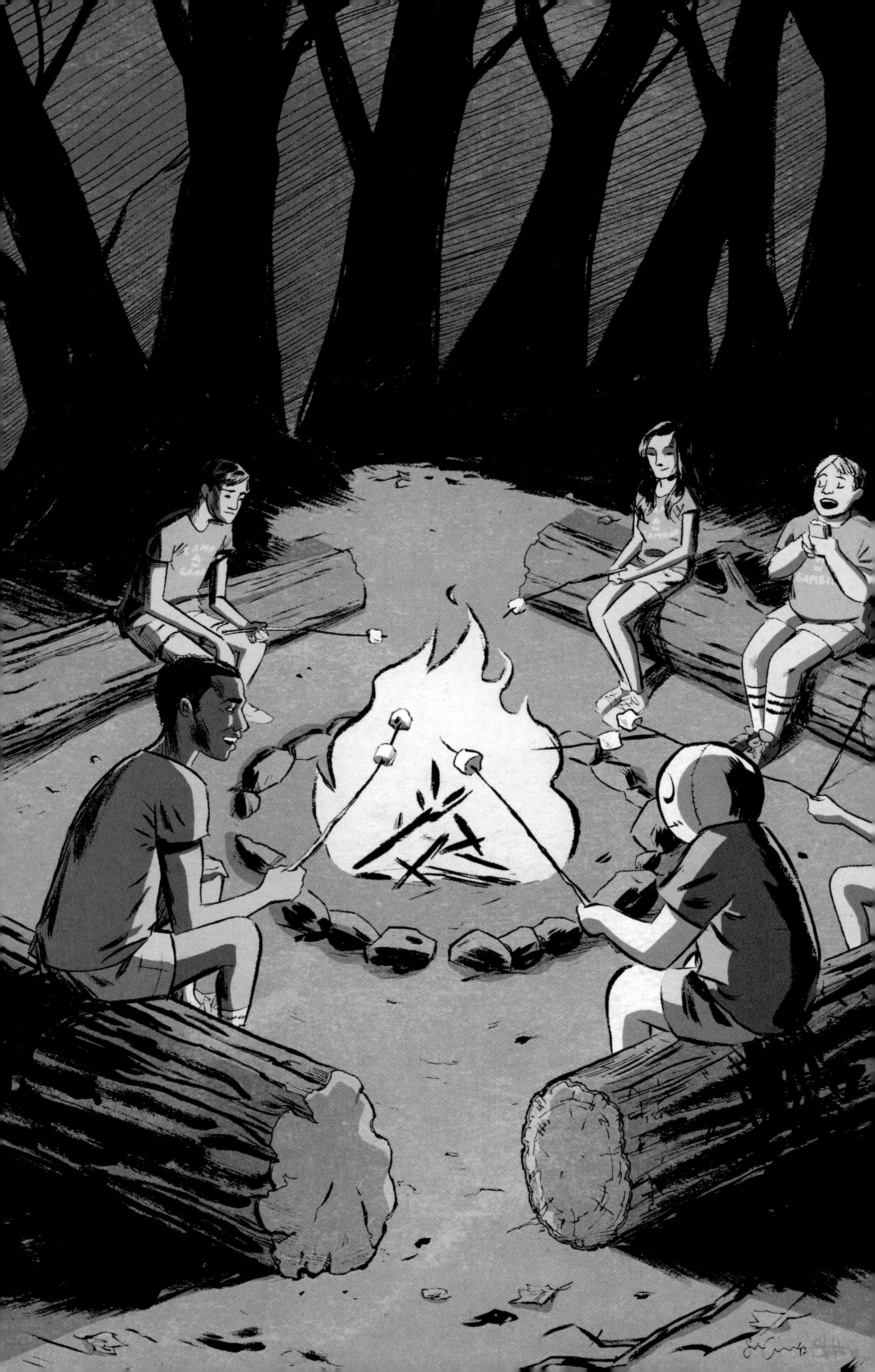

CHAPTER TWO:
"WORRIED SHOES"

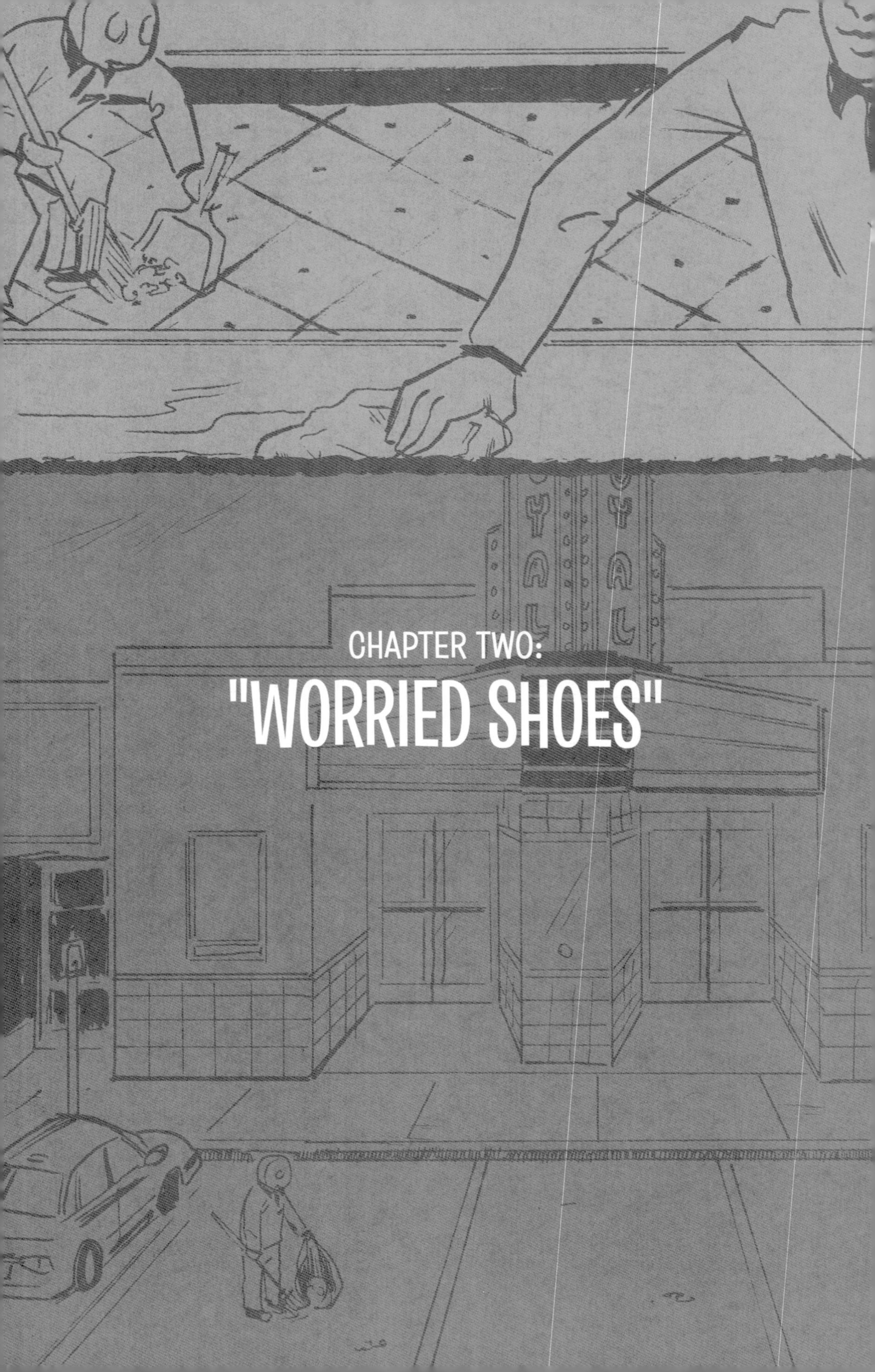

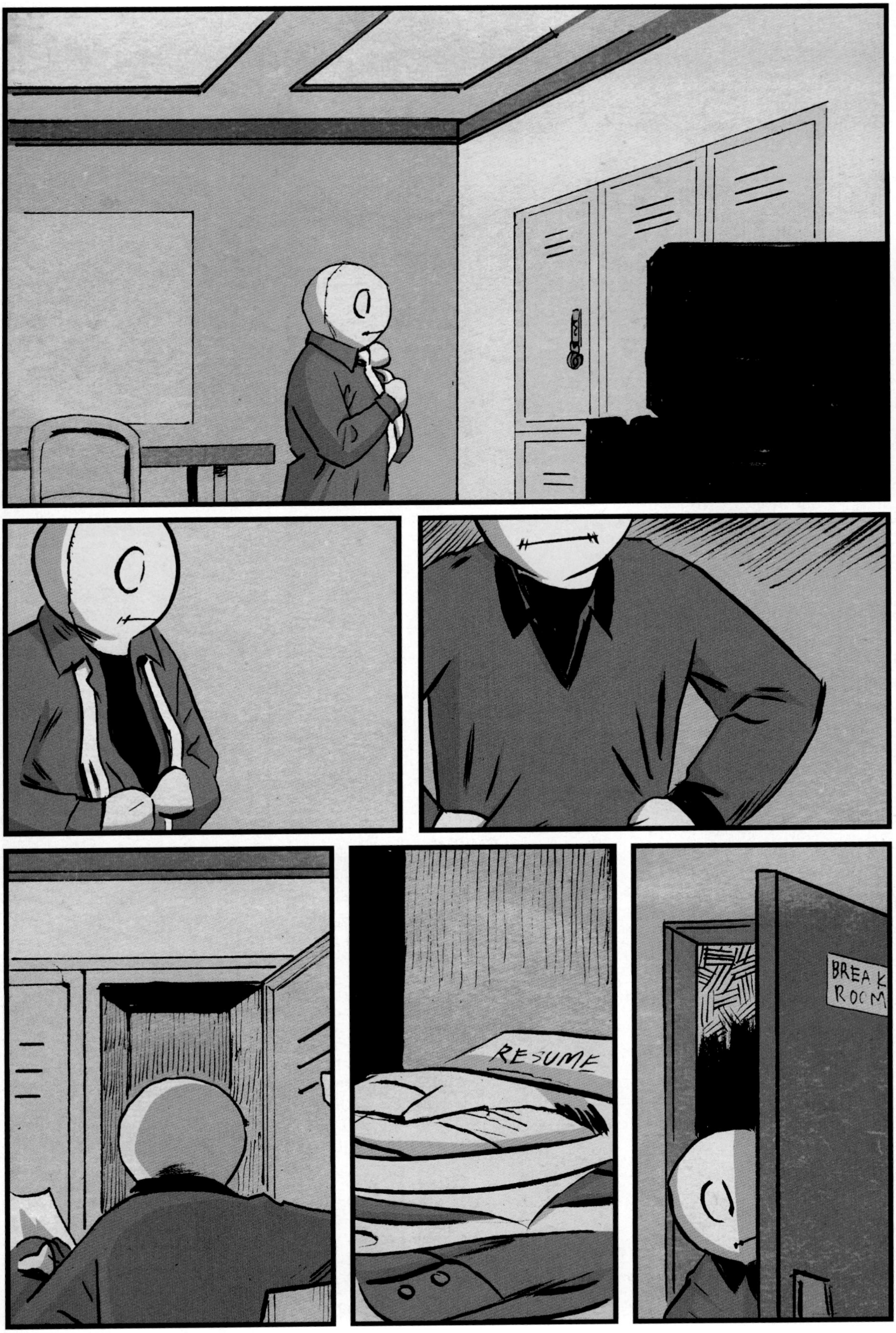
RESUME
BREAK ROOM

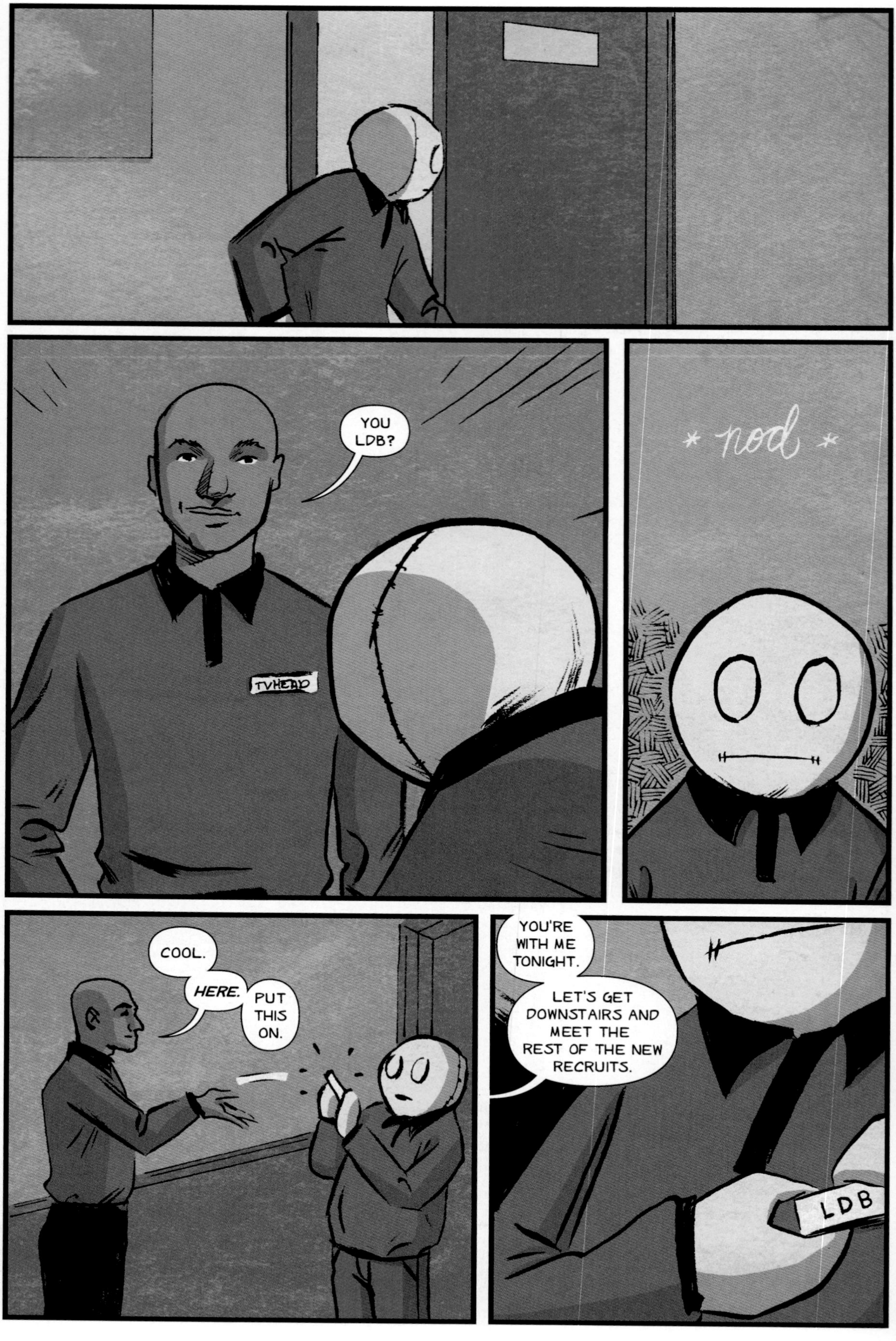
YOU LDB?
TVHEAD
* nod *
COOL.
HERE.
PUT THIS ON.
YOU'RE WITH ME TONIGHT.
LET'S GET DOWNSTAIRS AND MEET THE REST OF THE NEW RECRUITS.
LDB

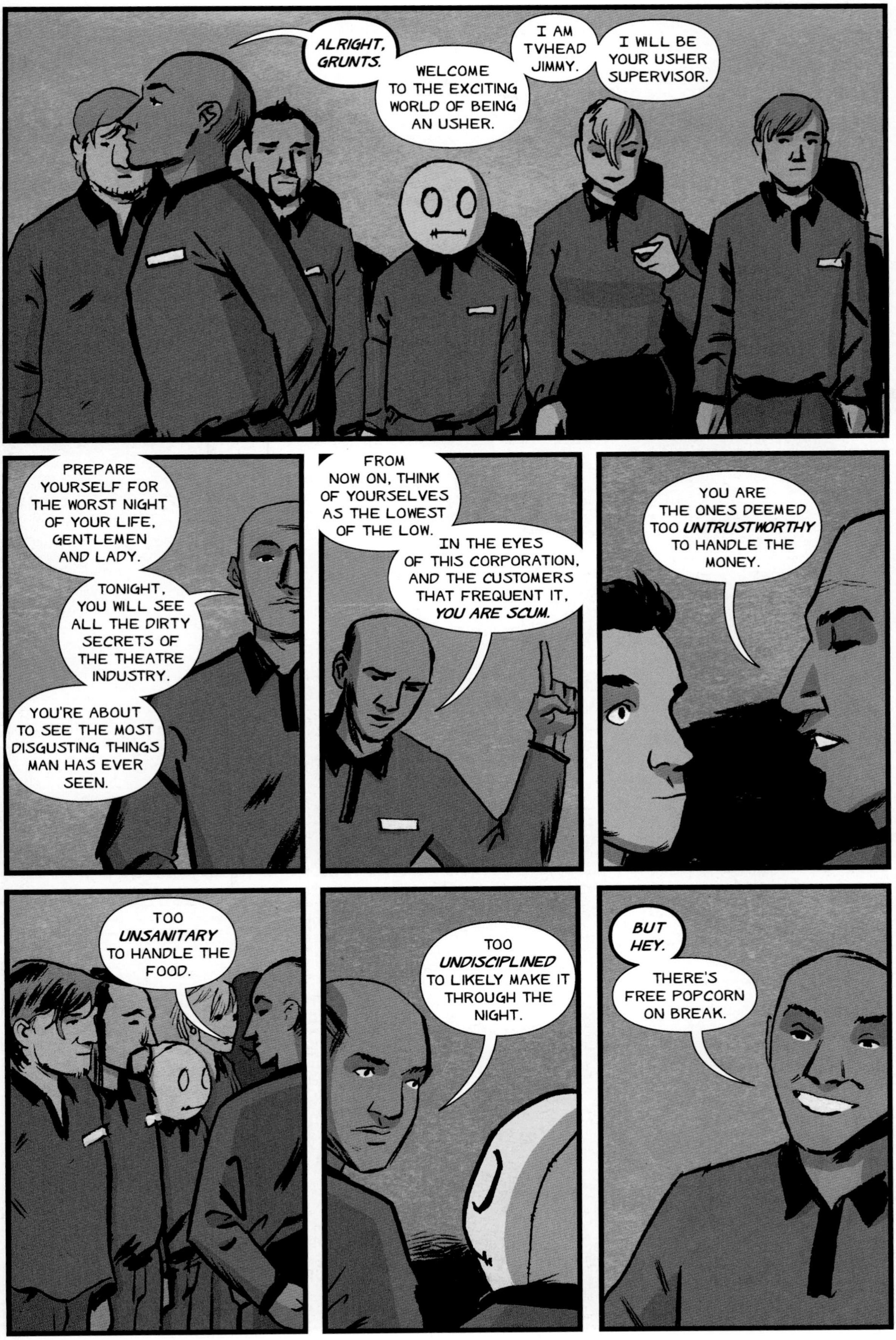
ALRIGHT, GRUNTS.
WELCOME TO THE EXCITING WORLD OF BEING AN USHER.
I AM TVHEAD JIMMY.
I WILL BE YOUR USHER SUPERVISOR.
PREPARE YOURSELF FOR THE WORST NIGHT OF YOUR LIFE, GENTLEMEN AND LADY.
TONIGHT, YOU WILL SEE ALL THE DIRTY SECRETS OF THE THEATRE INDUSTRY.
YOU'RE ABOUT TO SEE THE MOST DISGUSTING THINGS MAN HAS EVER SEEN.
FROM NOW ON, THINK OF YOURSELVES AS THE LOWEST OF THE LOW.
IN THE EYES OF THIS CORPORATION, AND THE CUSTOMERS THAT FREQUENT IT, YOU ARE SCUM.
YOU ARE THE ONES DEEMED TOO UNTRUSTWORTHY TO HANDLE THE MONEY.
TOO UNSANITARY TO HANDLE THE FOOD.
TOO UNDISCIPLINED TO LIKELY MAKE IT THROUGH THE NIGHT.
BUT HEY.
THERE'S FREE POPCORN ON BREAK.

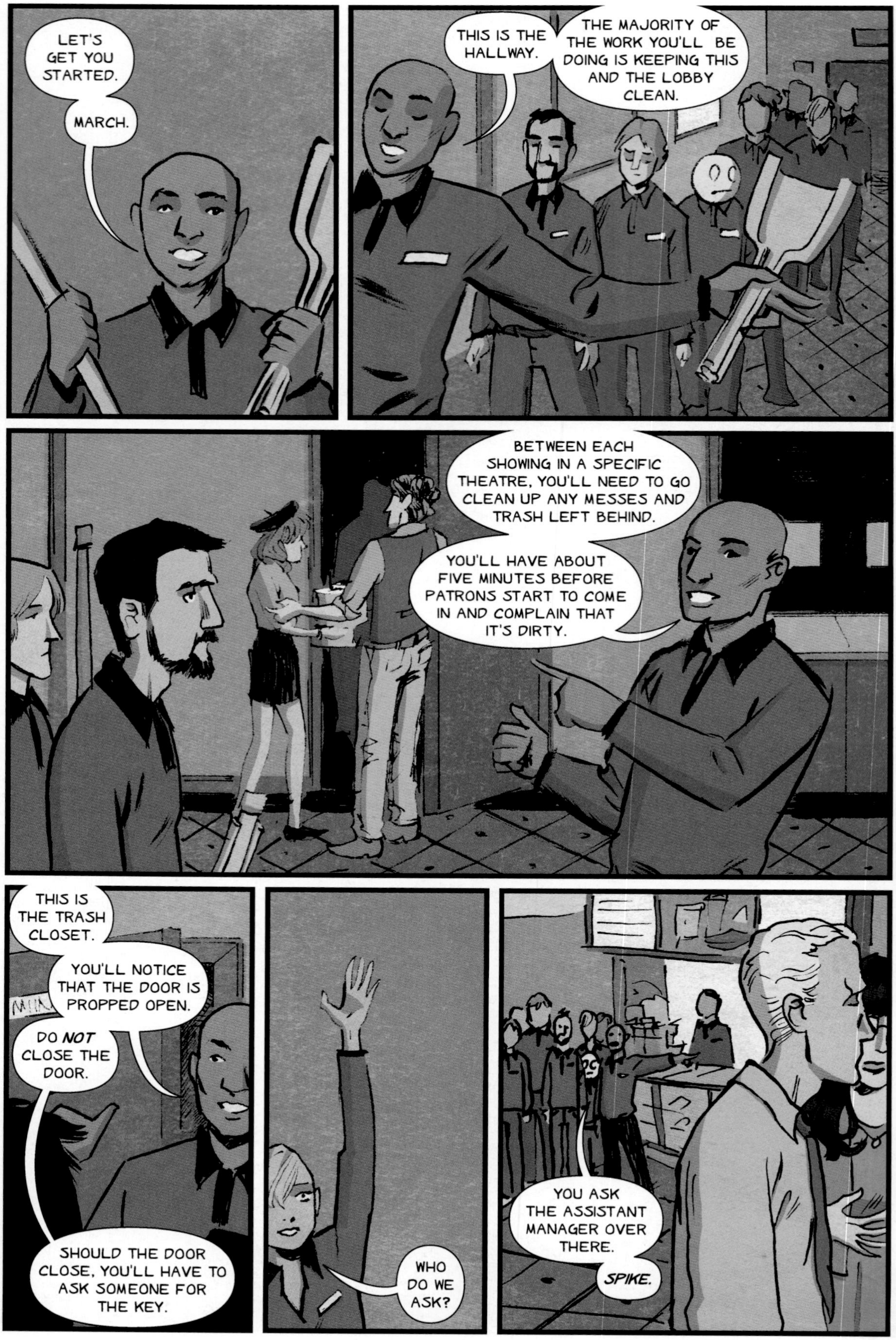
LET'S GET YOU STARTED.
MARCH.
THIS IS THE HALLWAY.
THE MAJORITY OF THE WORK YOU'LL BE DOING IS KEEPING THIS AND THE LOBBY CLEAN.
BETWEEN EACH SHOWING IN A SPECIFIC THEATRE, YOU'LL NEED TO GO CLEAN UP ANY MESSES AND TRASH LEFT BEHIND.
YOU'LL HAVE ABOUT FIVE MINUTES BEFORE PATRONS START TO COME IN AND COMPLAIN THAT IT'S DIRTY.
THIS IS THE TRASH CLOSET.
YOU'LL NOTICE THAT THE DOOR IS PROPPED OPEN.
DO ***NOT*** CLOSE THE DOOR.
SHOULD THE DOOR CLOSE, YOU'LL HAVE TO ASK SOMEONE FOR THE KEY.
WHO DO WE ASK?
YOU ASK THE ASSISTANT MANAGER OVER THERE.
SPIKE.

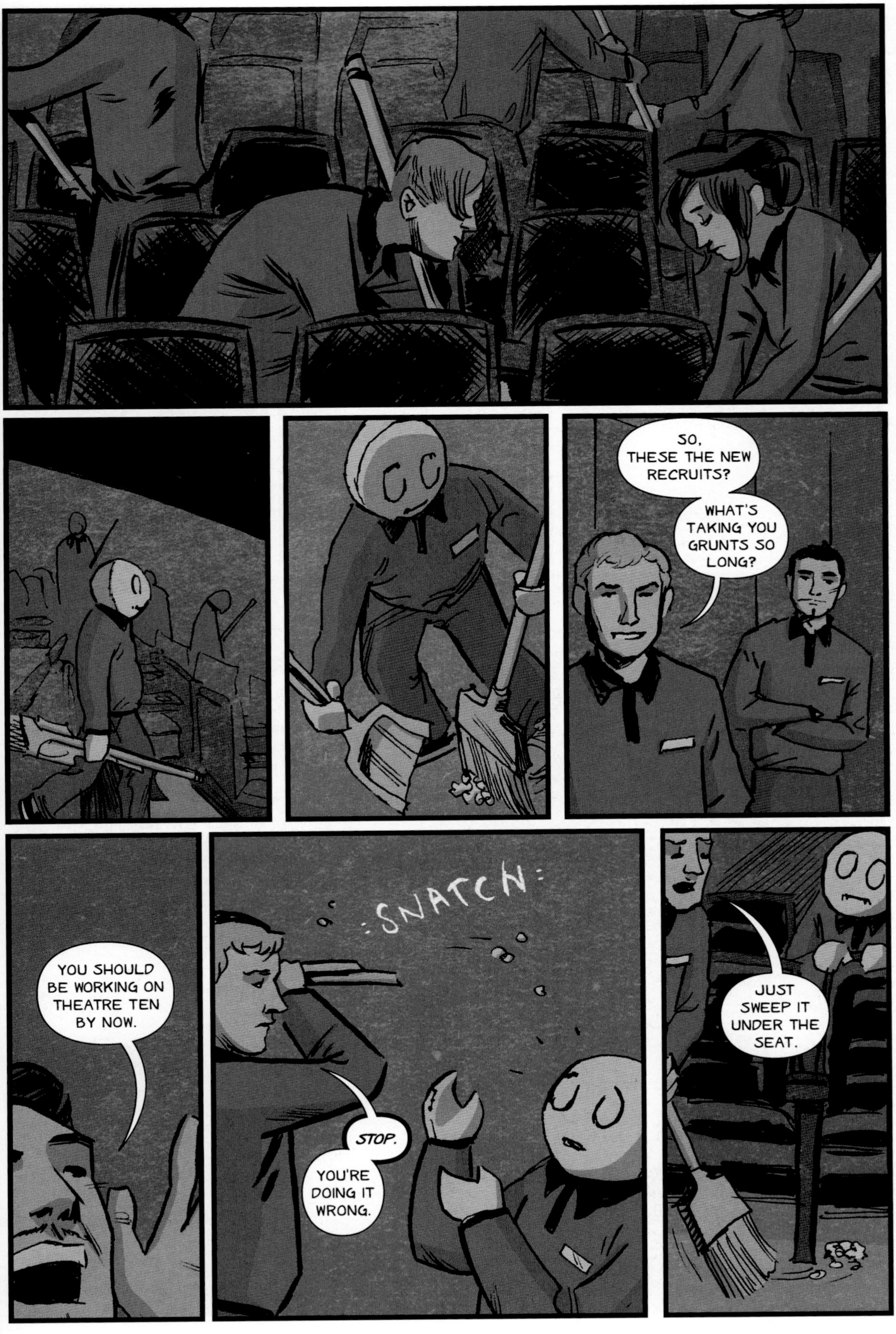
SO, THESE THE NEW RECRUITS?
WHAT'S TAKING YOU GRUNTS SO LONG?
YOU SHOULD BE WORKING ON THEATRE TEN BY NOW.
SNATCH
STOP.
YOU'RE DOING IT WRONG.
JUST SWEEP IT UNDER THE SEAT.

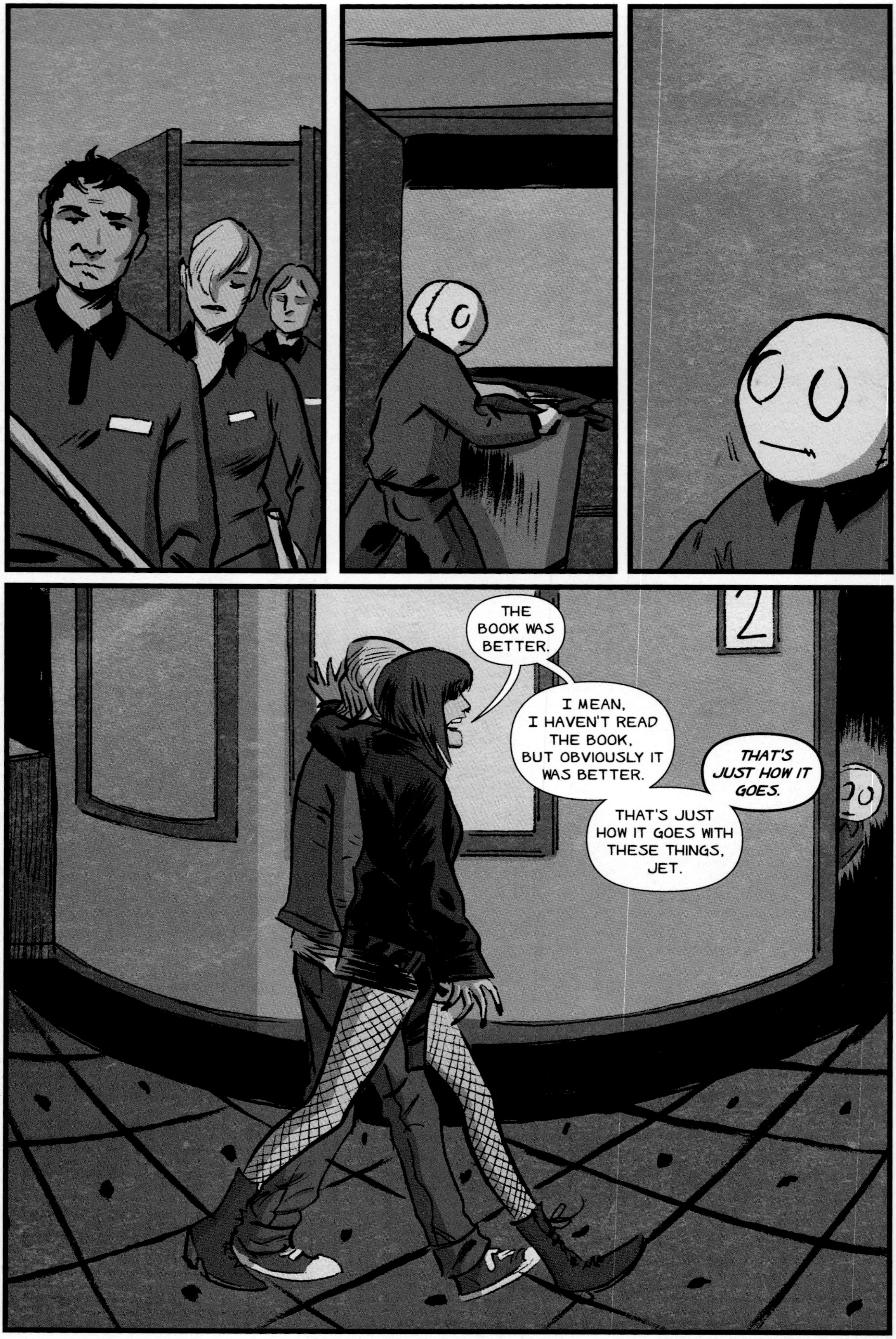
THE BOOK WAS BETTER.
I MEAN, I HAVEN'T READ THE BOOK, BUT OBVIOUSLY IT WAS BETTER.
THAT'S JUST HOW IT GOES WITH THESE THINGS, JET.
THAT'S JUST HOW IT GOES.
2

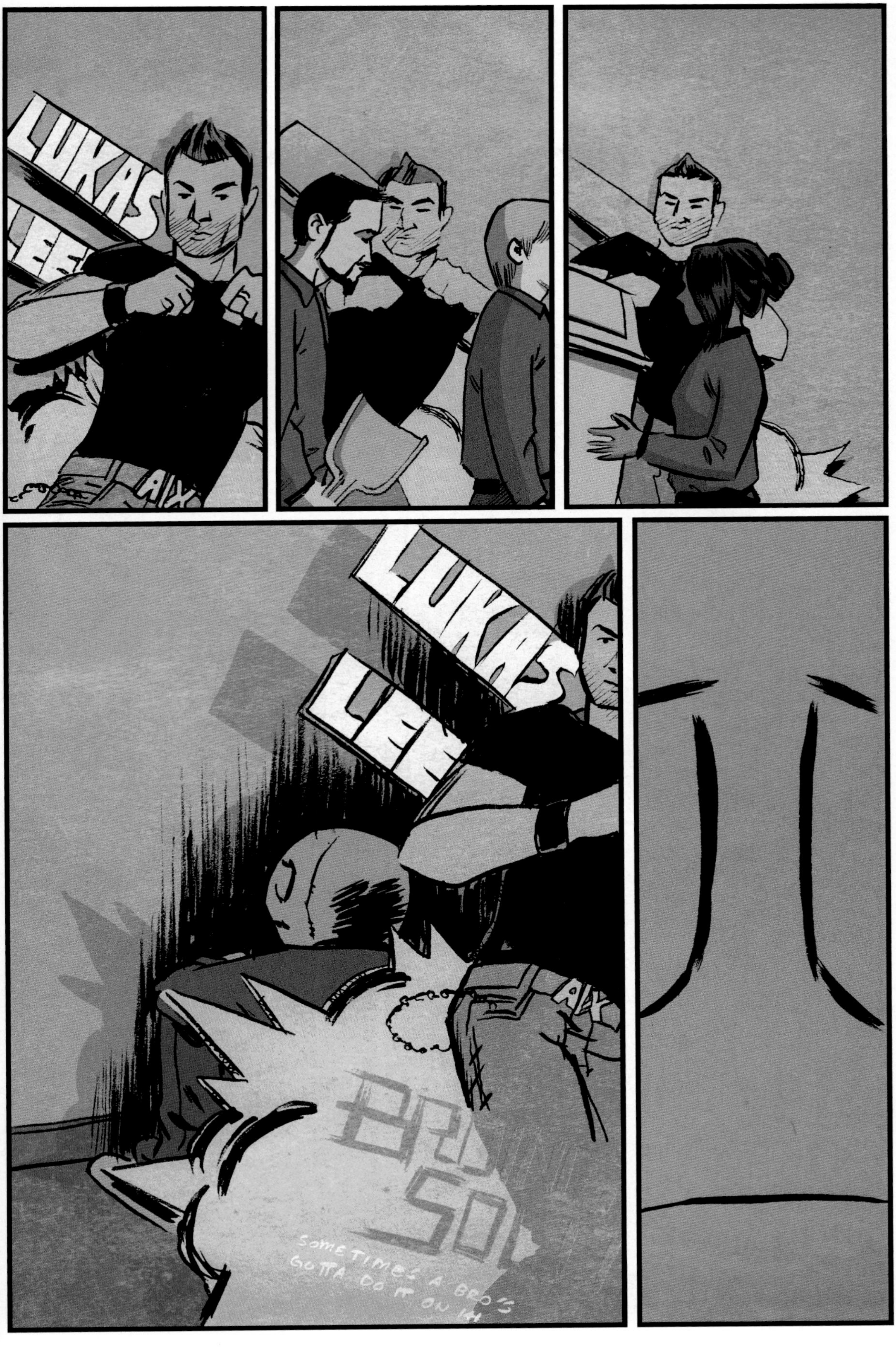
LUKAS
LEE
LUKAS
LEE
SOMETIMES A BRO'S
GOTTA DO IT ON

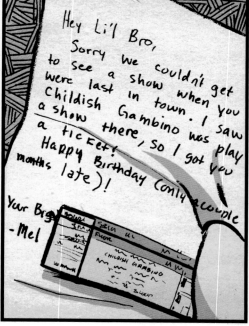

Hey Li'l Bro,
    Sorry we couldn't get
to see a show when you
were last in town. I saw
Childish Gambino was play
a show there, so I got you
a ticket!
    Happy Birthday (only a couple
months late)!

Your Bro
-Mel

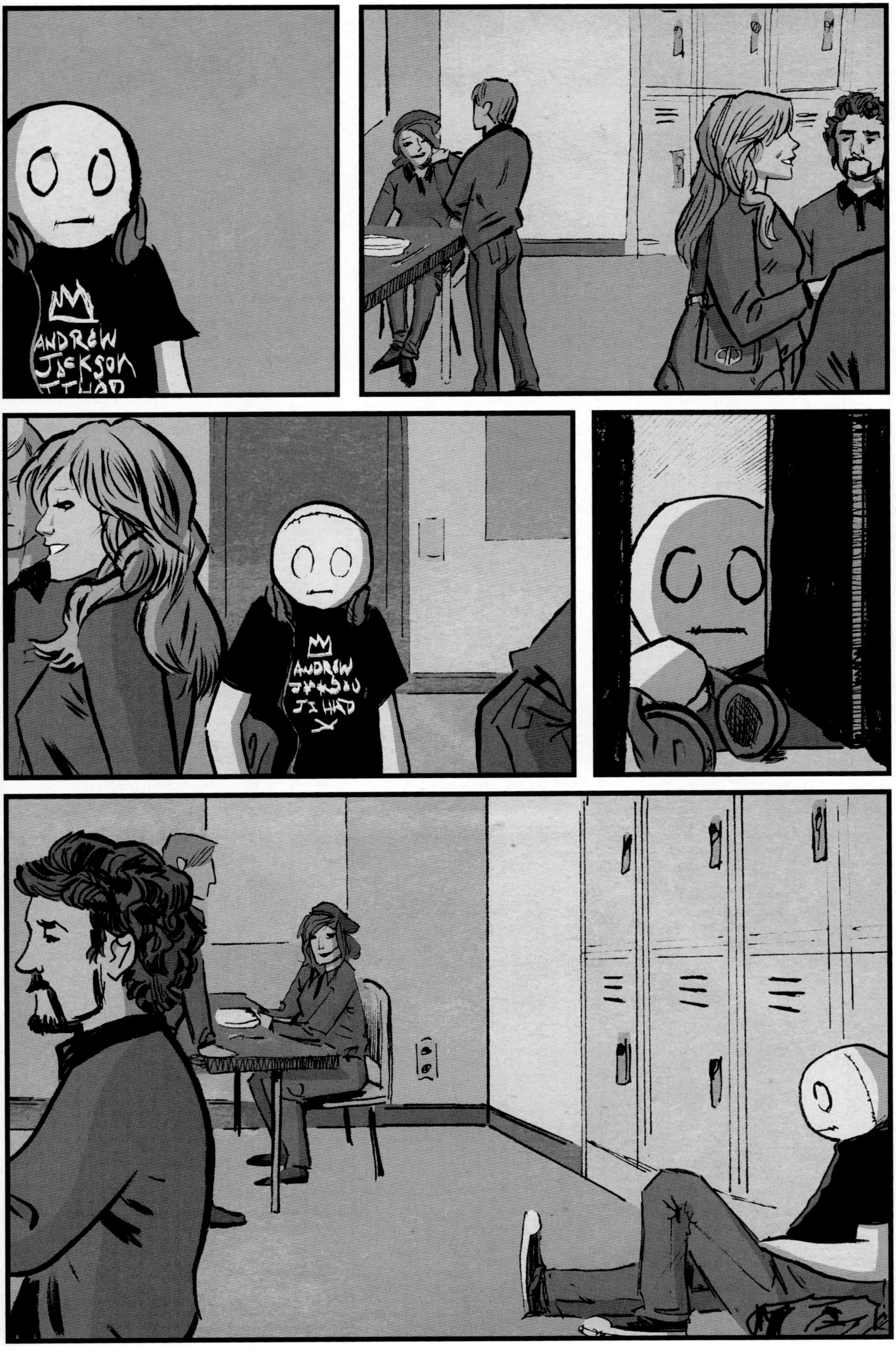
ANDREW
JACKSON

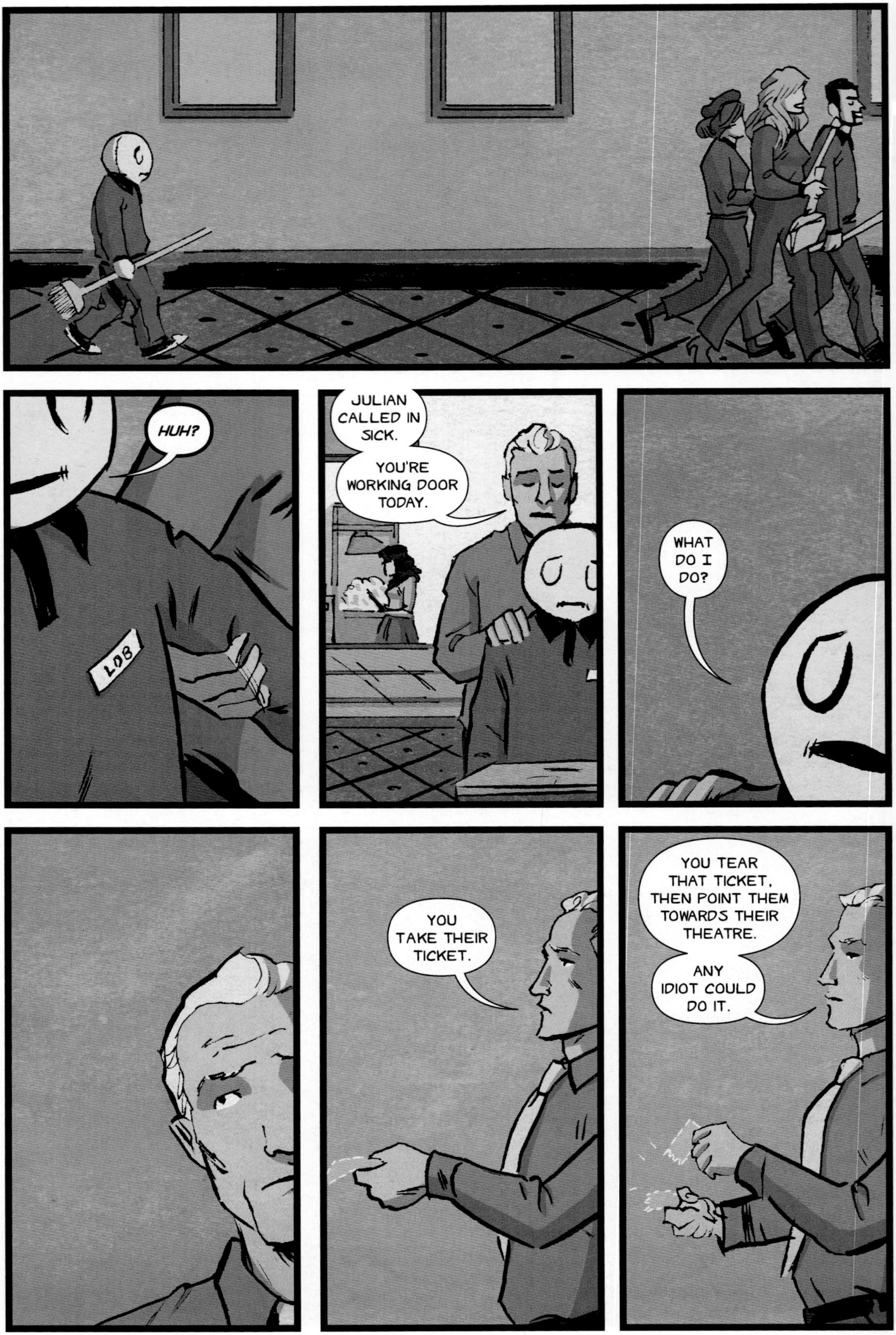
HUH?
LDB
JULIAN CALLED IN SICK.
YOU'RE WORKING DOOR TODAY.
WHAT DO I DO?
YOU TAKE THEIR TICKET.
YOU TEAR THAT TICKET, THEN POINT THEM TOWARDS THEIR THEATRE.
ANY IDIOT COULD DO IT.

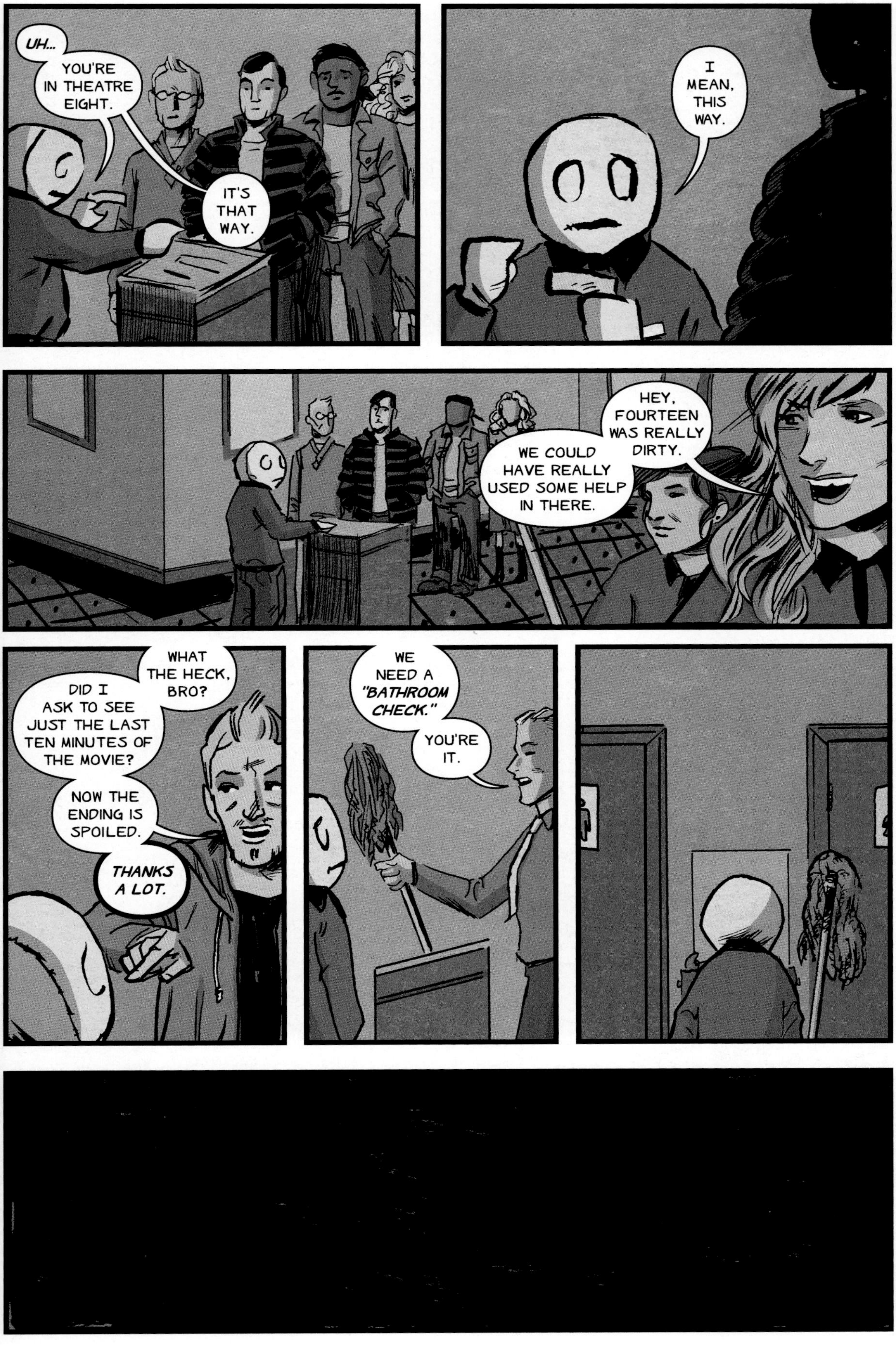
UH...
YOU'RE IN THEATRE EIGHT.
IT'S THAT WAY.
I MEAN, THIS WAY.
HEY, FOURTEEN WAS REALLY DIRTY.
WE COULD HAVE REALLY USED SOME HELP IN THERE.
WHAT THE HECK, BRO?
DID I ASK TO SEE JUST THE LAST TEN MINUTES OF THE MOVIE?
NOW THE ENDING IS SPOILED.
THANKS A LOT.
WE NEED A "BATHROOM CHECK."
YOU'RE IT.

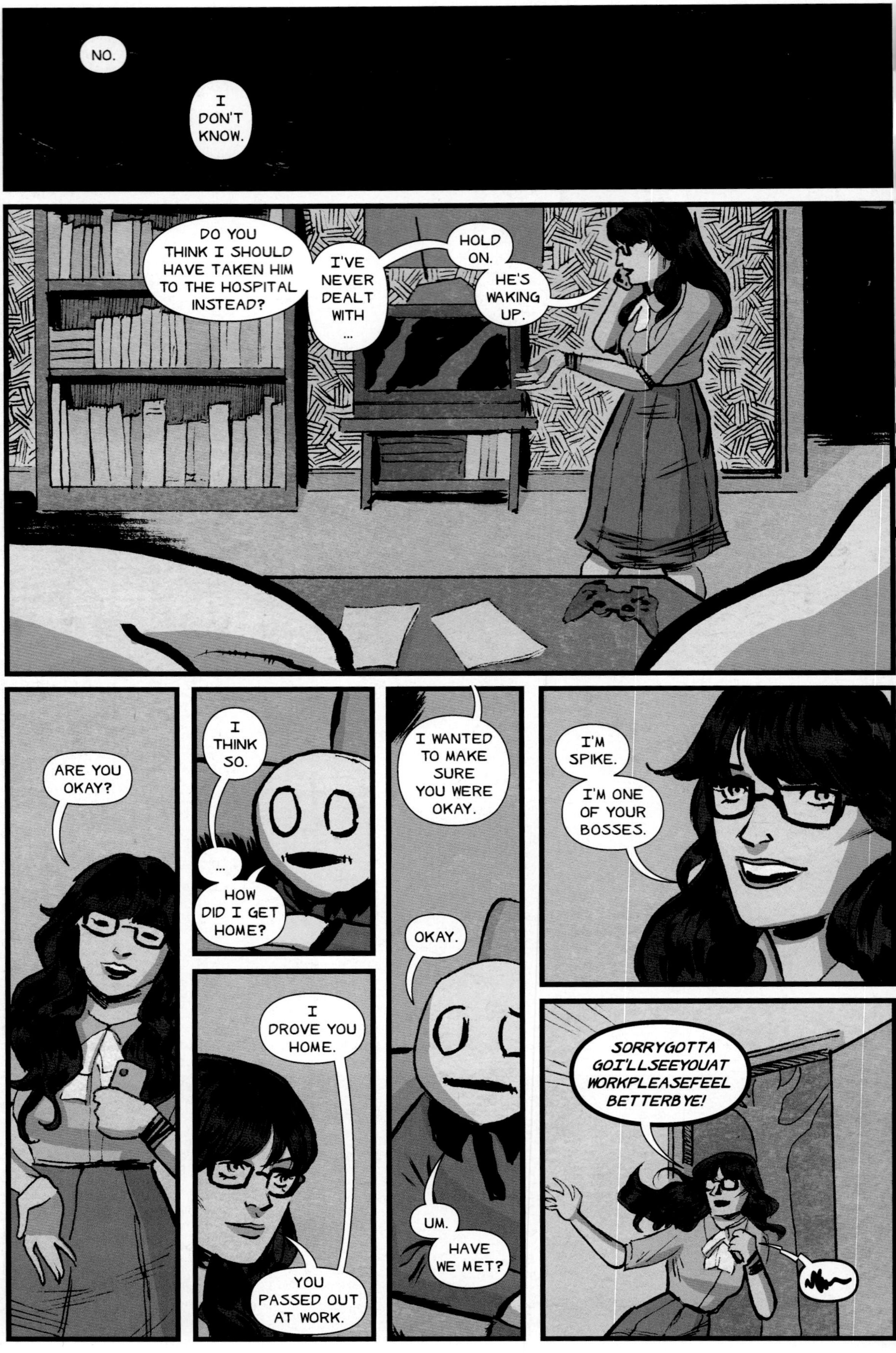

NO.
I DON'T KNOW.
DO YOU THINK I SHOULD HAVE TAKEN HIM TO THE HOSPITAL INSTEAD?
I'VE NEVER DEALT WITH ...
HOLD ON.
HE'S WAKING UP.
ARE YOU OKAY?
I THINK SO.
...
HOW DID I GET HOME?
I DROVE YOU HOME.
YOU PASSED OUT AT WORK.
I WANTED TO MAKE SURE YOU WERE OKAY.
OKAY.
UM.
HAVE WE MET?
I'M SPIKE.
I'M ONE OF YOUR BOSSES.
SORRYGOTTA GOI'LLSEEYOUAT WORKPLEASEFEEL BETTERBYE!

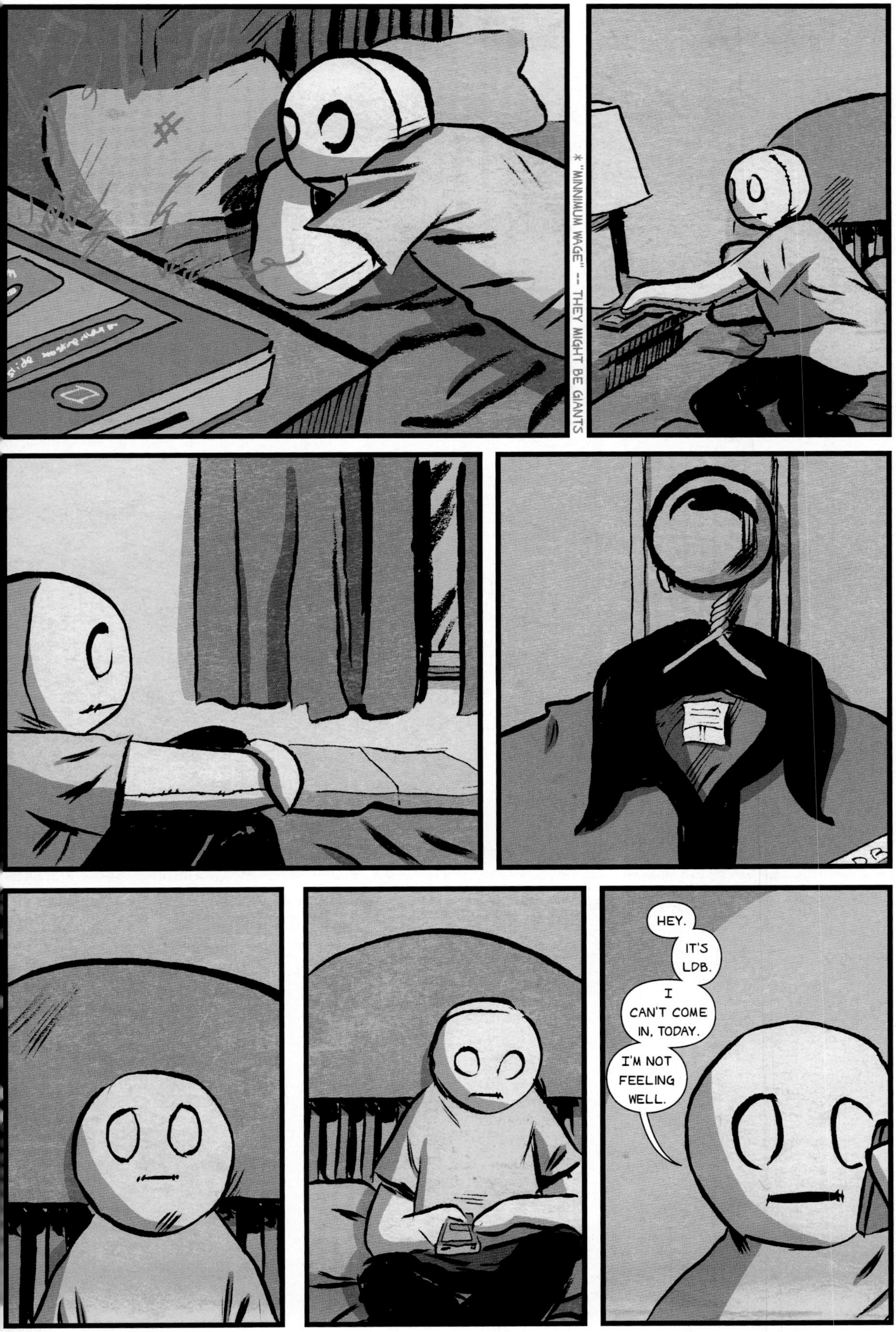

HEY.
IT'S LDB.
I CAN'T COME IN, TODAY.
I'M NOT FEELING WELL.

*"MINNIMUM WAGE" -- THEY MIGHT BE GIANTS

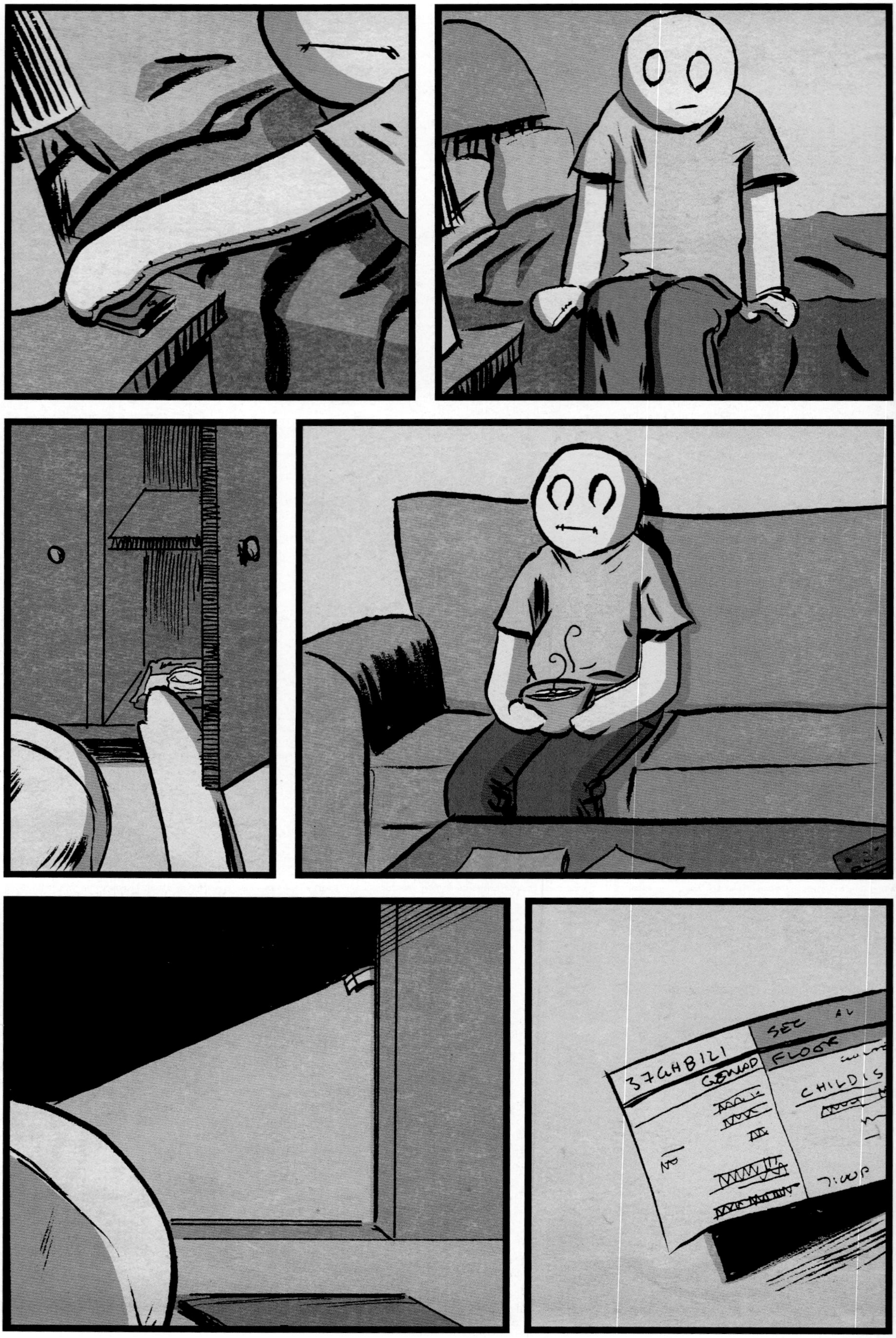
37GHB121
SEC
FLOOR
CHILDIS
7:00P

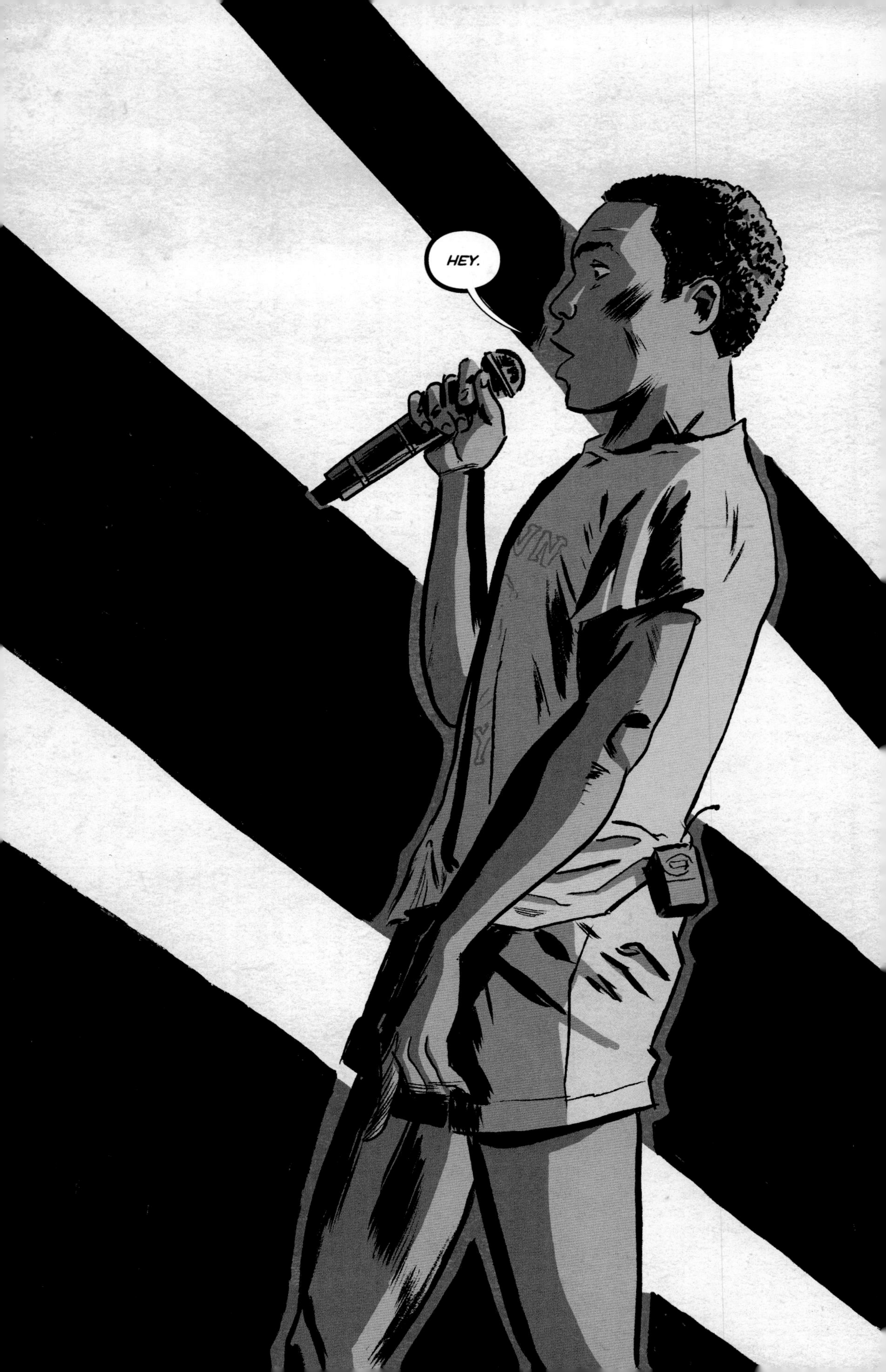
HEY.

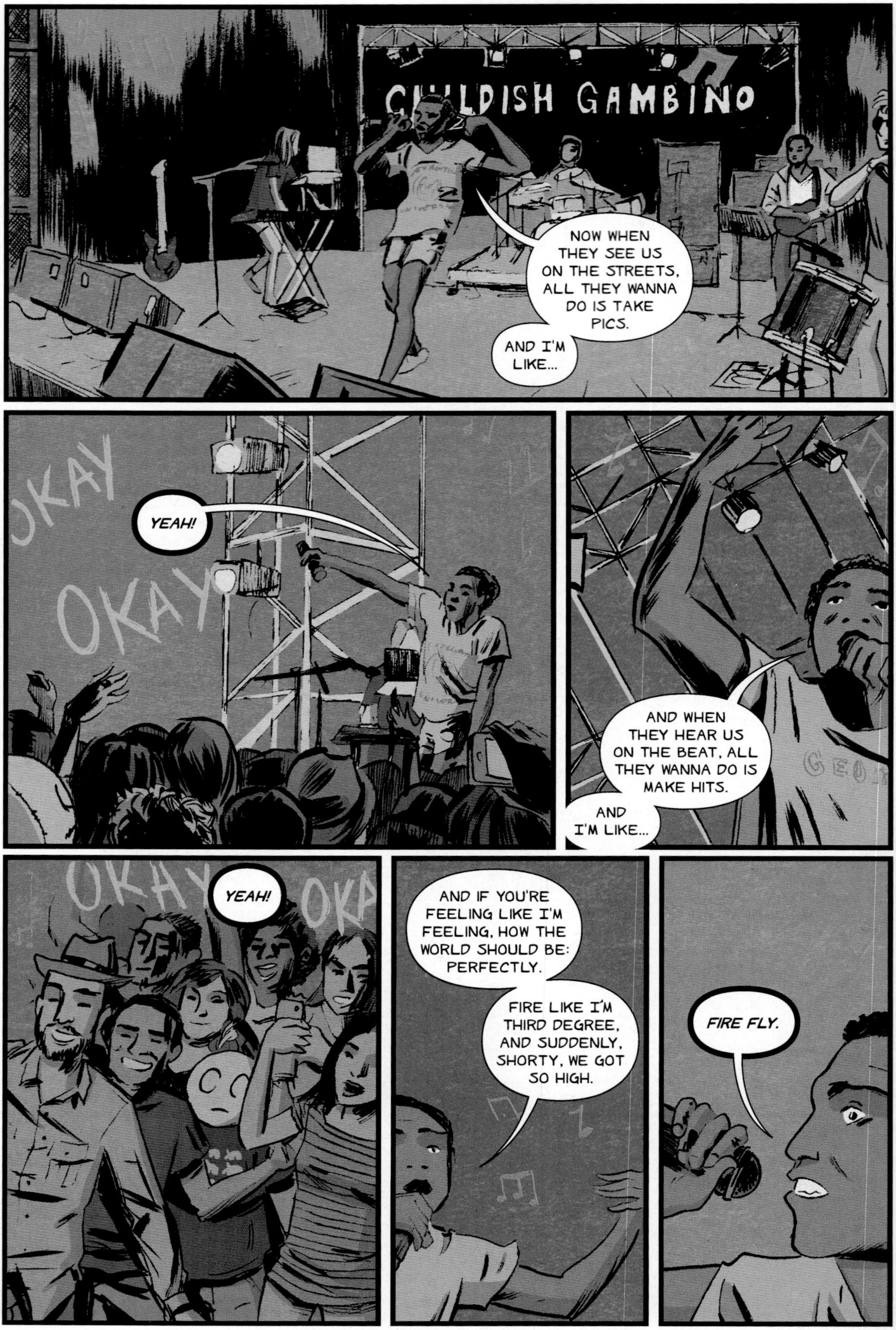
CHILDISH GAMBINO
NOW WHEN THEY SEE US ON THE STREETS, ALL THEY WANNA DO IS TAKE PICS.
AND I'M LIKE...
OKAY
OKAY
YEAH!
AND WHEN THEY HEAR US ON THE BEAT, ALL THEY WANNA DO IS MAKE HITS.
AND I'M LIKE...
OKAY
YEAH!
AND IF YOU'RE FEELING LIKE I'M FEELING, HOW THE WORLD SHOULD BE: PERFECTLY.
FIRE LIKE I'M THIRD DEGREE, AND SUDDENLY, SHORTY, WE GOT SO HIGH.
FIRE FLY.

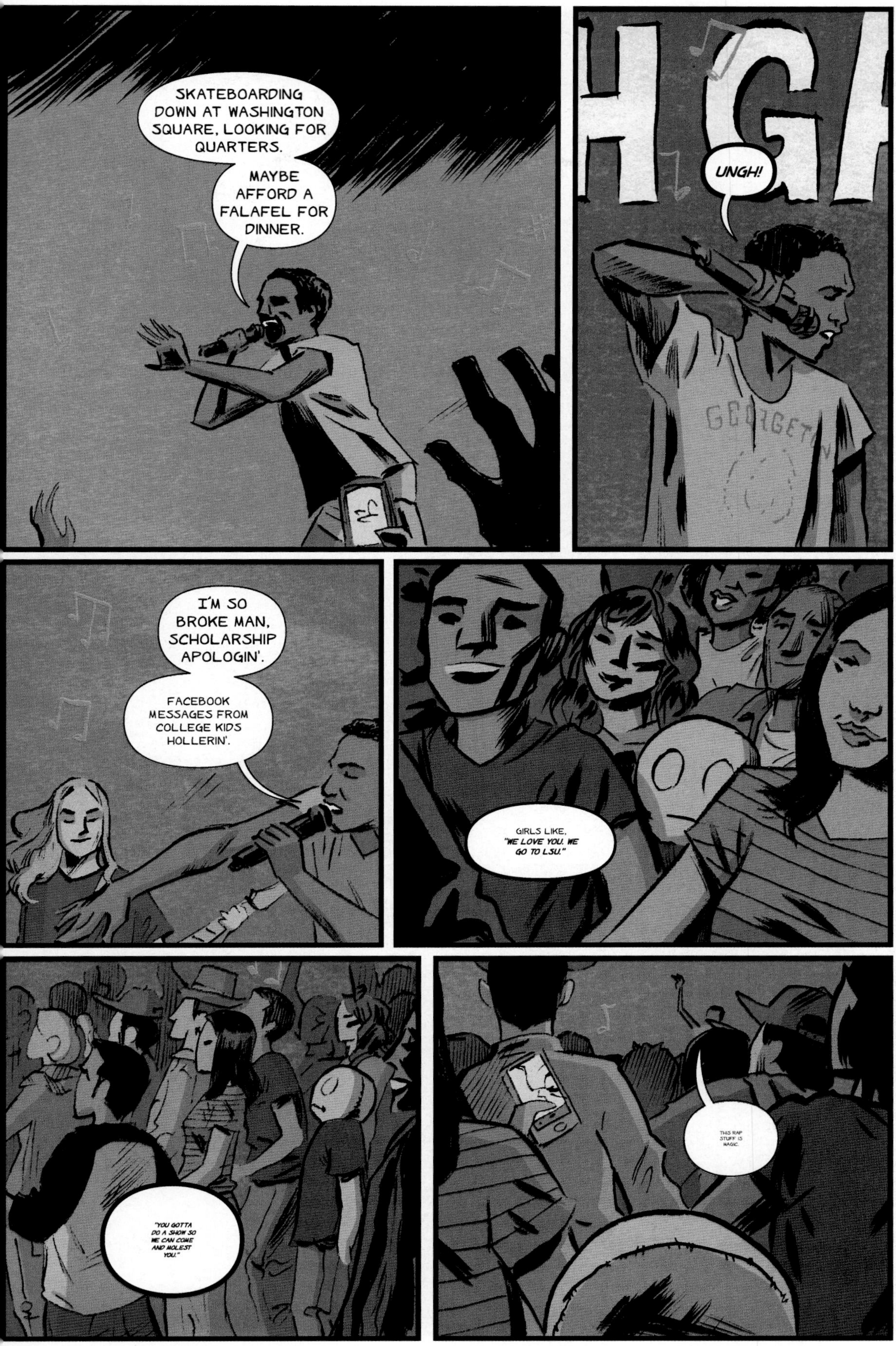
SKATEBOARDING DOWN AT WASHINGTON SQUARE, LOOKING FOR QUARTERS.
MAYBE AFFORD A FALAFEL FOR DINNER.
UNGH!
GEORGETOWN
I'M SO BROKE MAN, SCHOLARSHIP APOLOGIN'.
FACEBOOK MESSAGES FROM COLLEGE KIDS HOLLERIN'.
GIRLS LIKE, *"WE LOVE YOU. WE GO TO LSU."*
"YOU GOTTA DO A SHOW SO WE CAN COME AND MOLEST YOU."
THIS RAP STUFF IS MAGIC.

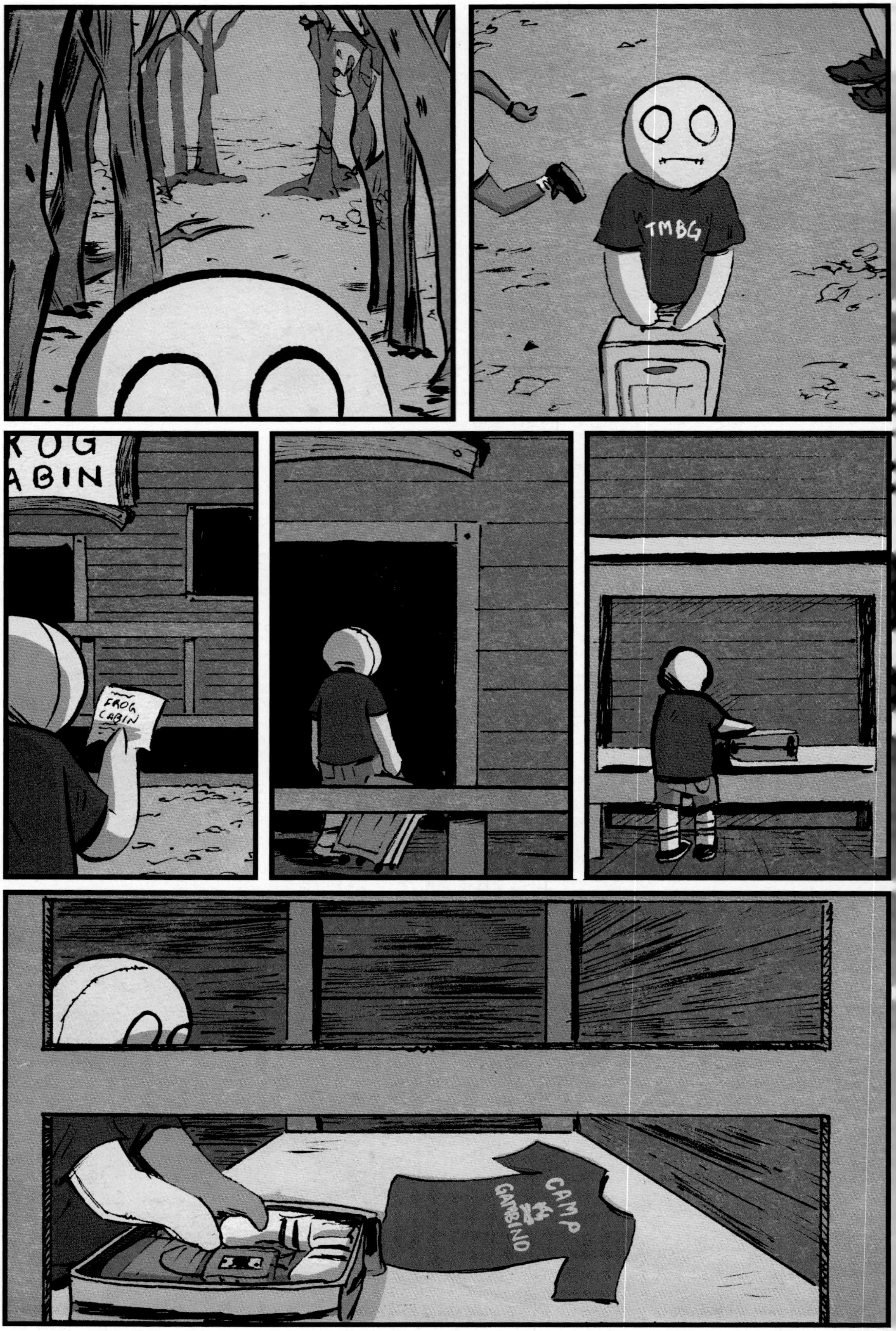
TMBG
ROG
ABIN
FROG
CABIN
CAMP
GAMBINO

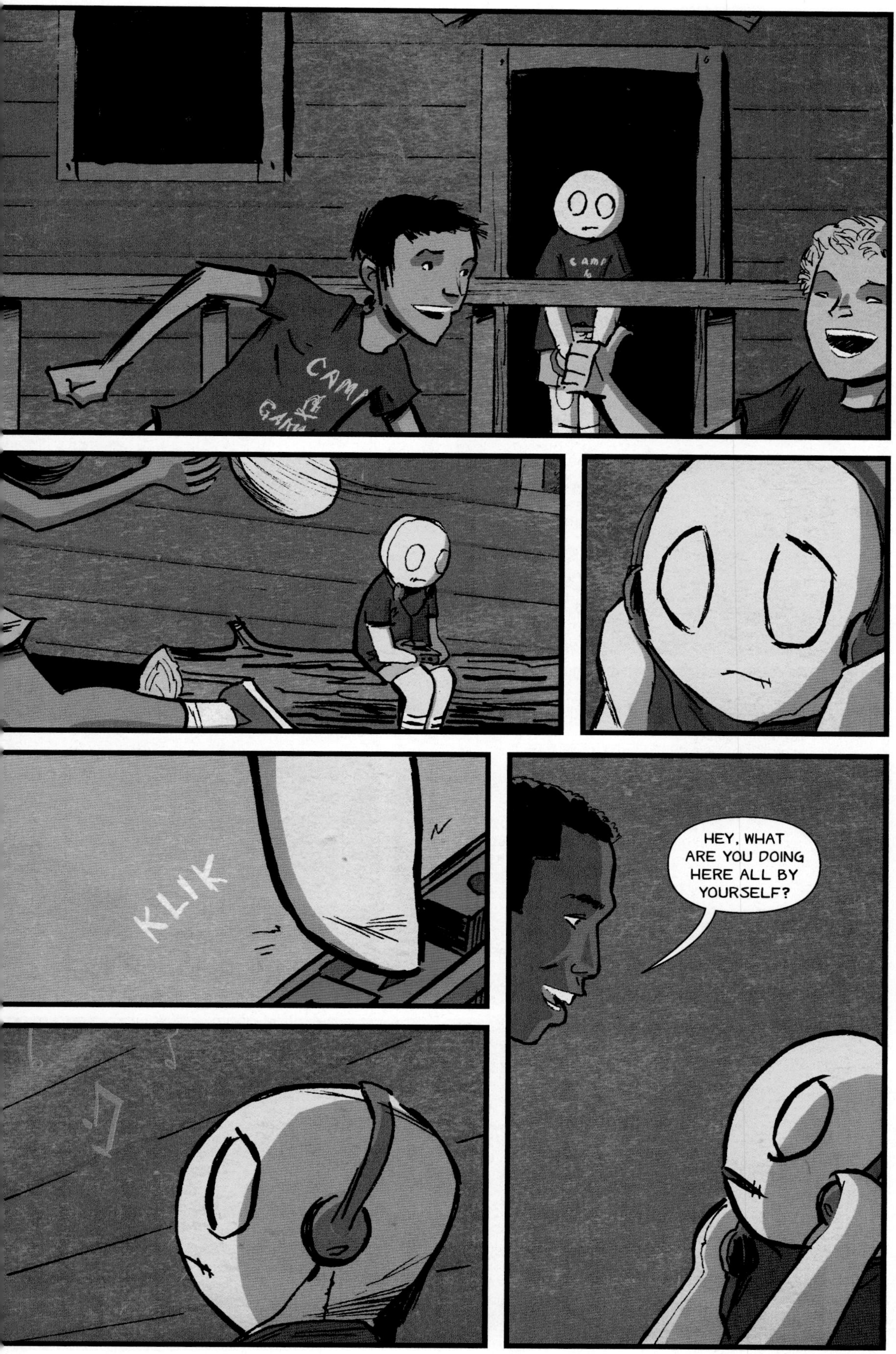
KLIK
HEY, WHAT ARE YOU DOING HERE ALL BY YOURSELF?

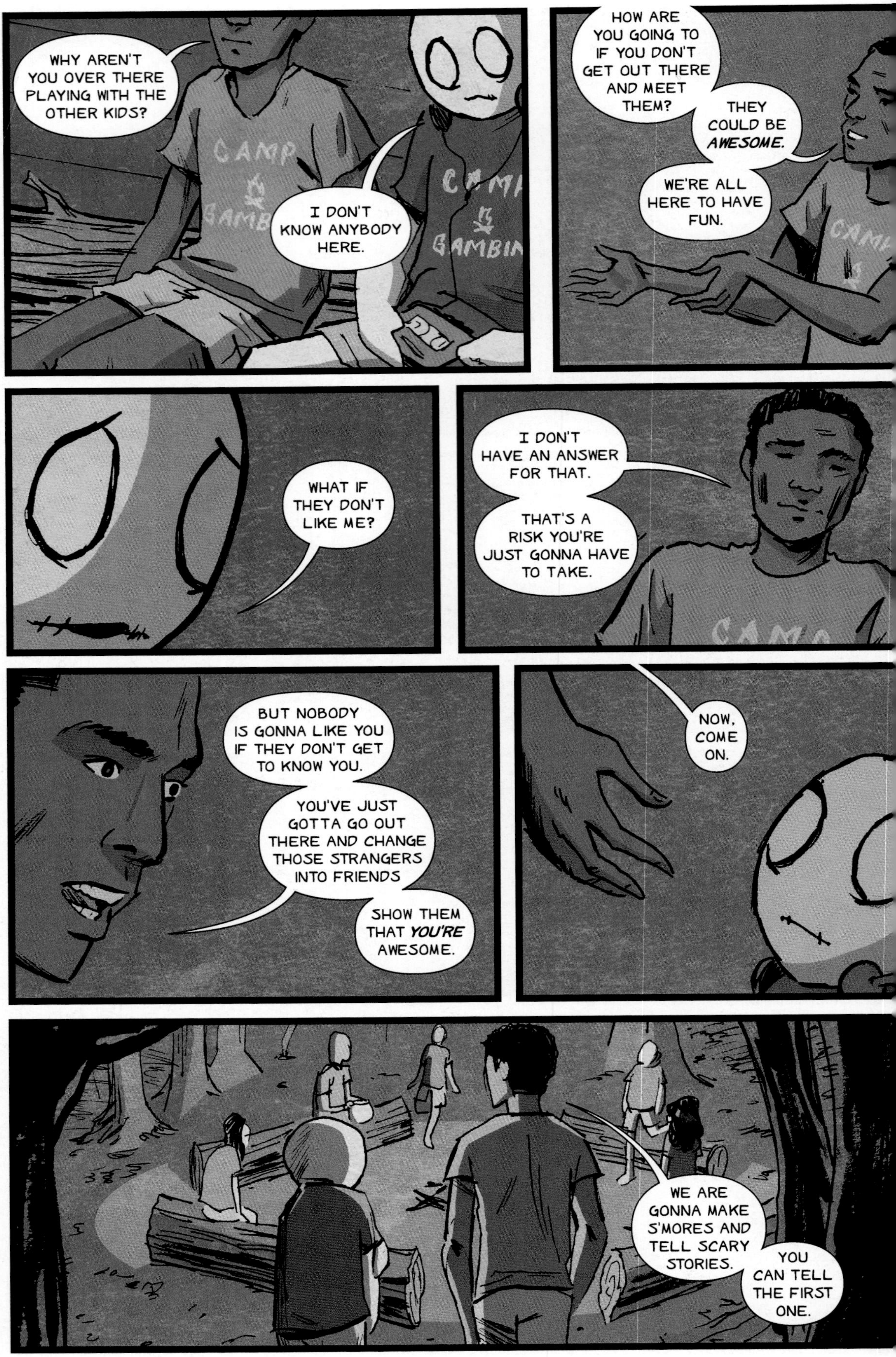
WHY AREN'T YOU OVER THERE PLAYING WITH THE OTHER KIDS?
CAMP GAMBINO
I DON'T KNOW ANYBODY HERE.
HOW ARE YOU GOING TO IF YOU DON'T GET OUT THERE AND MEET THEM?
THEY COULD BE *AWESOME.*
WE'RE ALL HERE TO HAVE FUN.
WHAT IF THEY DON'T LIKE ME?
I DON'T HAVE AN ANSWER FOR THAT.
THAT'S A RISK YOU'RE JUST GONNA HAVE TO TAKE.
BUT NOBODY IS GONNA LIKE YOU IF THEY DON'T GET TO KNOW YOU.
YOU'VE JUST GOTTA GO OUT THERE AND CHANGE THOSE STRANGERS INTO FRIENDS
SHOW THEM THAT *YOU'RE* AWESOME.
NOW, COME ON.
WE ARE GONNA MAKE S'MORES AND TELL SCARY STORIES.
YOU CAN TELL THE FIRST ONE.

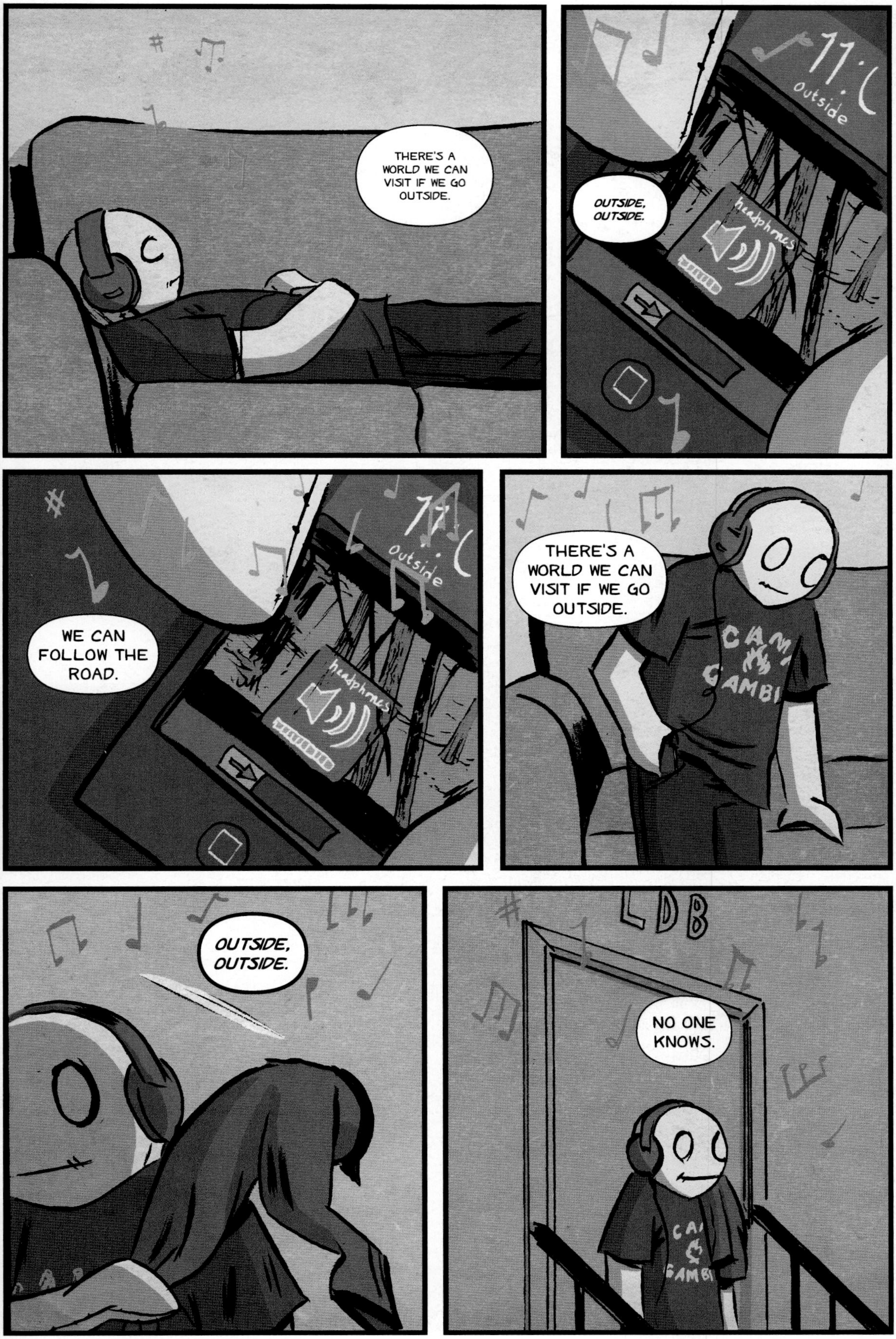
THERE'S A WORLD WE CAN VISIT IF WE GO OUTSIDE.
11:(
Outside
OUTSIDE, OUTSIDE.
headphones
WE CAN FOLLOW THE ROAD.
THERE'S A WORLD WE CAN VISIT IF WE GO OUTSIDE.
OUTSIDE, OUTSIDE.
LDB
NO ONE KNOWS.

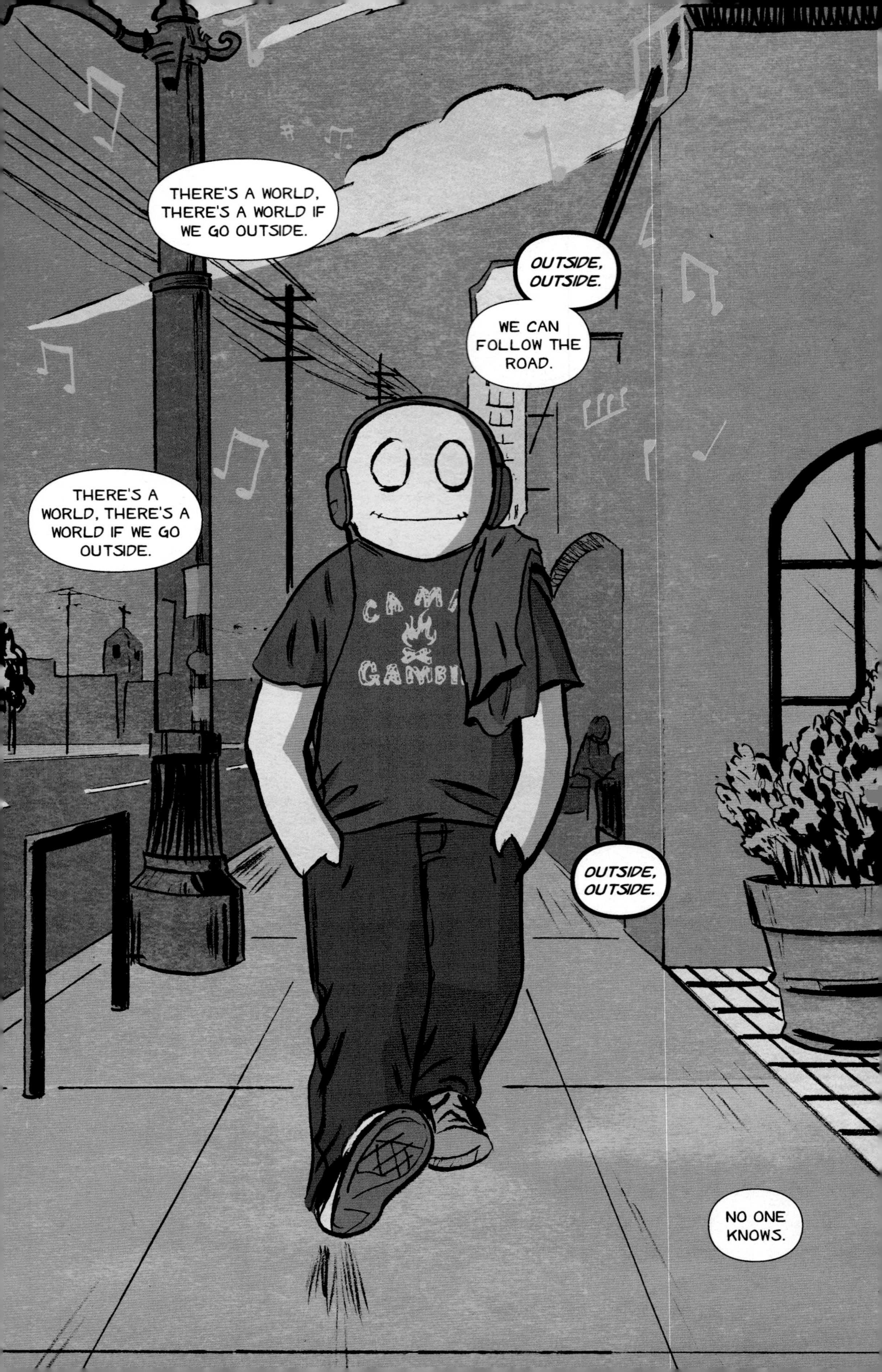
THERE'S A WORLD, THERE'S A WORLD IF WE GO OUTSIDE.
OUTSIDE, OUTSIDE.
WE CAN FOLLOW THE ROAD.
THERE'S A WORLD, THERE'S A WORLD IF WE GO OUTSIDE.
OUTSIDE, OUTSIDE.
NO ONE KNOWS.

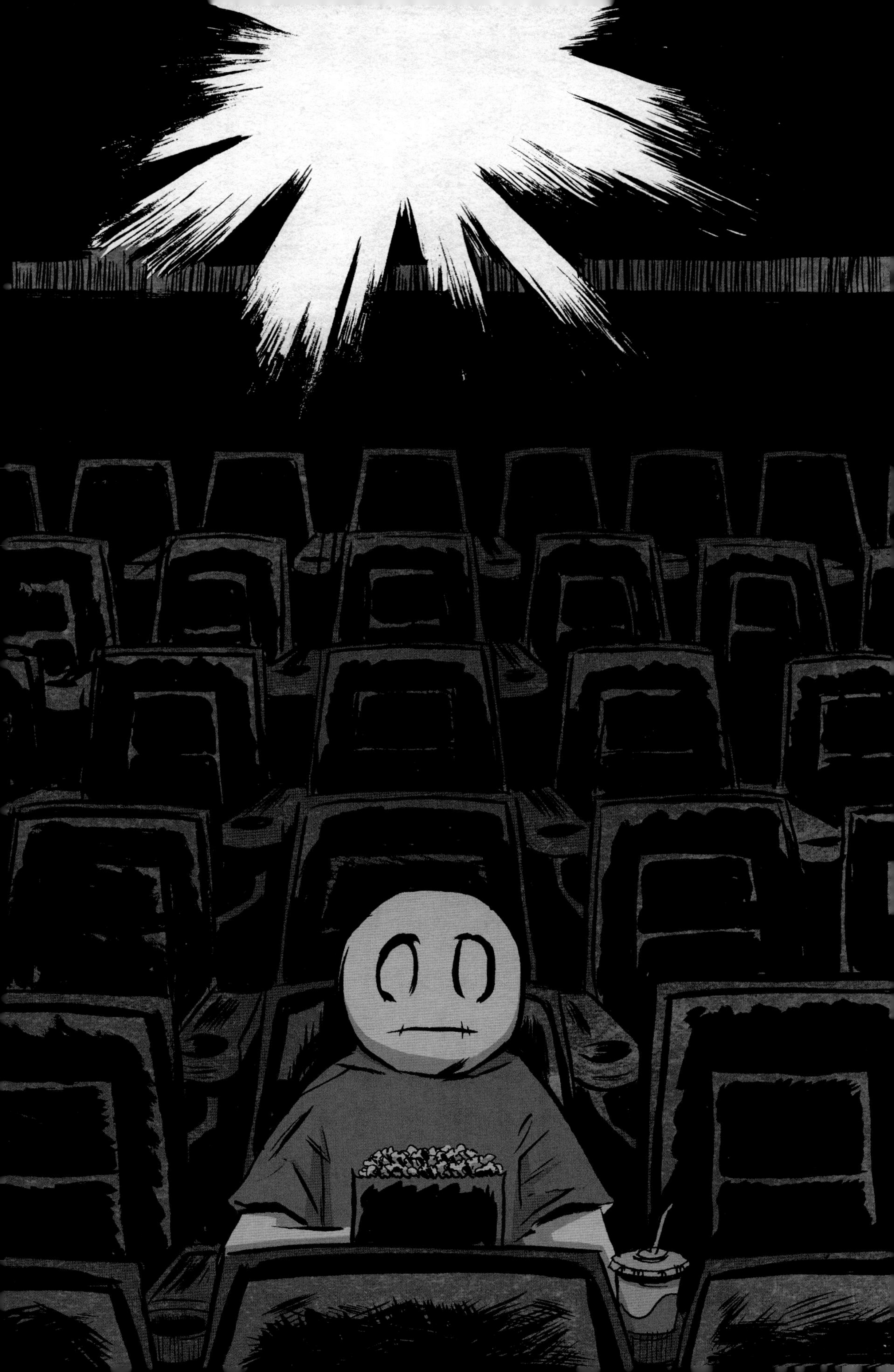

CHAPTER THREE:

"THREE SKETCHES OF A WORKPLACE CRUSH"

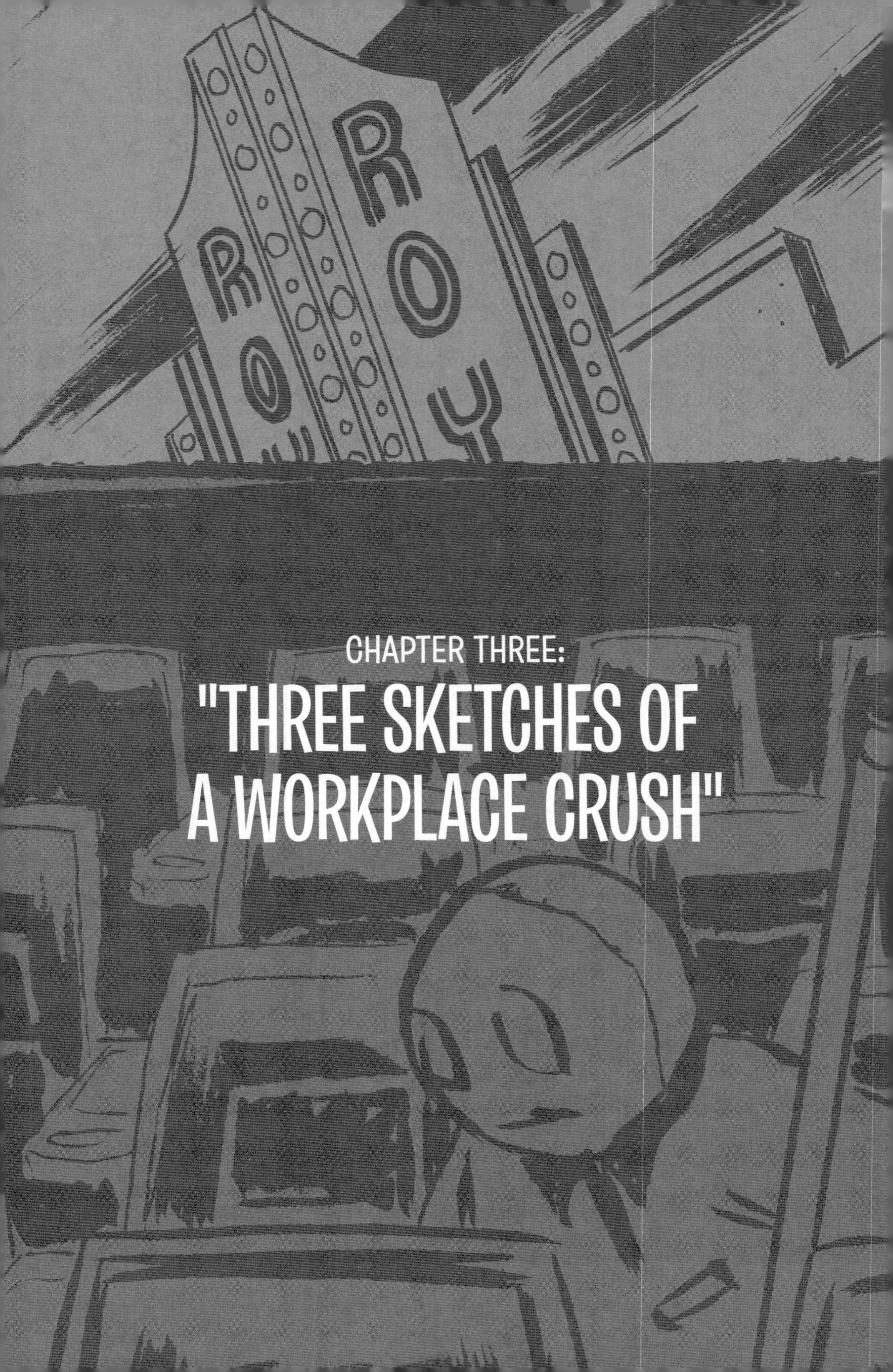

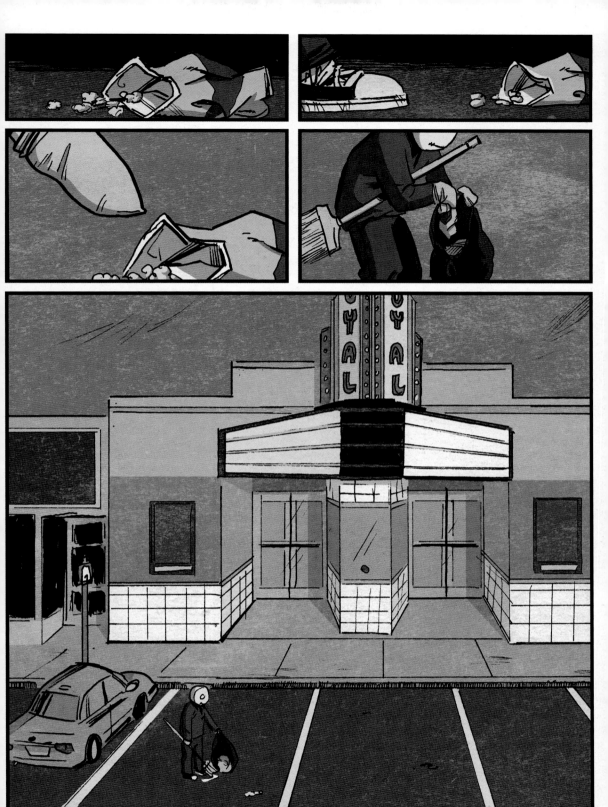

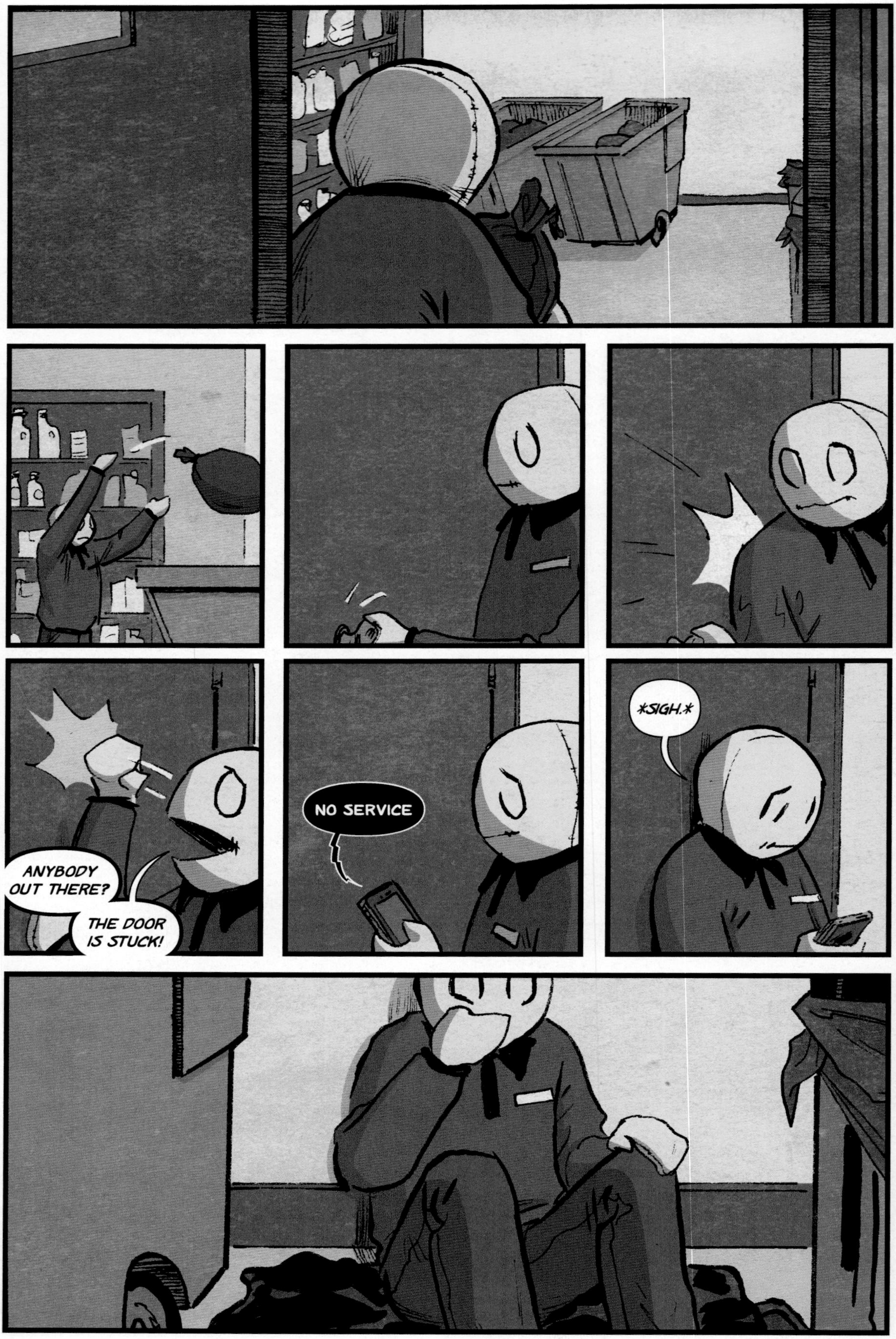
ANYBODY OUT THERE?
THE DOOR IS STUCK!
NO SERVICE
SIGH.

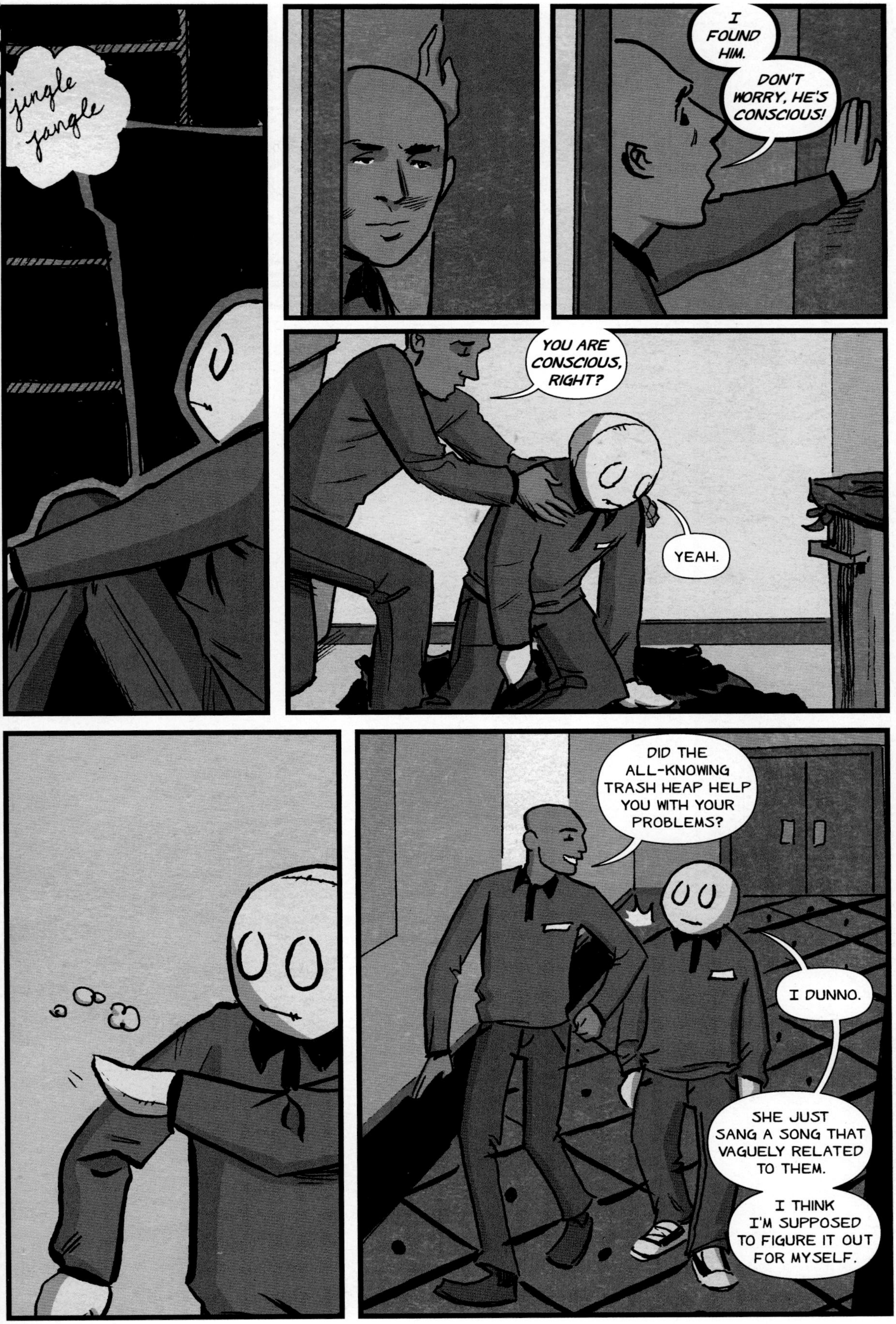
jingle jangle
I FOUND HIM.
DON'T WORRY, HE'S CONSCIOUS!
YOU ARE CONSCIOUS, RIGHT?
YEAH.
DID THE ALL-KNOWING TRASH HEAP HELP YOU WITH YOUR PROBLEMS?
I DUNNO.
SHE JUST SANG A SONG THAT VAGUELY RELATED TO THEM.
I THINK I'M SUPPOSED TO FIGURE IT OUT FOR MYSELF.

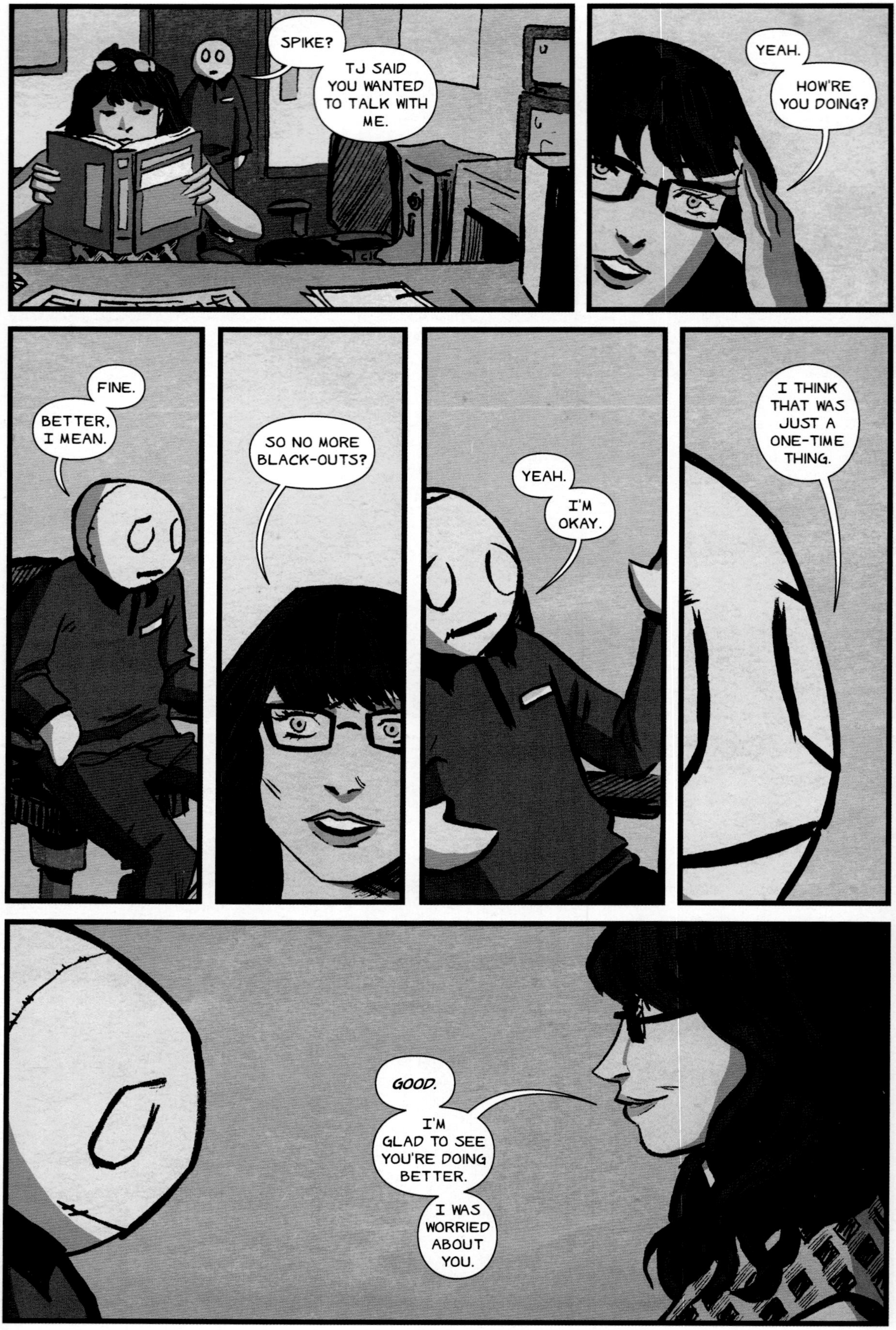
SPIKE?
TJ SAID YOU WANTED TO TALK WITH ME.
YEAH.
HOW'RE YOU DOING?
FINE.
BETTER, I MEAN.
SO NO MORE BLACK-OUTS?
YEAH.
I'M OKAY.
I THINK THAT WAS JUST A ONE-TIME THING.
GOOD.
I'M GLAD TO SEE YOU'RE DOING BETTER.
I WAS WORRIED ABOUT YOU.

IS THAT ALL?

I SHOULD PROBABLY GO HELP CLEAN THEATRE SEVEN.

THANKS FOR GETTING ME HOME THE OTHER NIGHT.

NO PROBLEM.

I'M JUST GLAD YOU'RE ALRIGHT.

SNF
SNF

GET STUCK IN THE TRASH CLOSET?

YEAH...

WE'RE NOT SUPPOSED TO GIVE YOU MORE THAN ONE OF THESE.

SO YOU DIDN'T GET THIS FROM ME OKAY?

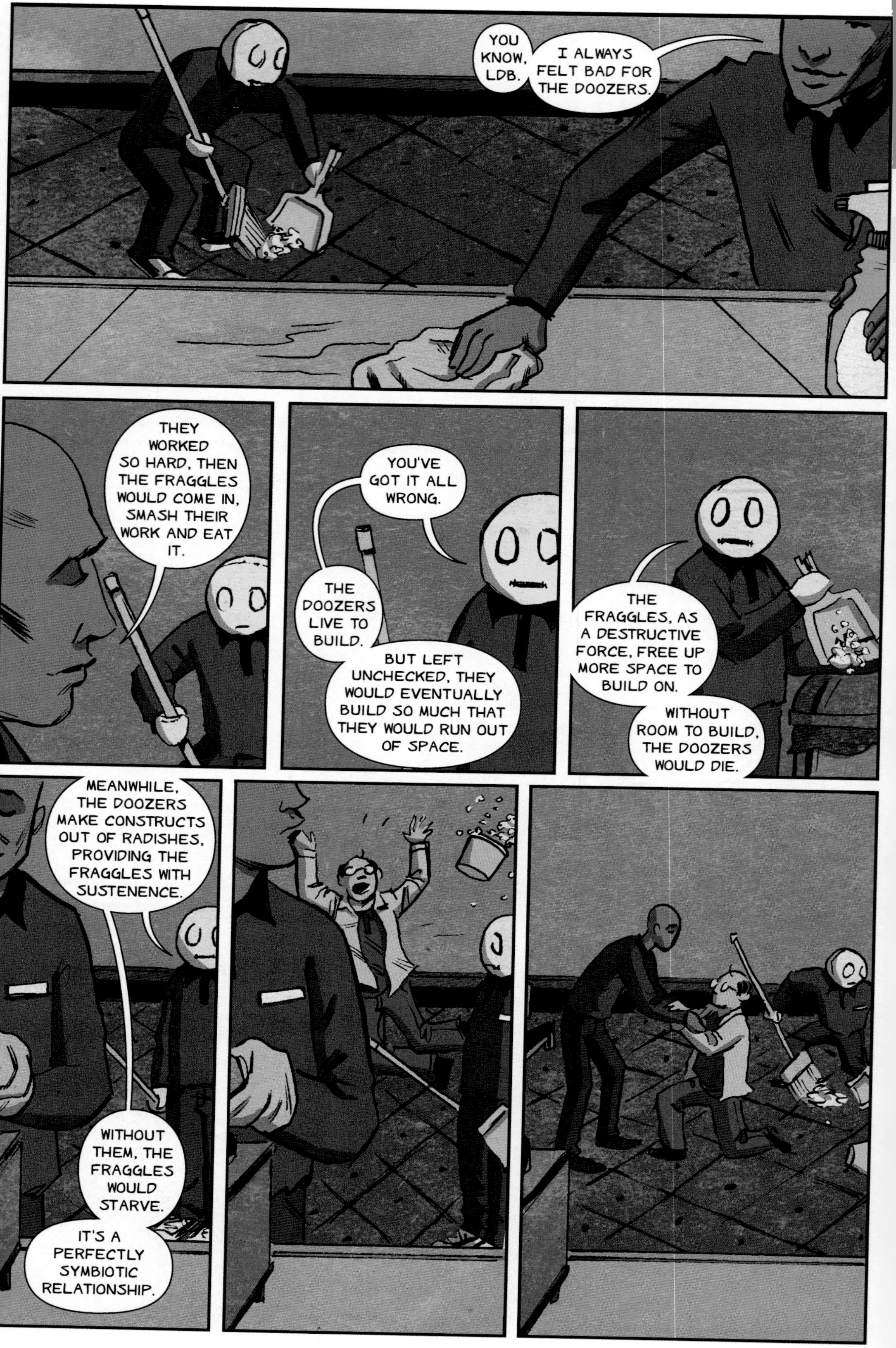
YOU KNOW, LDB.
I ALWAYS FELT BAD FOR THE DOOZERS.
THEY WORKED SO HARD, THEN THE FRAGGLES WOULD COME IN, SMASH THEIR WORK AND EAT IT.
YOU'VE GOT IT ALL WRONG.
THE DOOZERS LIVE TO BUILD.
BUT LEFT UNCHECKED, THEY WOULD EVENTUALLY BUILD SO MUCH THAT THEY WOULD RUN OUT OF SPACE.
THE FRAGGLES, AS A DESTRUCTIVE FORCE, FREE UP MORE SPACE TO BUILD ON.
WITHOUT ROOM TO BUILD, THE DOOZERS WOULD DIE.
MEANWHILE, THE DOOZERS MAKE CONSTRUCTS OUT OF RADISHES, PROVIDING THE FRAGGLES WITH SUSTENENCE.
WITHOUT THEM, THE FRAGGLES WOULD STARVE.
IT'S A PERFECTLY SYMBIOTIC RELATIONSHIP.

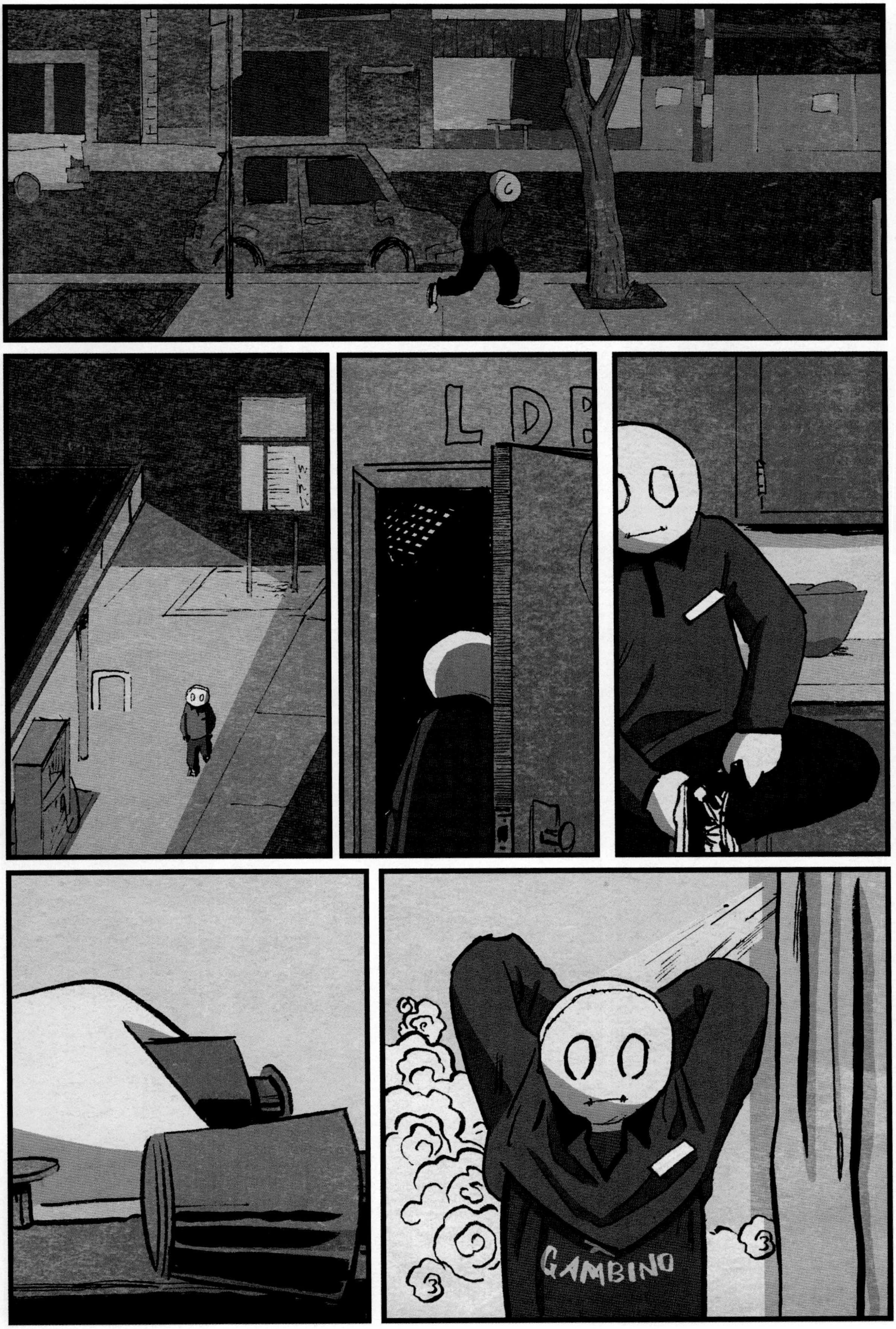
GAMBINO

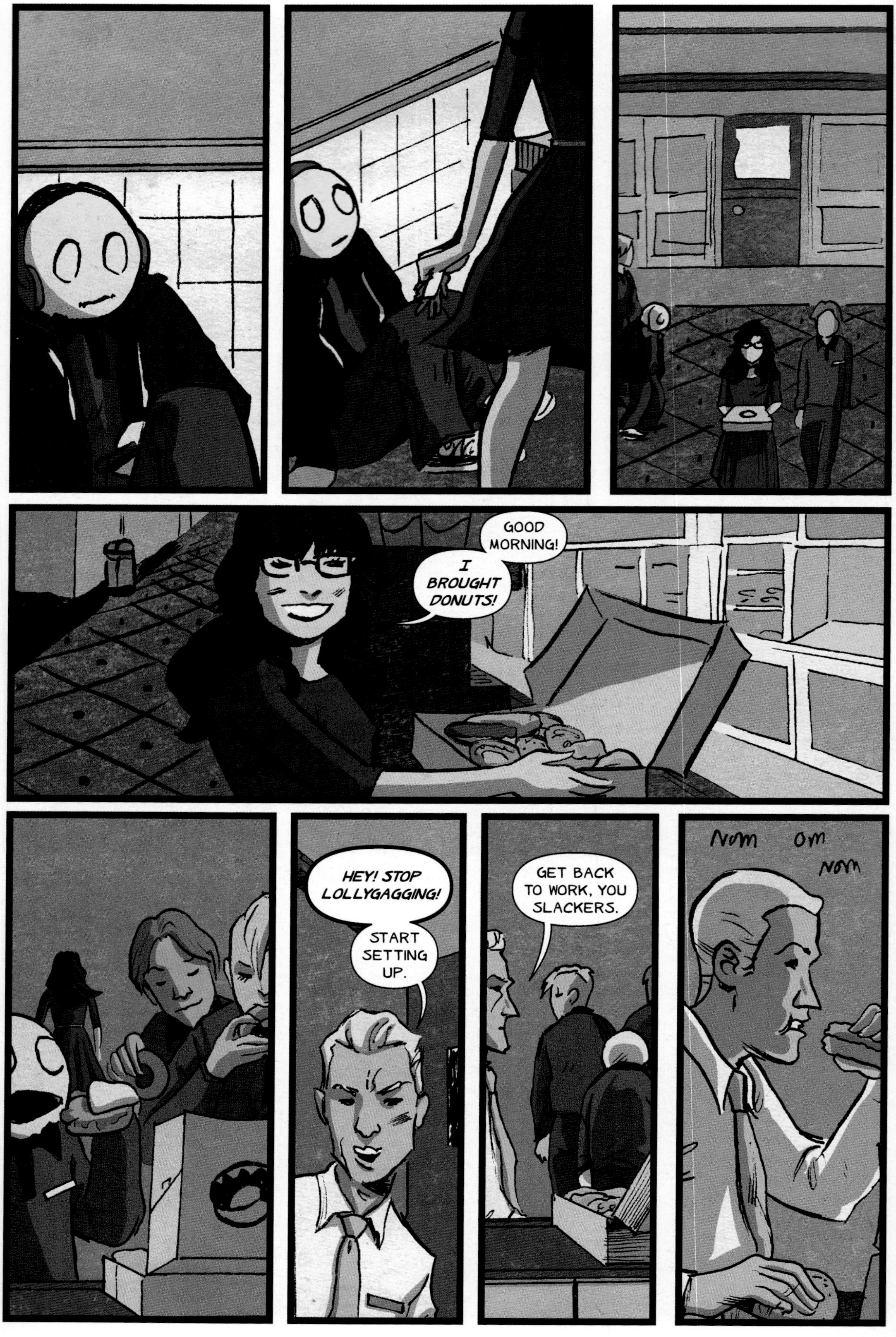
GOOD MORNING!
I BROUGHT DONUTS!
HEY! STOP LOLLYGAGGING!
START SETTING UP.
GET BACK TO WORK, YOU SLACKERS.
Nom om Nom

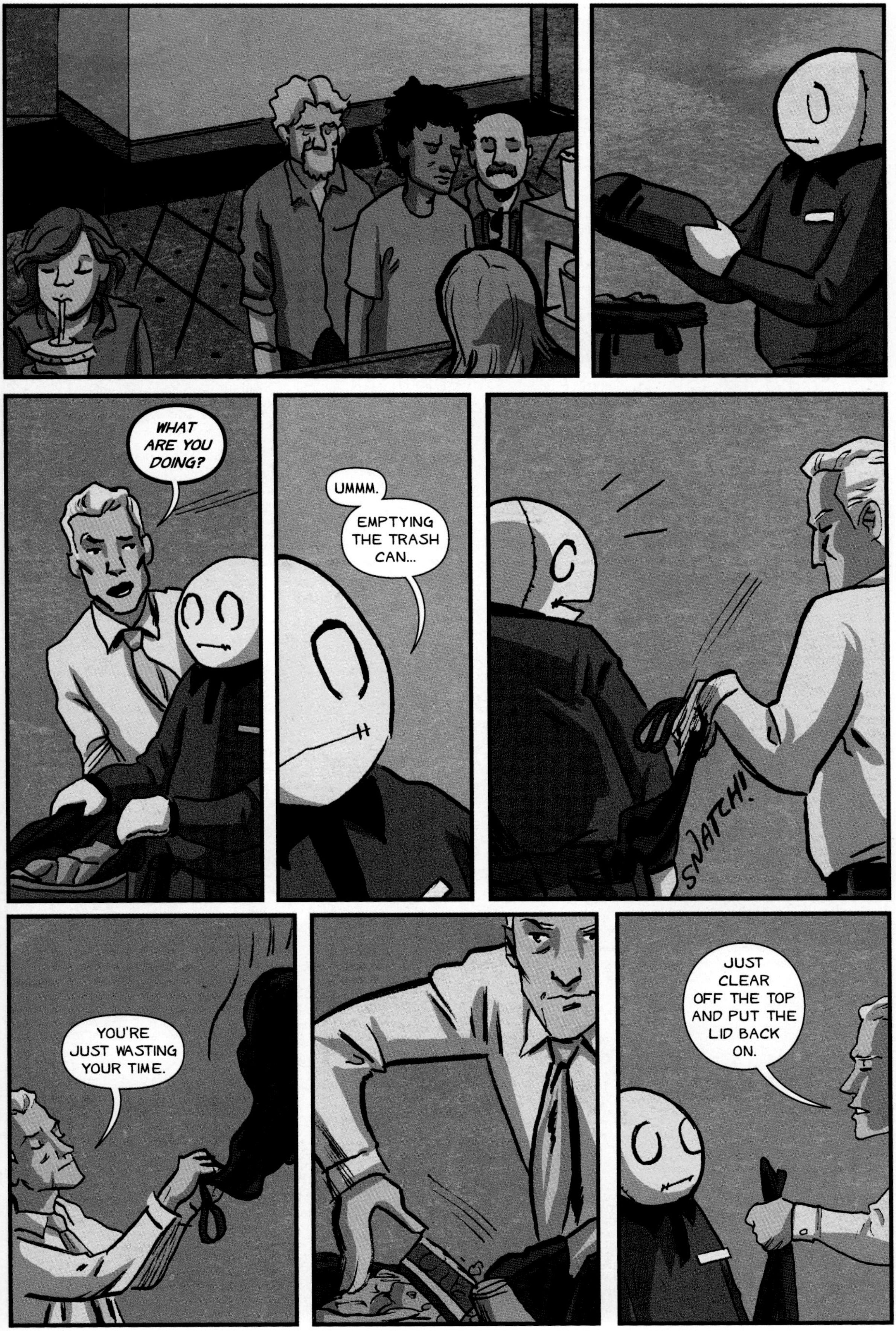
WHAT ARE YOU DOING?
UMMM.
EMPTYING THE TRASH CAN...
SNATCH!
YOU'RE JUST WASTING YOUR TIME.
JUST CLEAR OFF THE TOP AND PUT THE LID BACK ON.

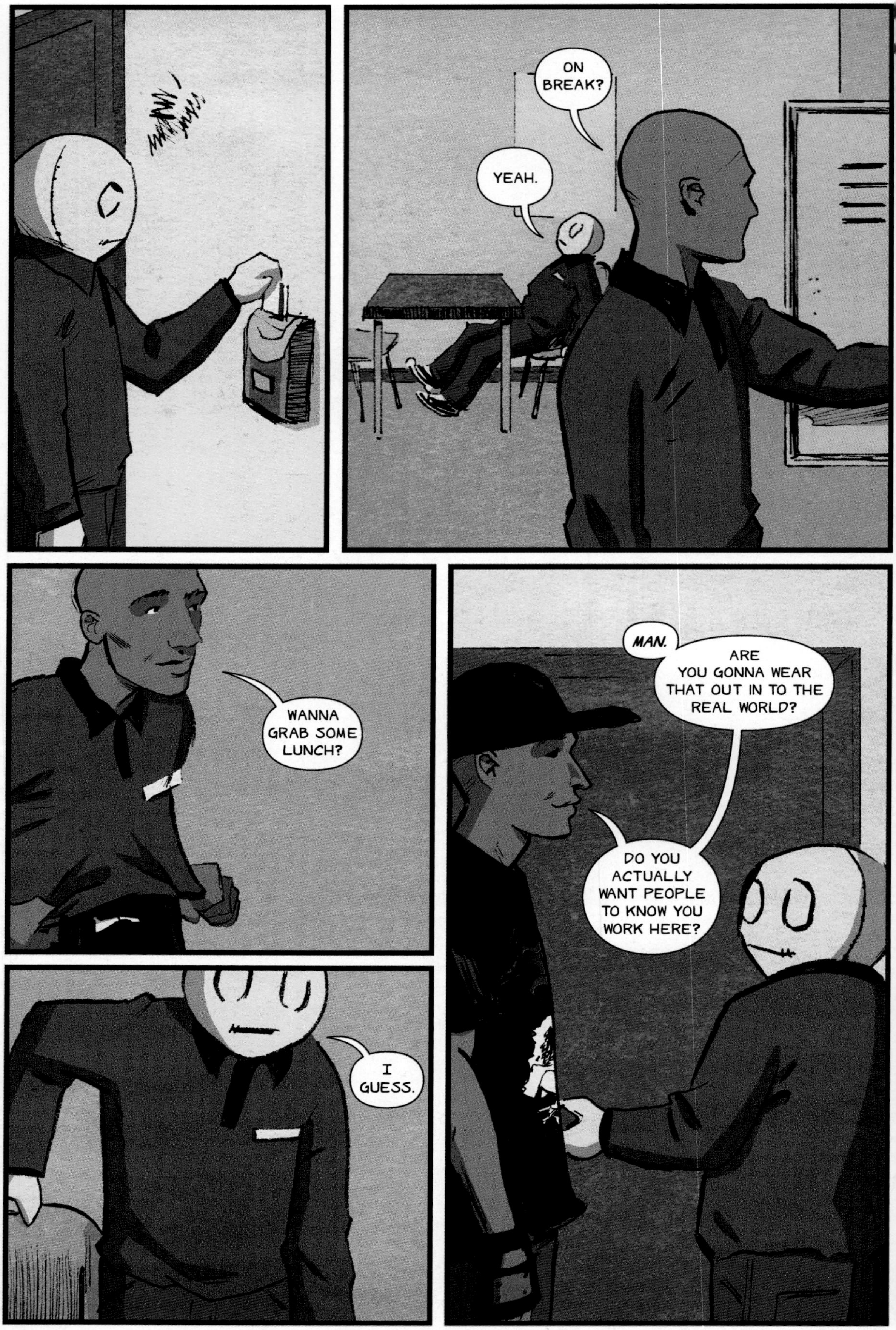
ON BREAK?
YEAH.
WANNA GRAB SOME LUNCH?
I GUESS.
MAN.
ARE YOU GONNA WEAR THAT OUT IN TO THE REAL WORLD?
DO YOU ACTUALLY WANT PEOPLE TO KNOW YOU WORK HERE?

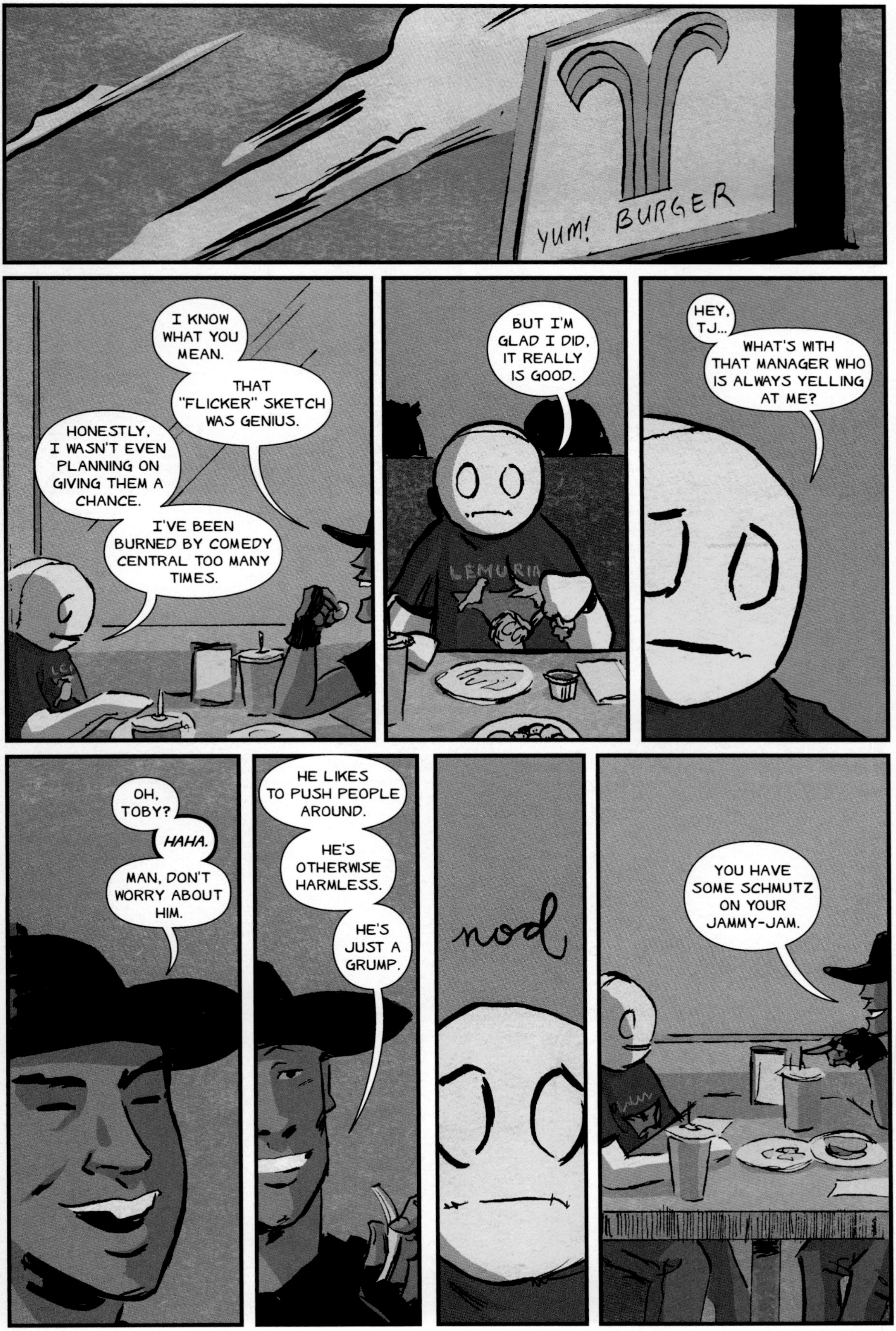
YUM! BURGER
I KNOW WHAT YOU MEAN.
THAT "FLICKER" SKETCH WAS GENIUS.
HONESTLY, I WASN'T EVEN PLANNING ON GIVING THEM A CHANCE.
I'VE BEEN BURNED BY COMEDY CENTRAL TOO MANY TIMES.
LEMURIA
BUT I'M GLAD I DID, IT REALLY IS GOOD.
HEY, TJ...
WHAT'S WITH THAT MANAGER WHO IS ALWAYS YELLING AT ME?
OH, TOBY?
HAHA.
MAN, DON'T WORRY ABOUT HIM.
HE LIKES TO PUSH PEOPLE AROUND.
HE'S OTHERWISE HARMLESS.
HE'S JUST A GRUMP.
nod
YOU HAVE SOME SCHMUTZ ON YOUR JAMMY-JAM.

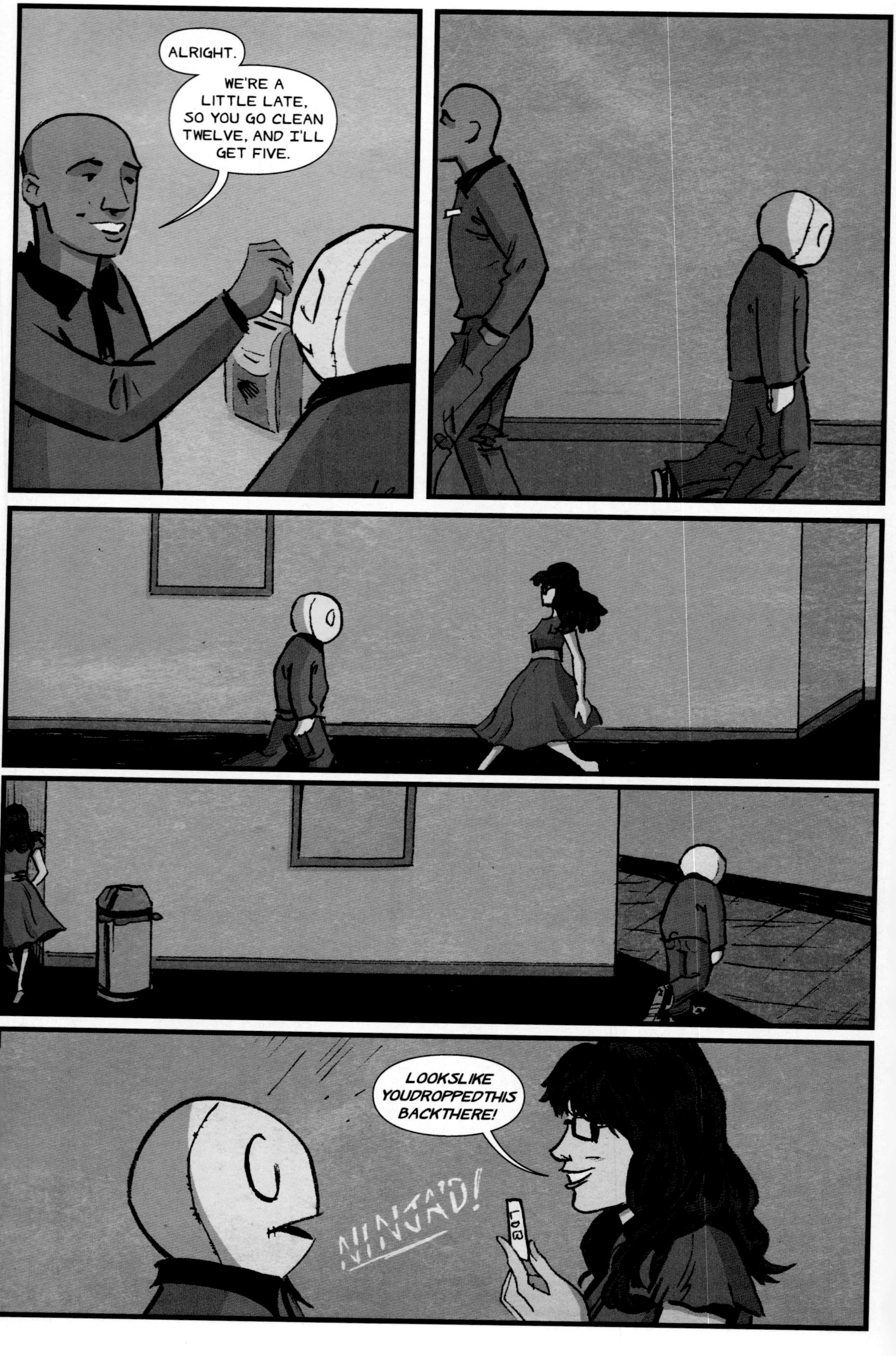
ALRIGHT.
WE'RE A LITTLE LATE, SO YOU GO CLEAN TWELVE, AND I'LL GET FIVE.
LOOKSLIKE YOUDROPPEDTHIS BACKTHERE!
NINJA'D!

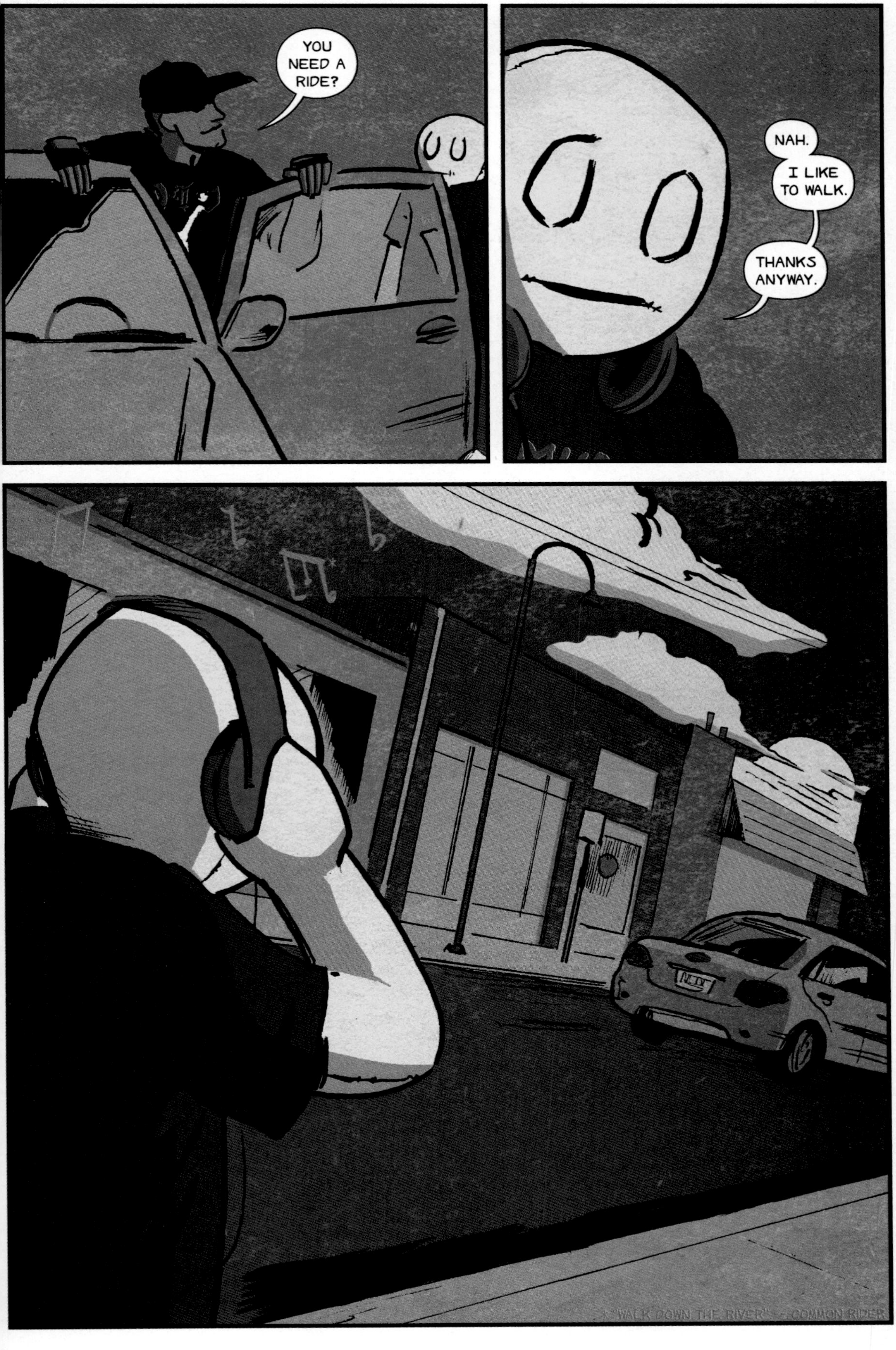
YOU NEED A RIDE?
NAH.
I LIKE TO WALK.
THANKS ANYWAY.
* "WALK DOWN THE RIVER" -- COMMON RIDER

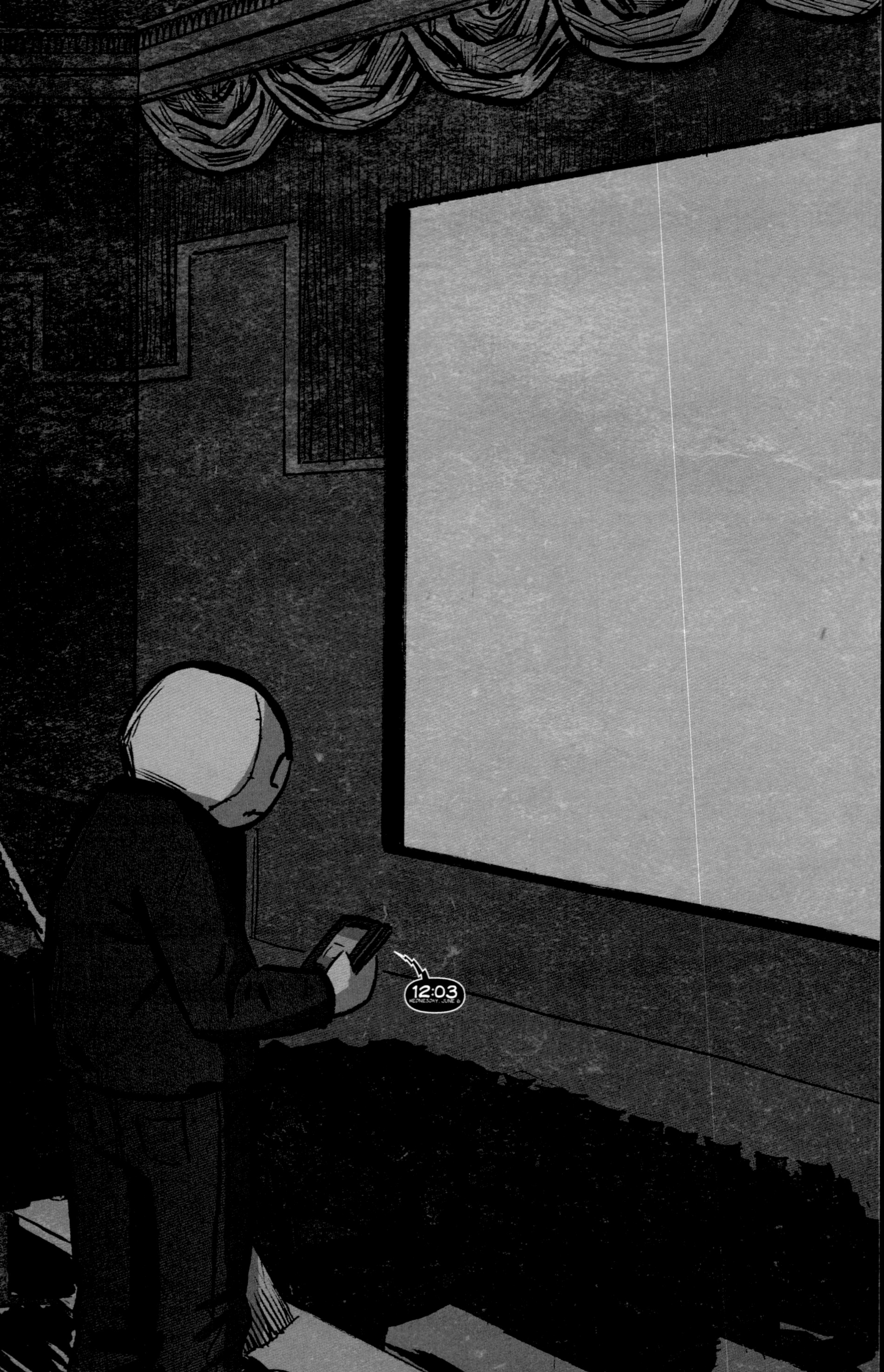
12:03
WEDNESDAY, JUNE 6

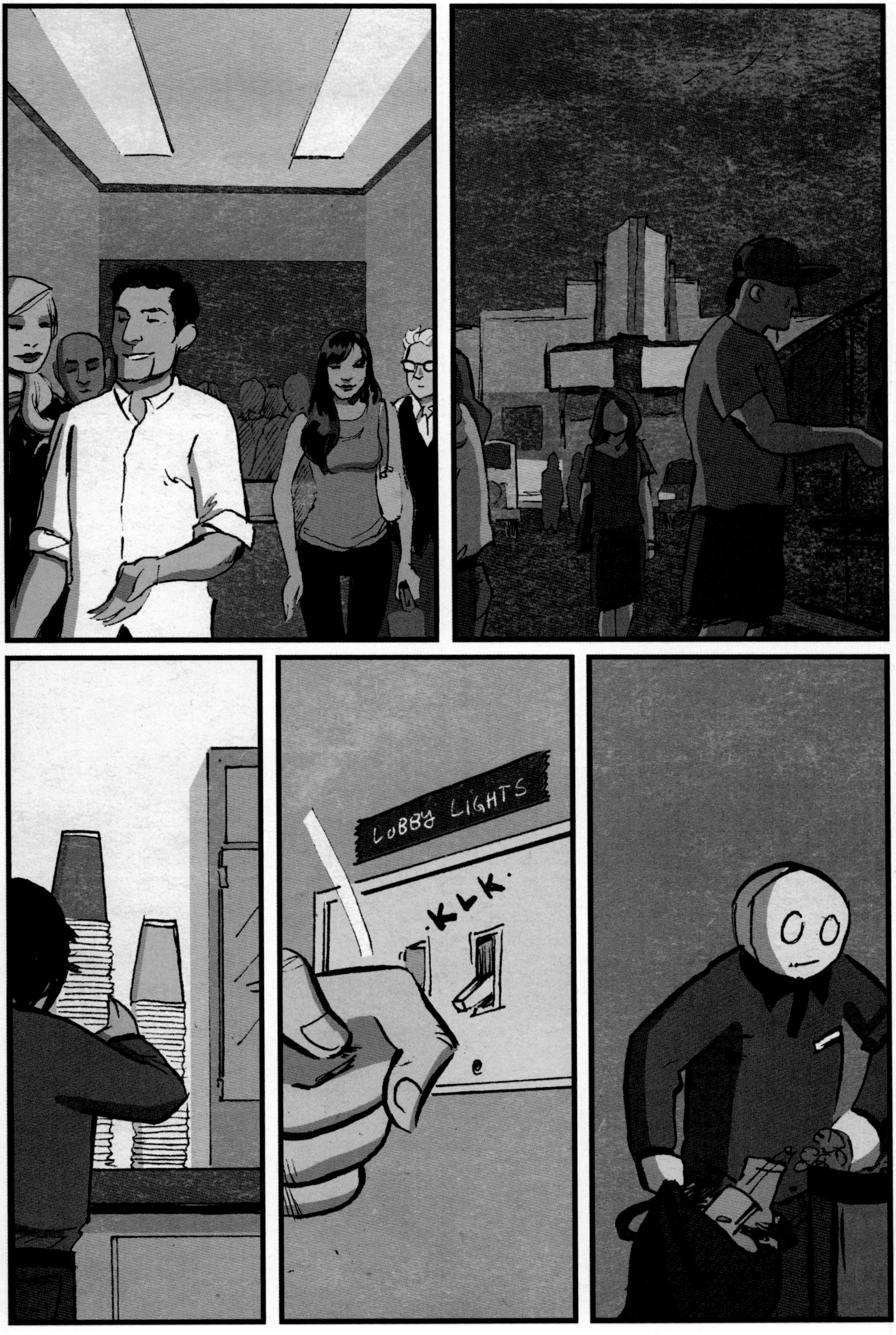
LOBBY LIGHTS
KLK

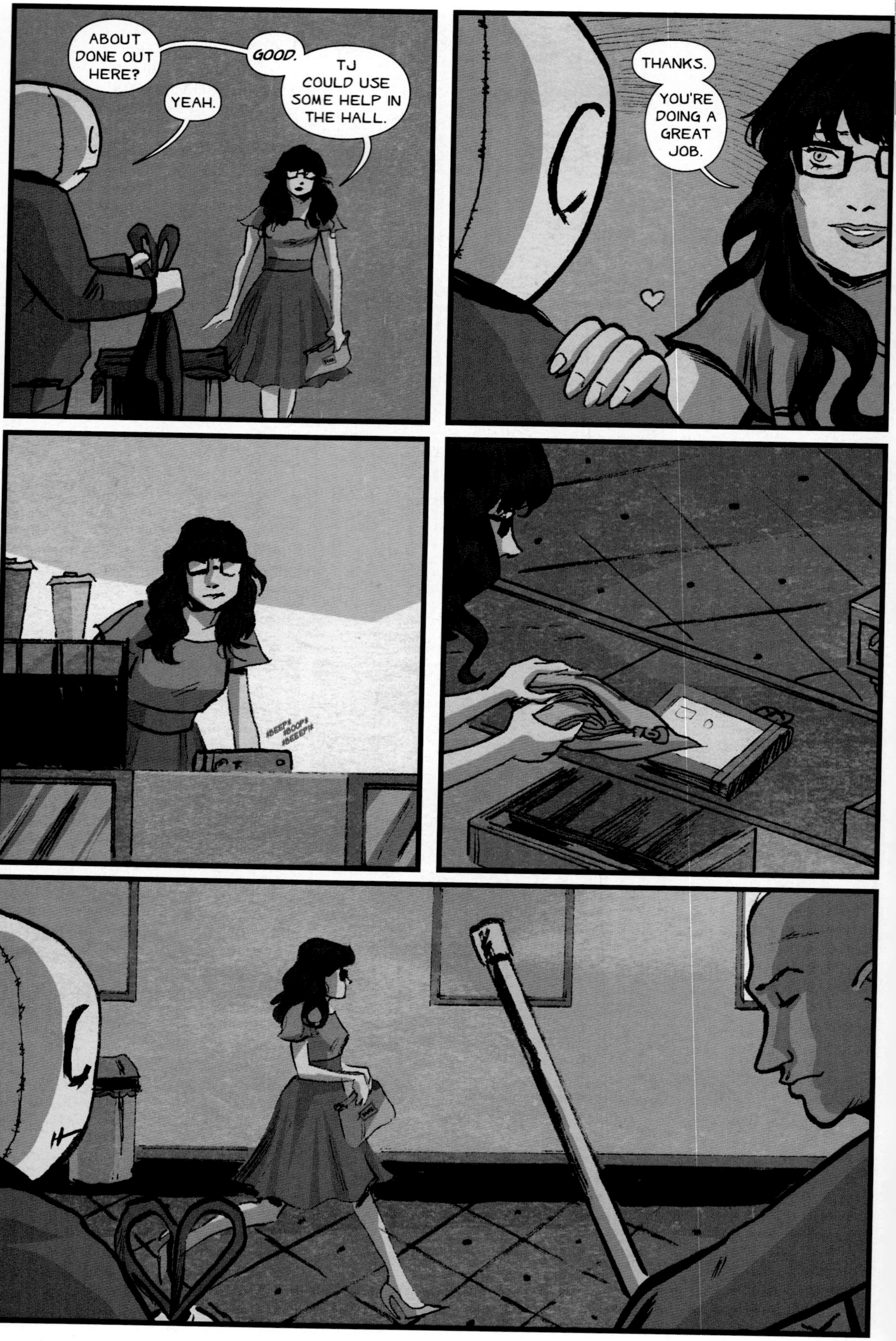
ABOUT DONE OUT HERE?
YEAH.
GOOD.
TJ COULD USE SOME HELP IN THE HALL.
THANKS.
YOU'RE DOING A GREAT JOB.
BEEP
BOOP
BEEEP

HUH?

OH YEAH, SURE.

NO PROBLEM.

THANKS, MAN!

I'LL TAKE SOLO DUMPSTER DUTY FOR YOU TOMORROW.

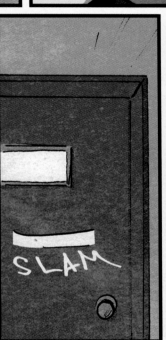

SLAM

HNH.

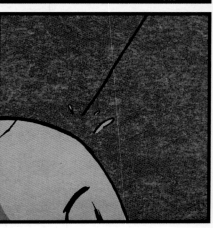

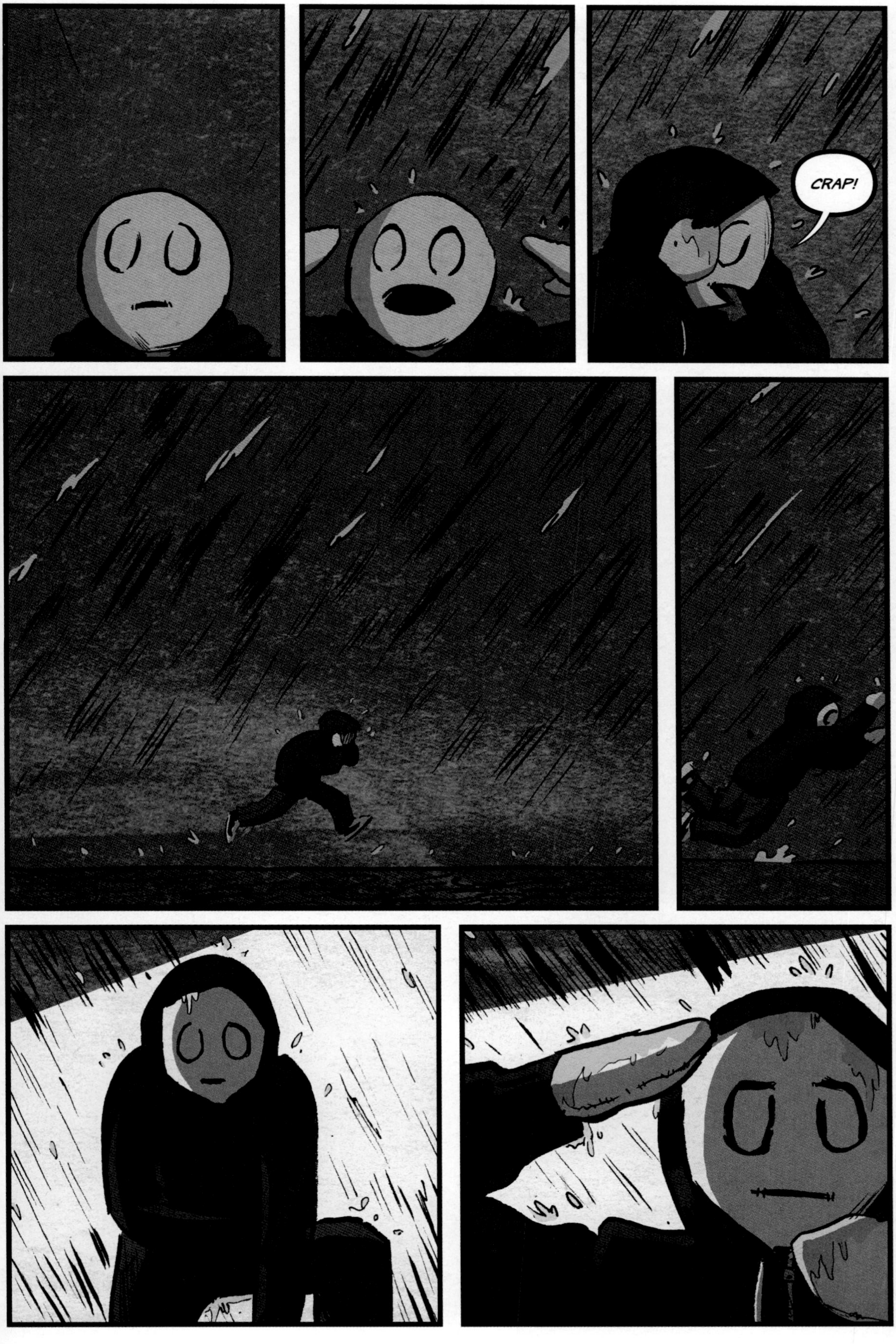
CRAP!

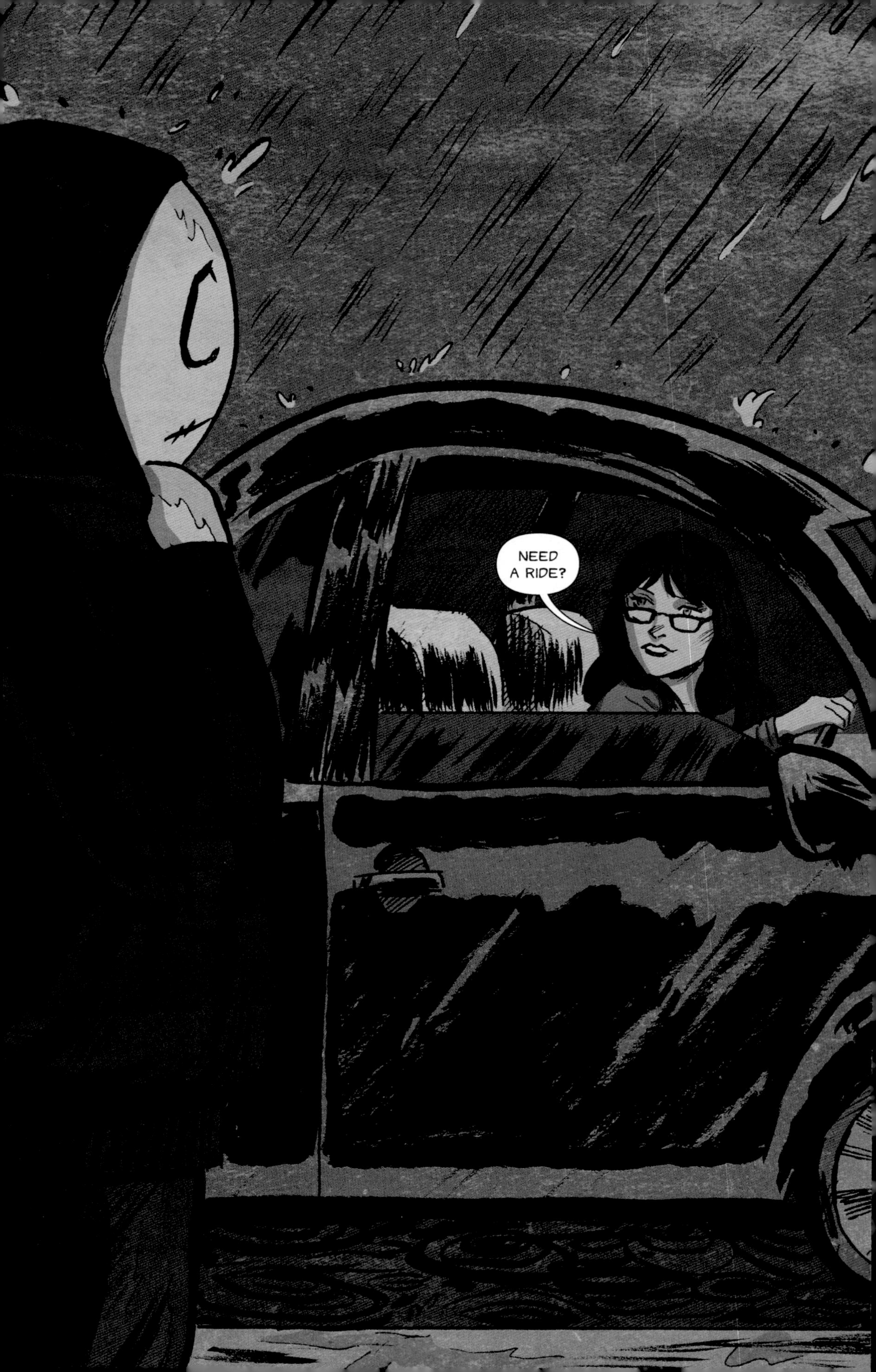
NEED A RIDE?

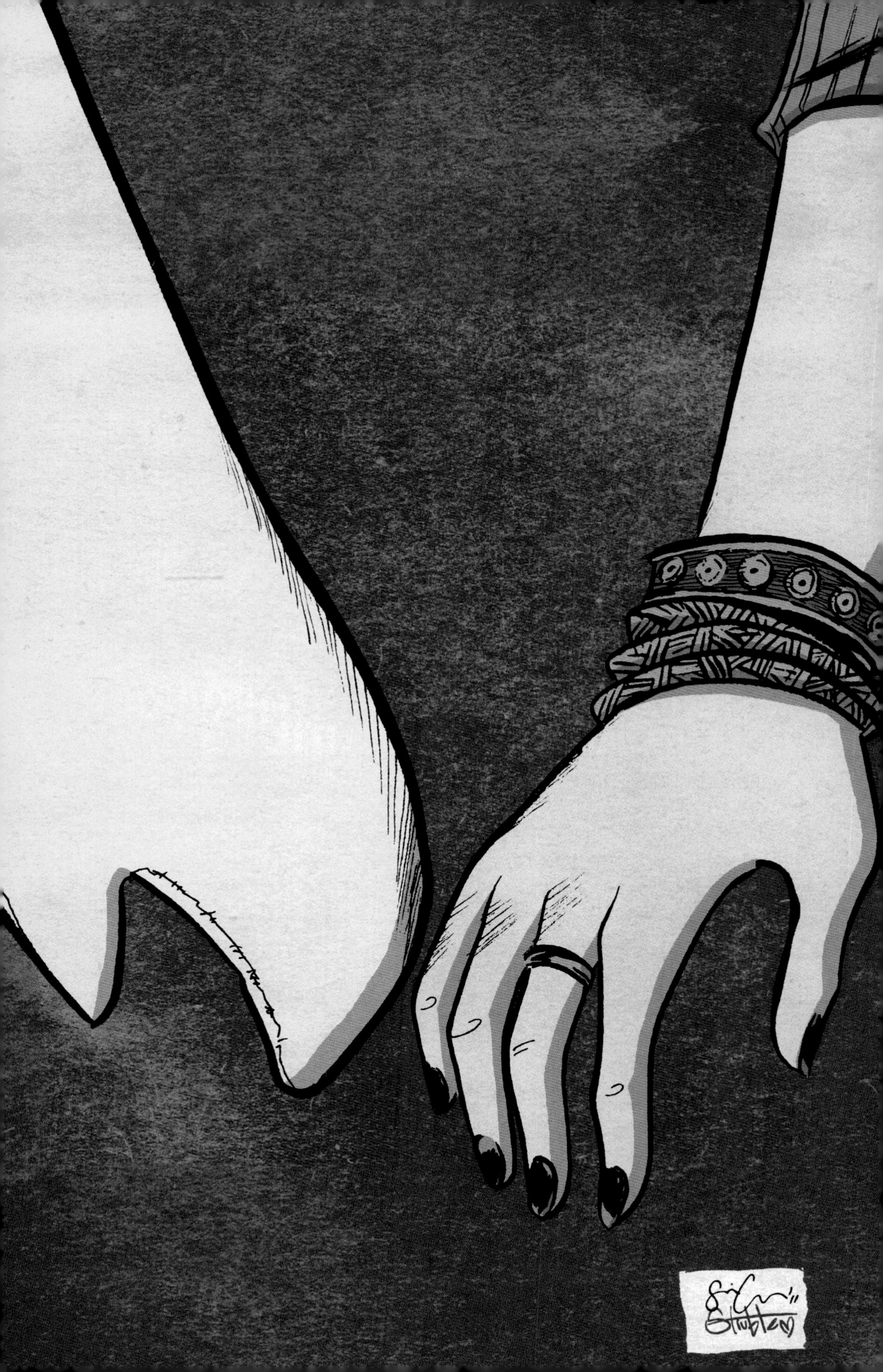

CHAPTER FOUR:
"BRAND NEW SHOES"

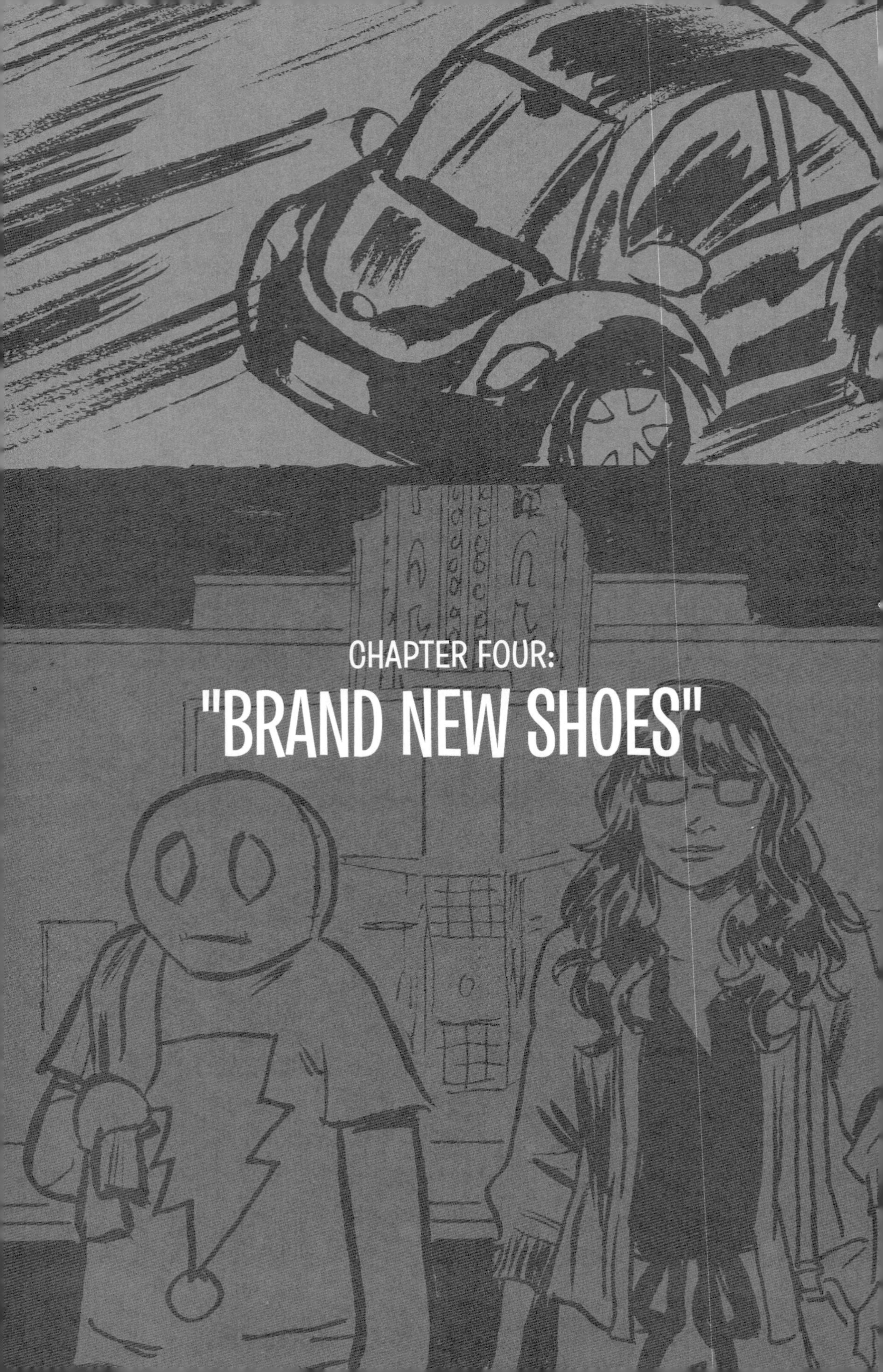

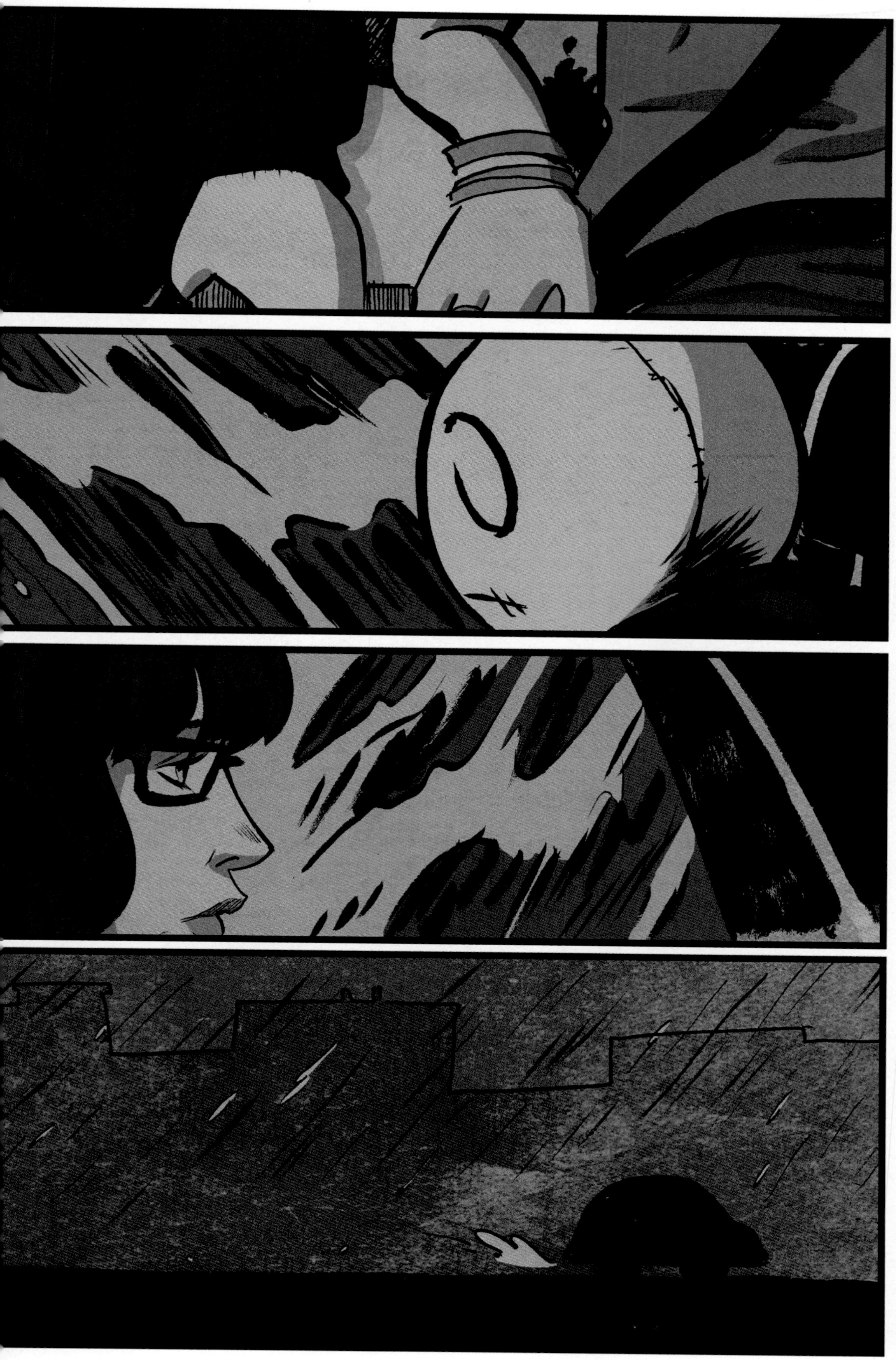

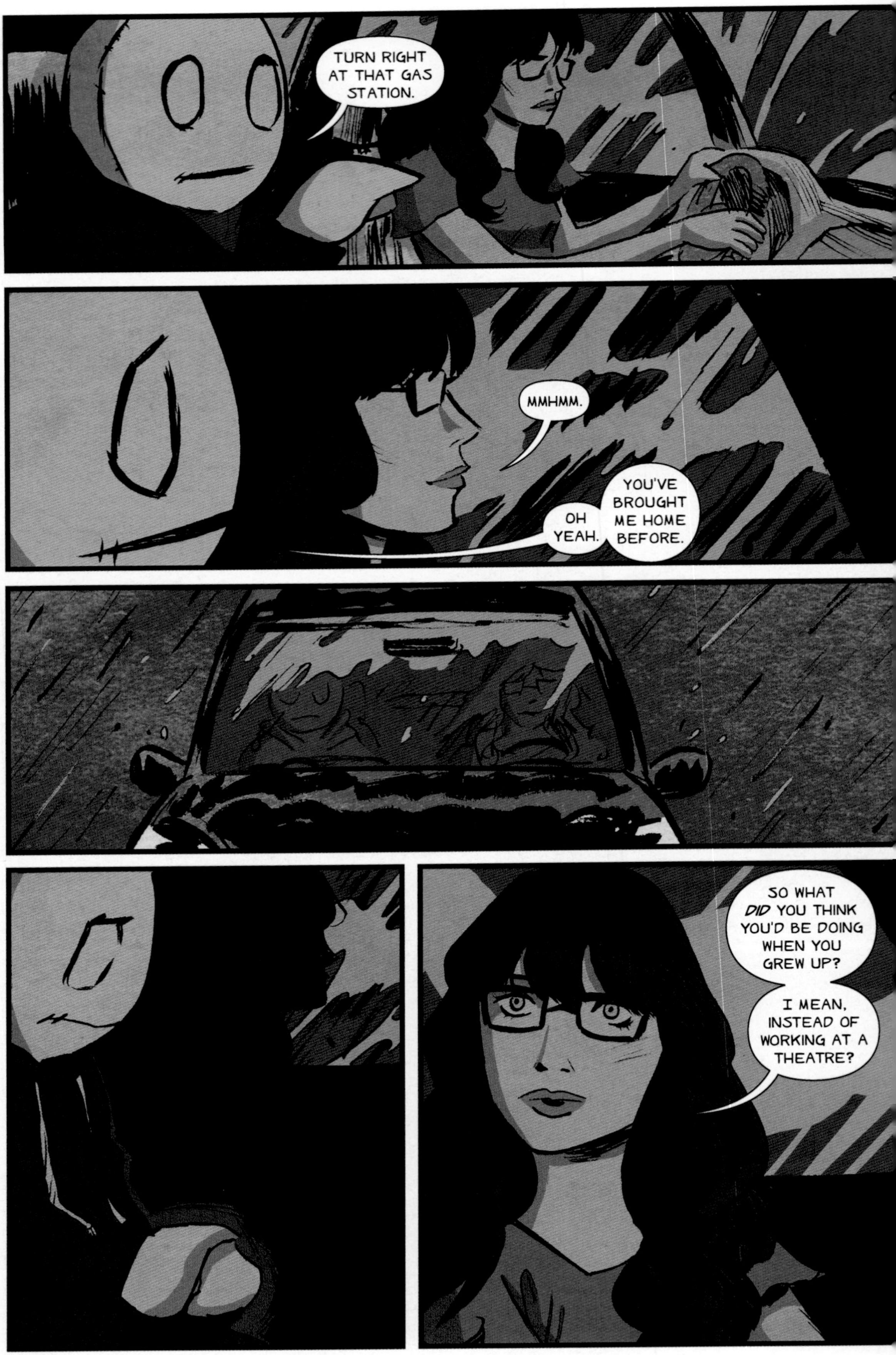
TURN RIGHT AT THAT GAS STATION.
MMHMM.
OH YEAH.
YOU'VE BROUGHT ME HOME BEFORE.
SO WHAT *DID* YOU THINK YOU'D BE DOING WHEN YOU GREW UP?
I MEAN, INSTEAD OF WORKING AT A THEATRE?

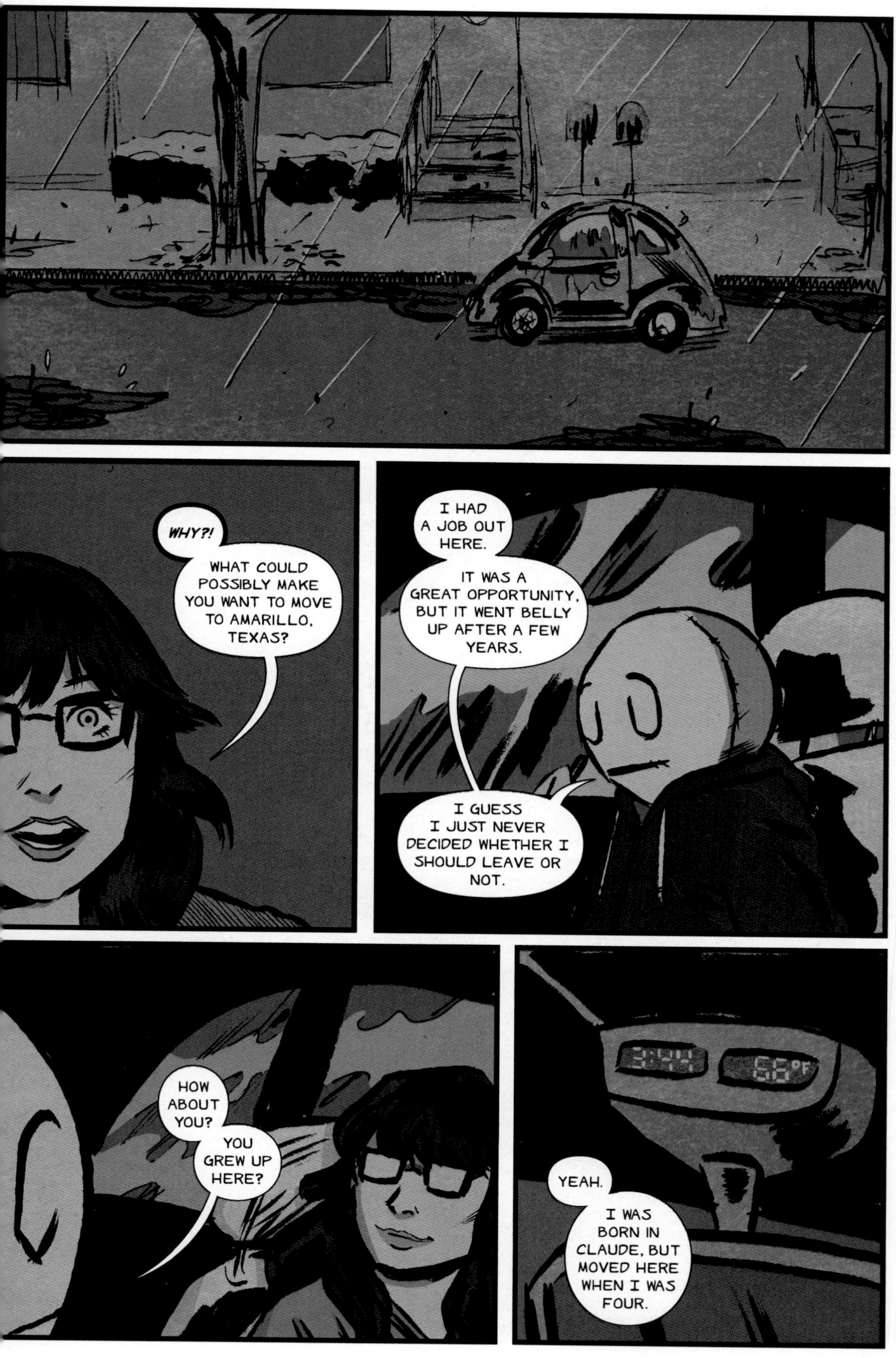
WHY?!
WHAT COULD POSSIBLY MAKE YOU WANT TO MOVE TO AMARILLO, TEXAS?
I HAD A JOB OUT HERE.
IT WAS A GREAT OPPORTUNITY, BUT IT WENT BELLY UP AFTER A FEW YEARS.
I GUESS I JUST NEVER DECIDED WHETHER I SHOULD LEAVE OR NOT.
HOW ABOUT YOU?
YOU GREW UP HERE?
YEAH.
I WAS BORN IN CLAUDE, BUT MOVED HERE WHEN I WAS FOUR.

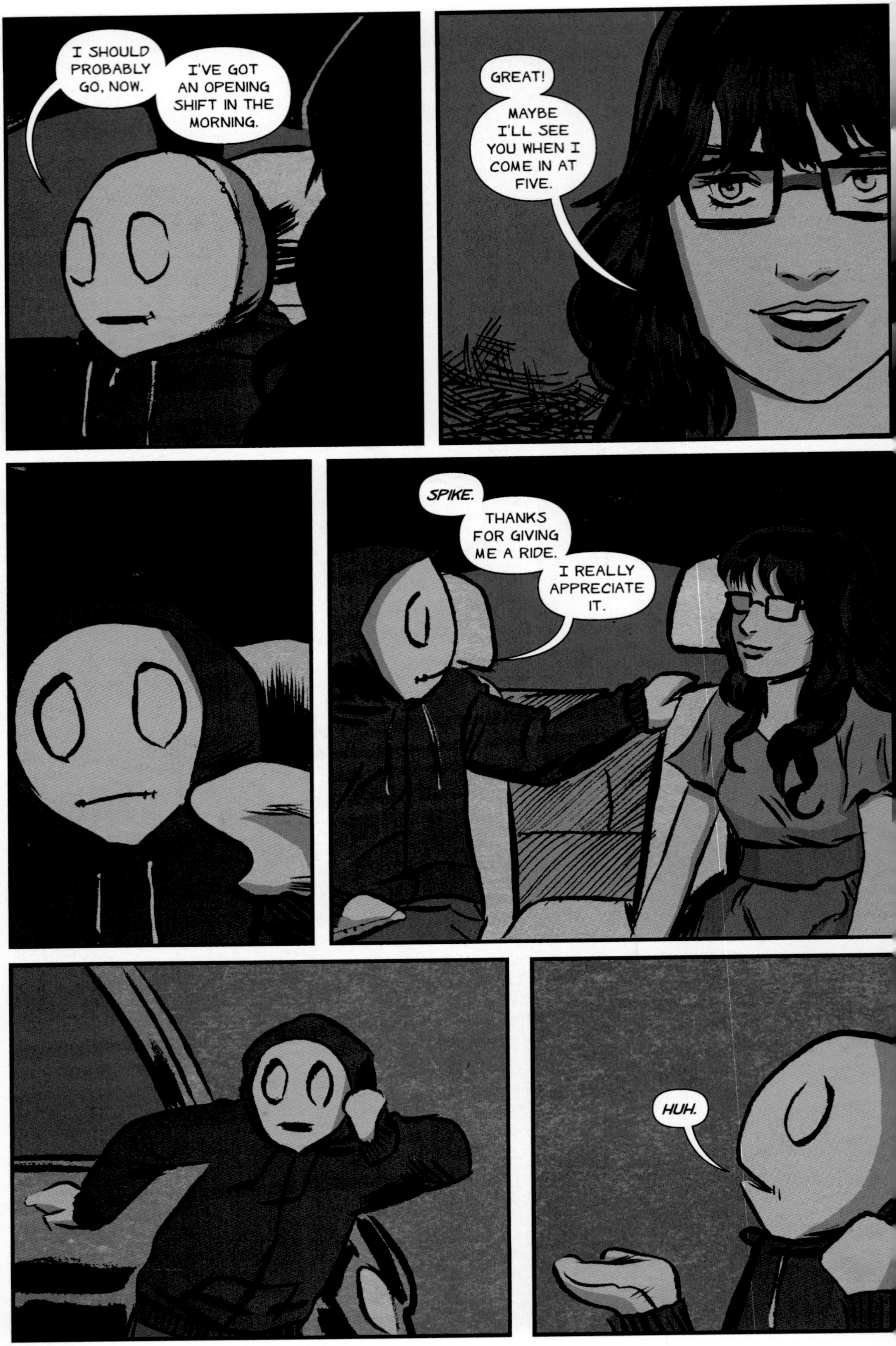
I SHOULD PROBABLY GO, NOW.
I'VE GOT AN OPENING SHIFT IN THE MORNING.
GREAT!
MAYBE I'LL SEE YOU WHEN I COME IN AT FIVE.
SPIKE.
THANKS FOR GIVING ME A RIDE.
I REALLY APPRECIATE IT.
HUH.

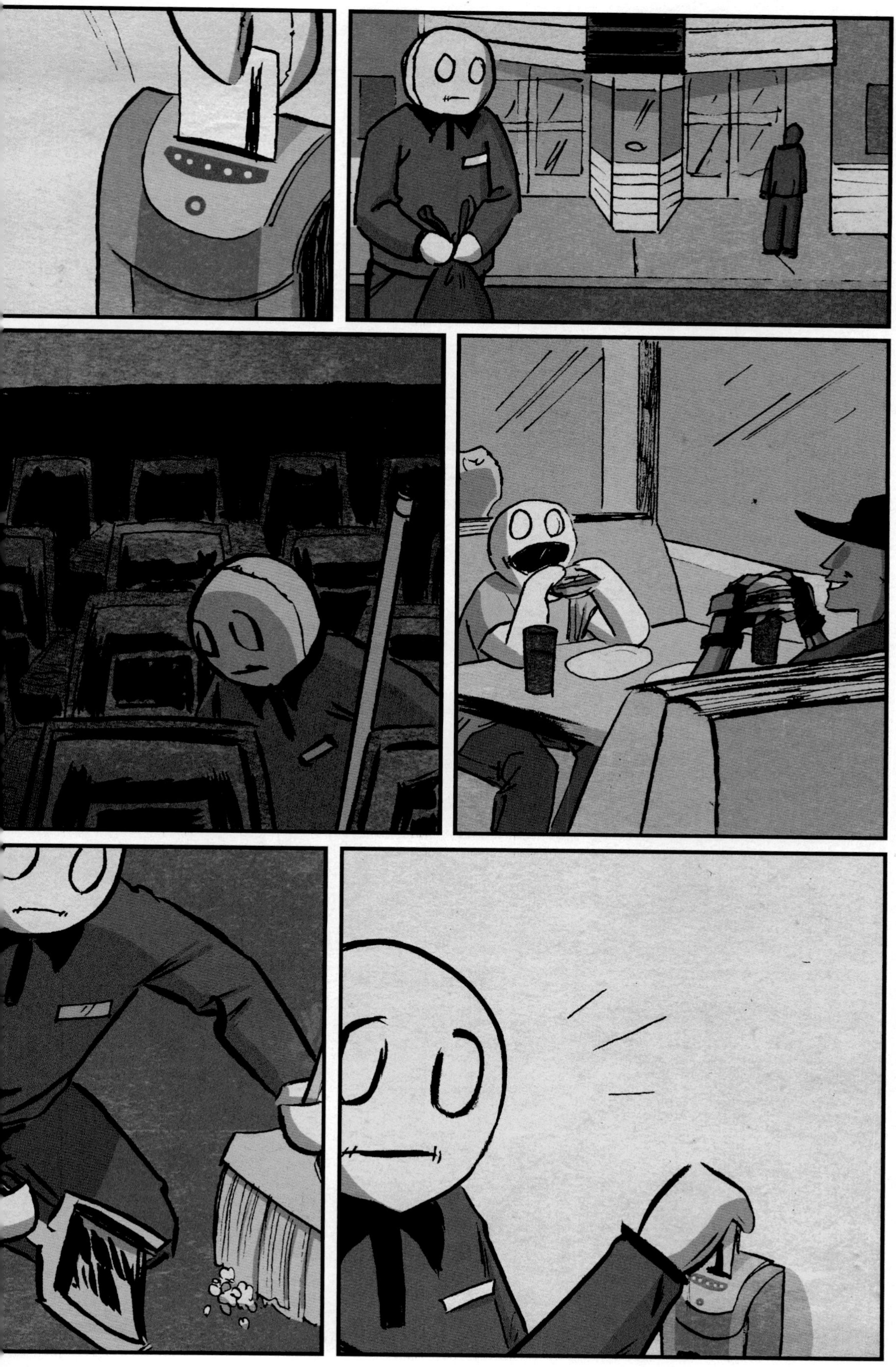

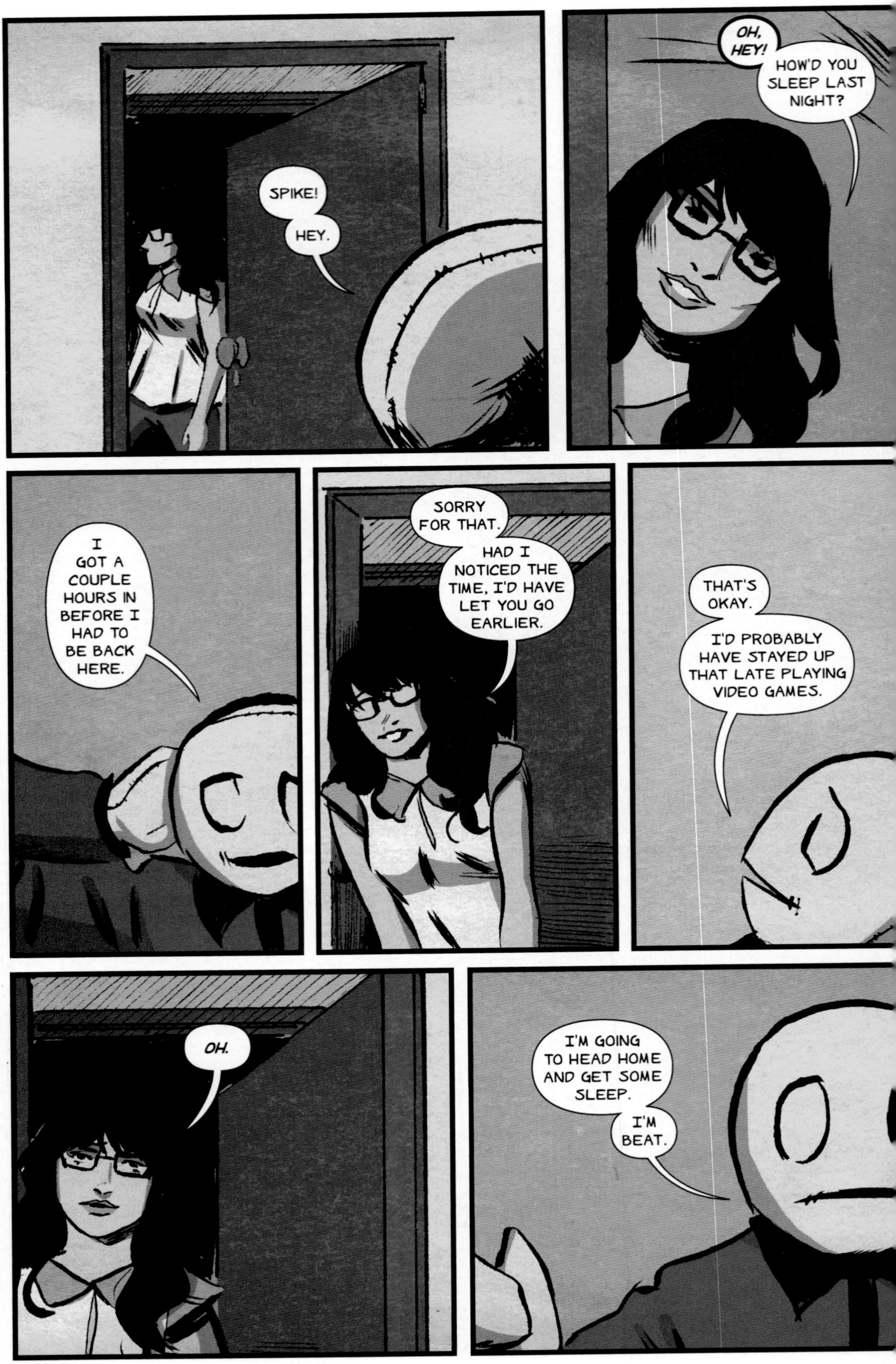
SPIKE!
HEY.
OH, HEY!
HOW'D YOU SLEEP LAST NIGHT?
I GOT A COUPLE HOURS IN BEFORE I HAD TO BE BACK HERE.
SORRY FOR THAT.
HAD I NOTICED THE TIME, I'D HAVE LET YOU GO EARLIER.
THAT'S OKAY.
I'D PROBABLY HAVE STAYED UP THAT LATE PLAYING VIDEO GAMES.
OH.
I'M GOING TO HEAD HOME AND GET SOME SLEEP.
I'M BEAT.

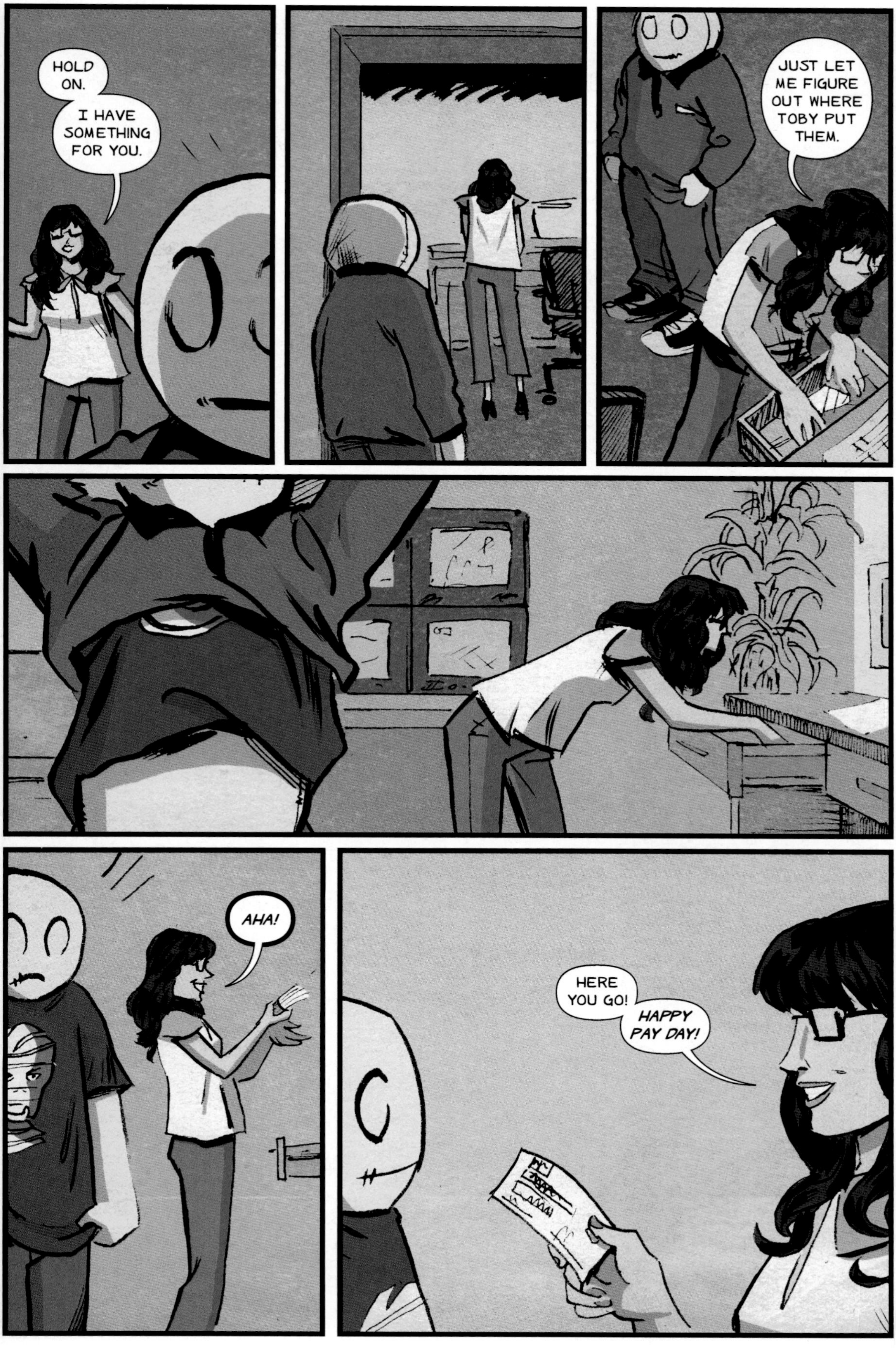
HOLD ON.
I HAVE SOMETHING FOR YOU.
JUST LET ME FIGURE OUT WHERE TOBY PUT THEM.
AHA!
HERE YOU GO!
HAPPY PAY DAY!

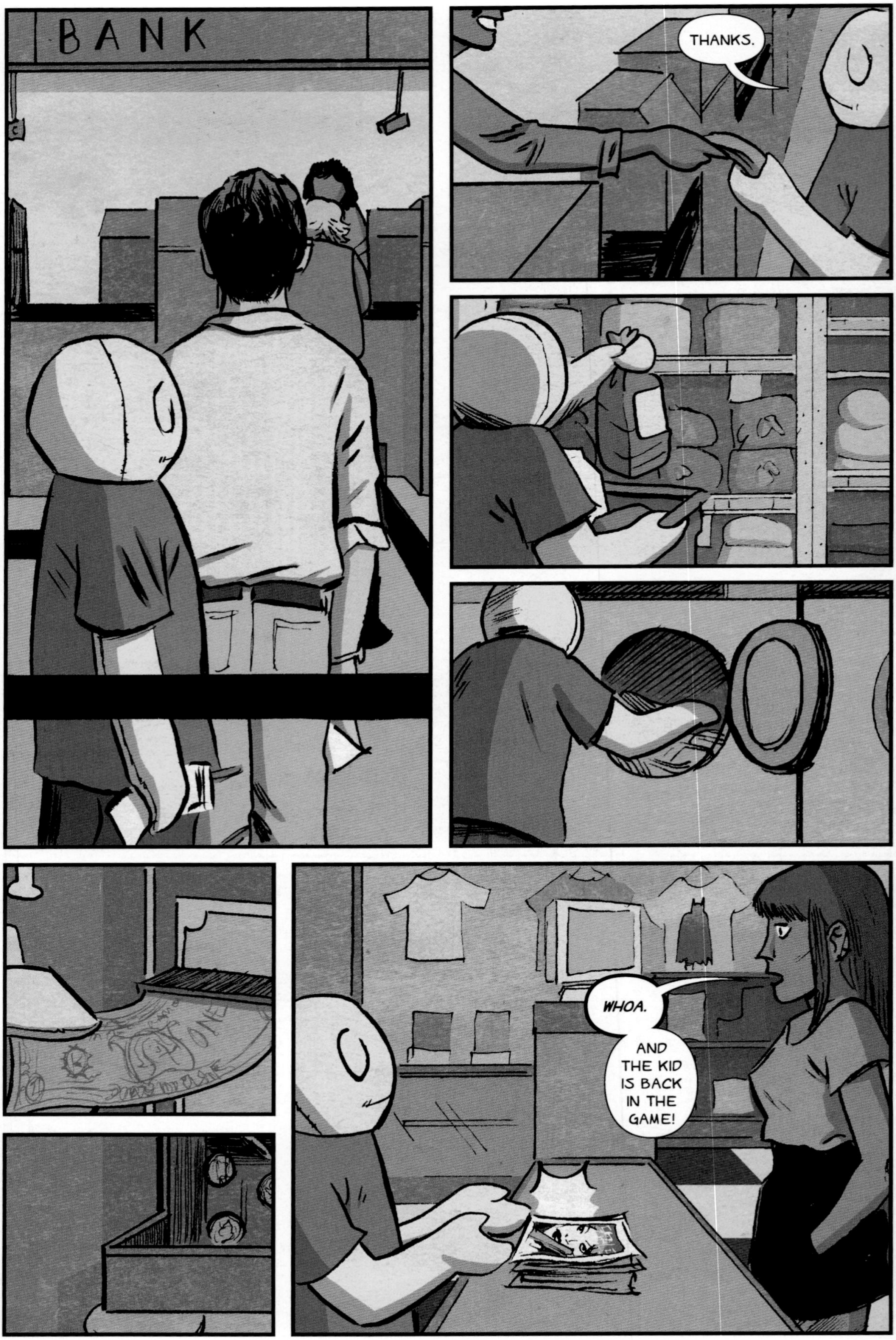
BANK
THANKS.
WHOA.
AND THE KID IS BACK IN THE GAME!

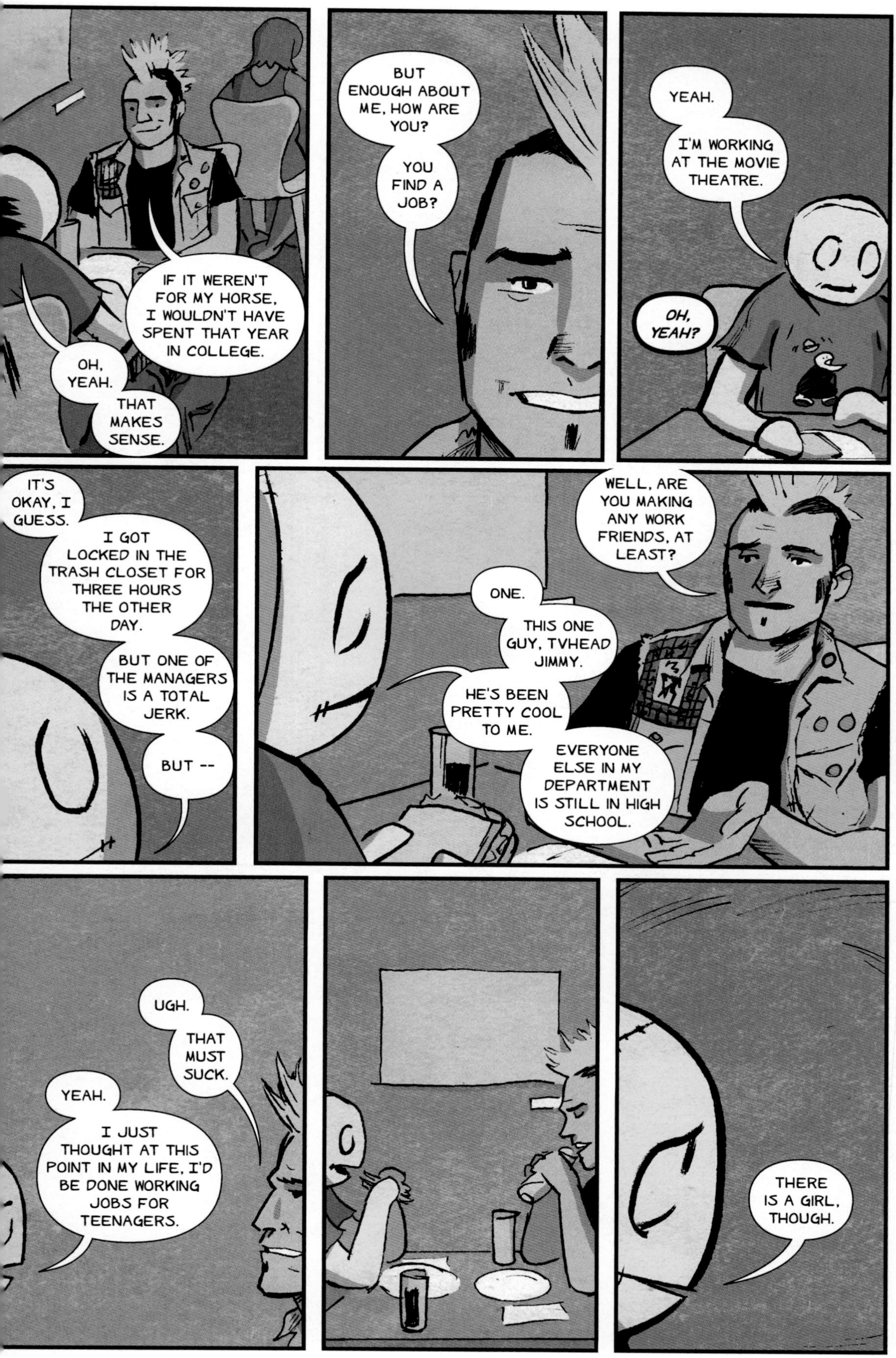
IF IT WEREN'T FOR MY HORSE, I WOULDN'T HAVE SPENT THAT YEAR IN COLLEGE.
OH, YEAH.
THAT MAKES SENSE.
BUT ENOUGH ABOUT ME, HOW ARE YOU?
YOU FIND A JOB?
YEAH.
I'M WORKING AT THE MOVIE THEATRE.
OH, YEAH?
IT'S OKAY, I GUESS.
I GOT LOCKED IN THE TRASH CLOSET FOR THREE HOURS THE OTHER DAY.
BUT ONE OF THE MANAGERS IS A TOTAL JERK.
BUT --
WELL, ARE YOU MAKING ANY WORK FRIENDS, AT LEAST?
ONE.
THIS ONE GUY, TVHEAD JIMMY.
HE'S BEEN PRETTY COOL TO ME.
EVERYONE ELSE IN MY DEPARTMENT IS STILL IN HIGH SCHOOL.
UGH.
THAT MUST SUCK.
YEAH.
I JUST THOUGHT AT THIS POINT IN MY LIFE, I'D BE DONE WORKING JOBS FOR TEENAGERS.
THERE IS A GIRL, THOUGH.

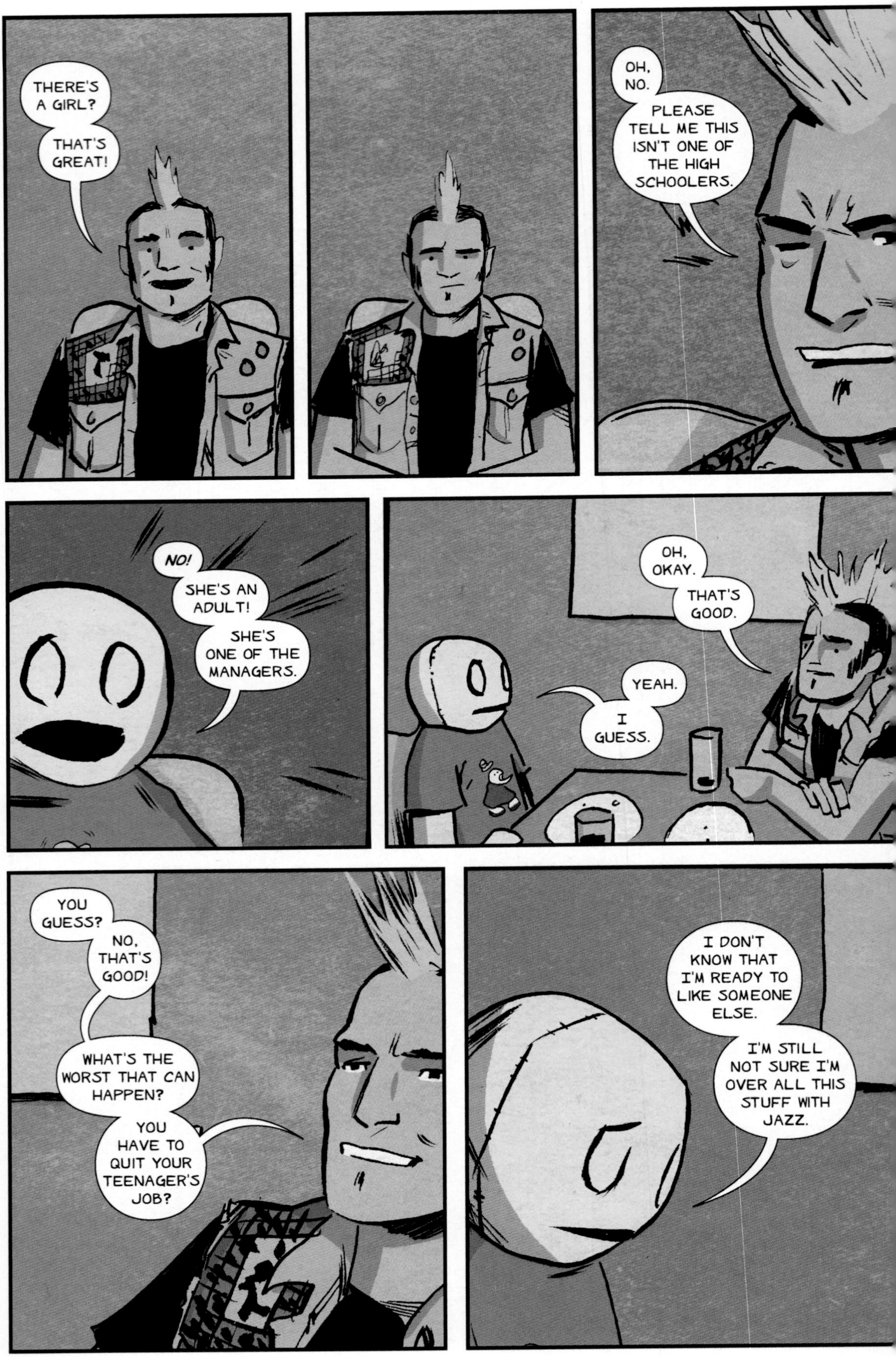
THERE'S A GIRL?
THAT'S GREAT!
OH, NO.
PLEASE TELL ME THIS ISN'T ONE OF THE HIGH SCHOOLERS.
NO!
SHE'S AN ADULT!
SHE'S ONE OF THE MANAGERS.
OH, OKAY.
THAT'S GOOD.
YEAH.
I GUESS.
YOU GUESS?
NO, THAT'S GOOD!
WHAT'S THE WORST THAT CAN HAPPEN?
YOU HAVE TO QUIT YOUR TEENAGER'S JOB?
I DON'T KNOW THAT I'M READY TO LIKE SOMEONE ELSE.
I'M STILL NOT SURE I'M OVER ALL THIS STUFF WITH JAZZ.

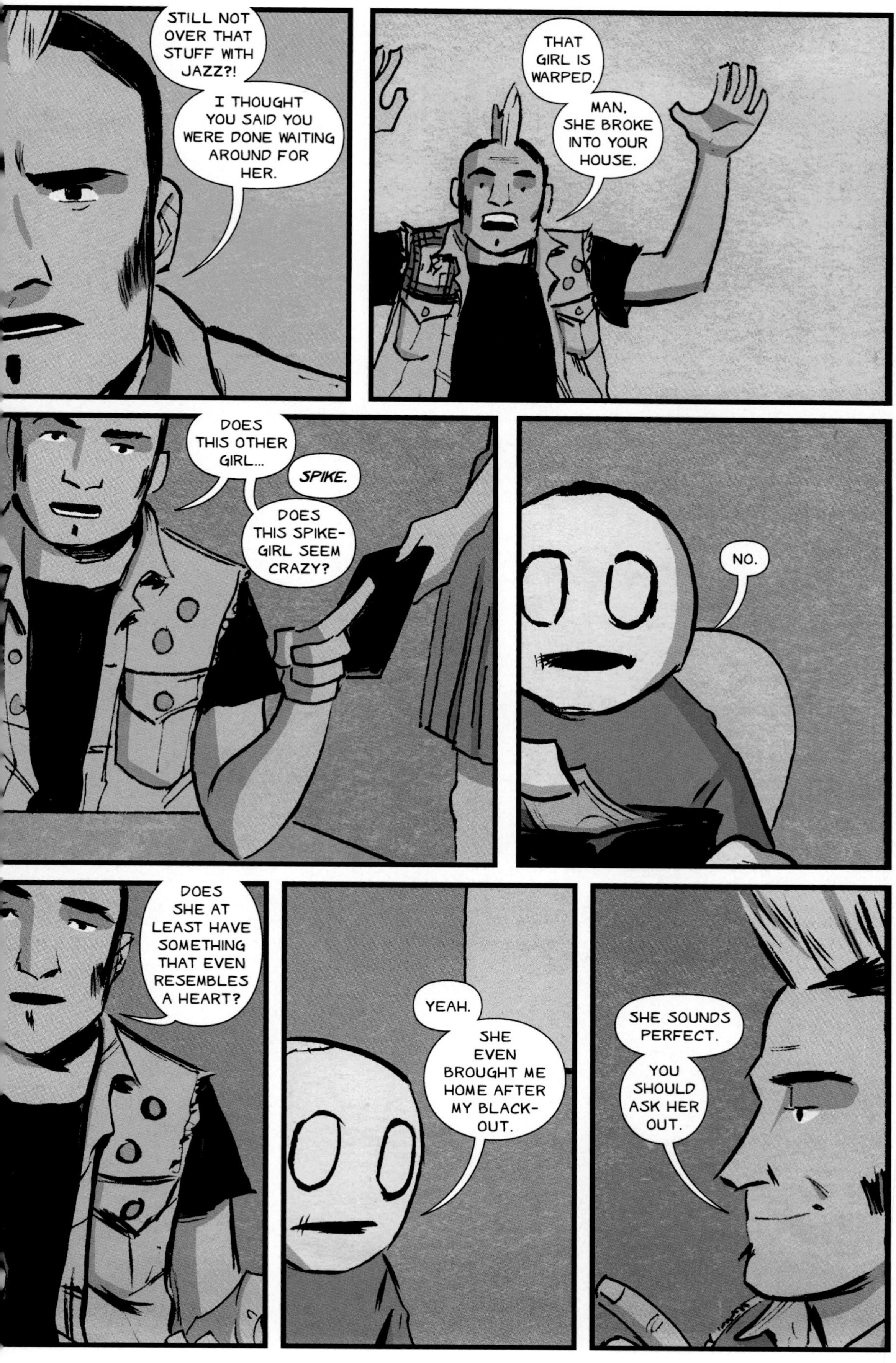
STILL NOT OVER THAT STUFF WITH JAZZ?!
I THOUGHT YOU SAID YOU WERE DONE WAITING AROUND FOR HER.
THAT GIRL IS WARPED.
MAN, SHE BROKE INTO YOUR HOUSE.
DOES THIS OTHER GIRL...
SPIKE.
DOES THIS SPIKE-GIRL SEEM CRAZY?
NO.
DOES SHE AT LEAST HAVE SOMETHING THAT EVEN RESEMBLES A HEART?
YEAH.
SHE EVEN BROUGHT ME HOME AFTER MY BLACK-OUT.
SHE SOUNDS PERFECT.
YOU SHOULD ASK HER OUT.

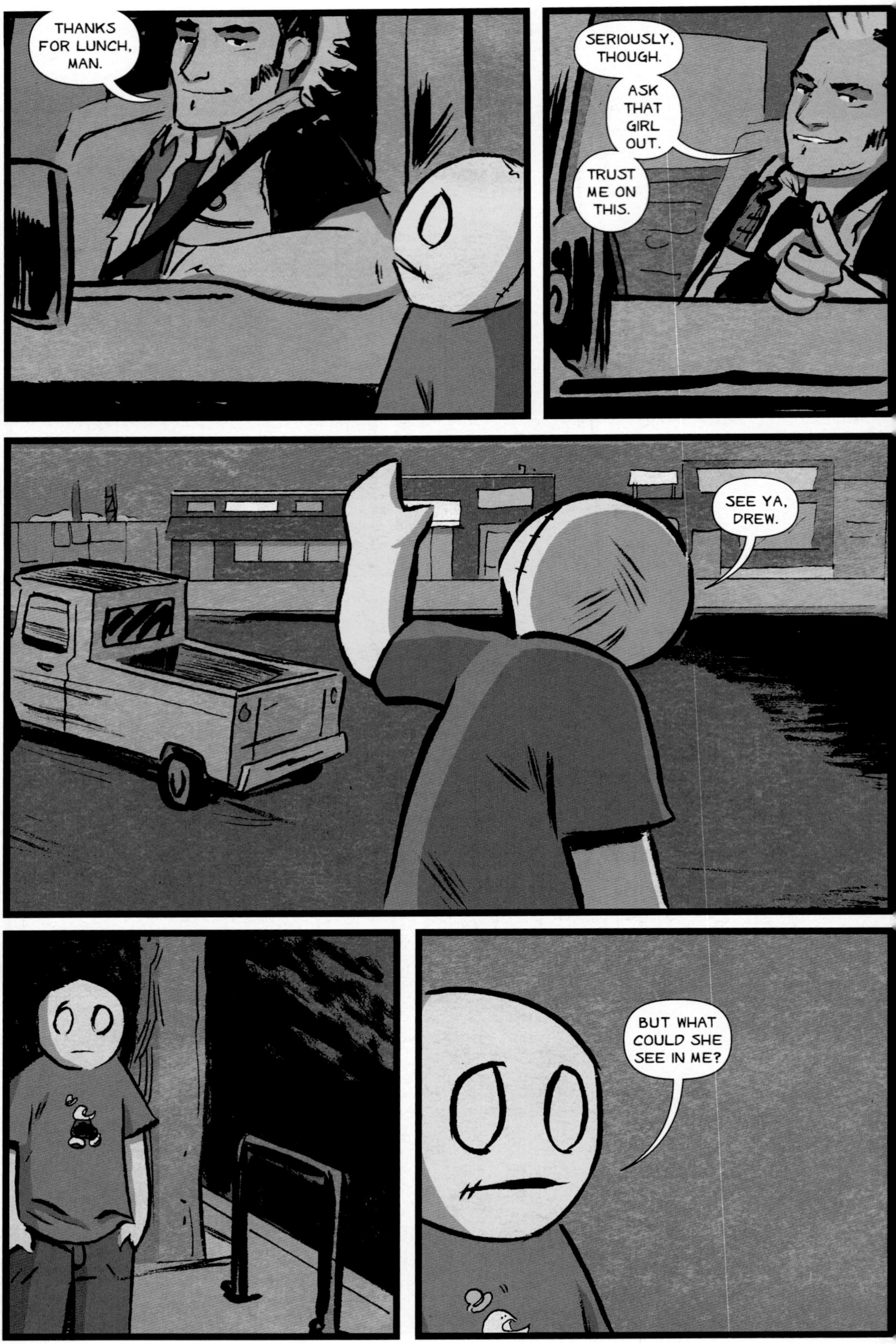
THANKS FOR LUNCH, MAN.
SERIOUSLY, THOUGH.
ASK THAT GIRL OUT.
TRUST ME ON THIS.
SEE YA, DREW.
BUT WHAT COULD SHE SEE IN ME?

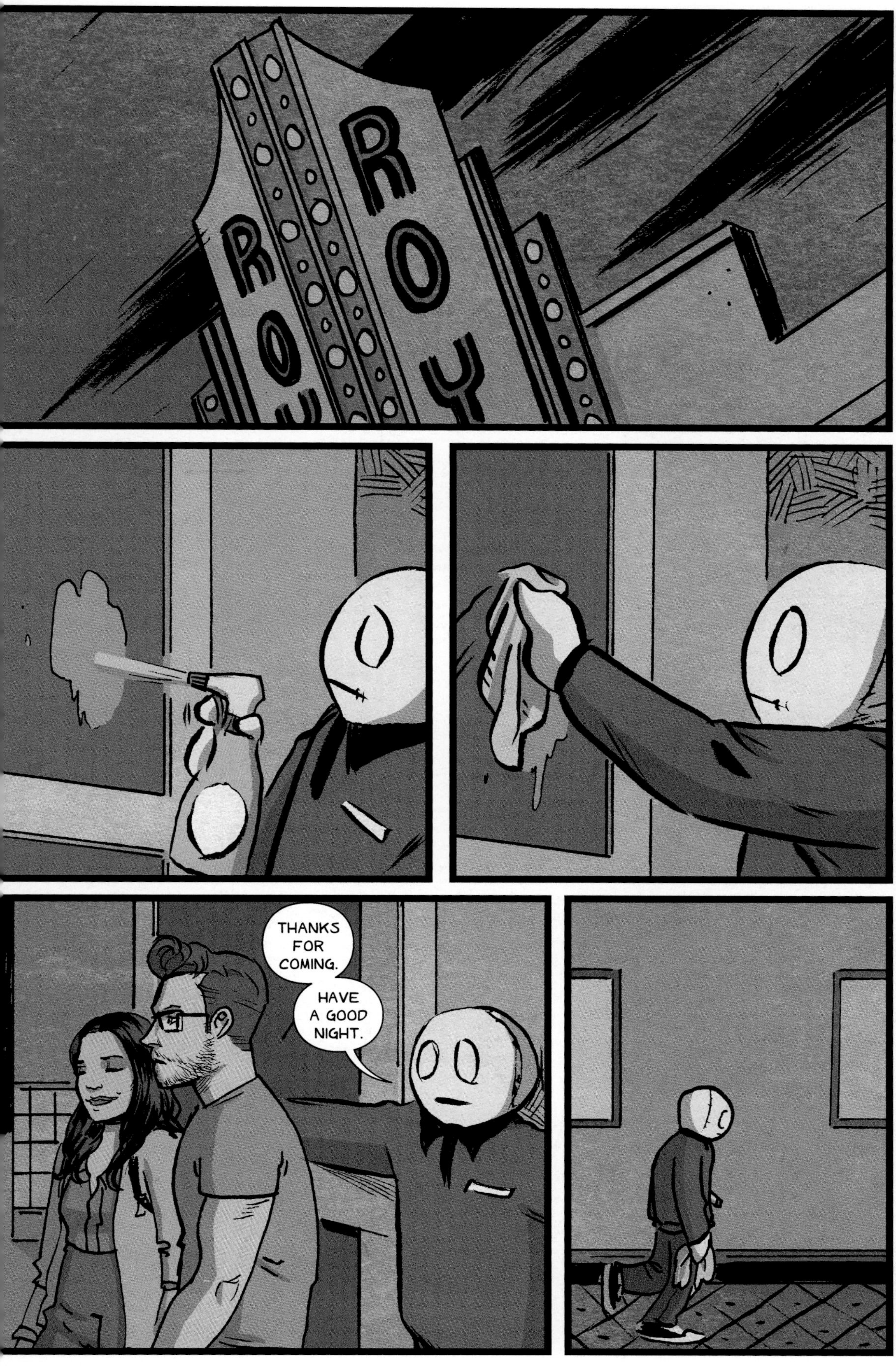
ROXY
THANKS FOR COMING.
HAVE A GOOD NIGHT.

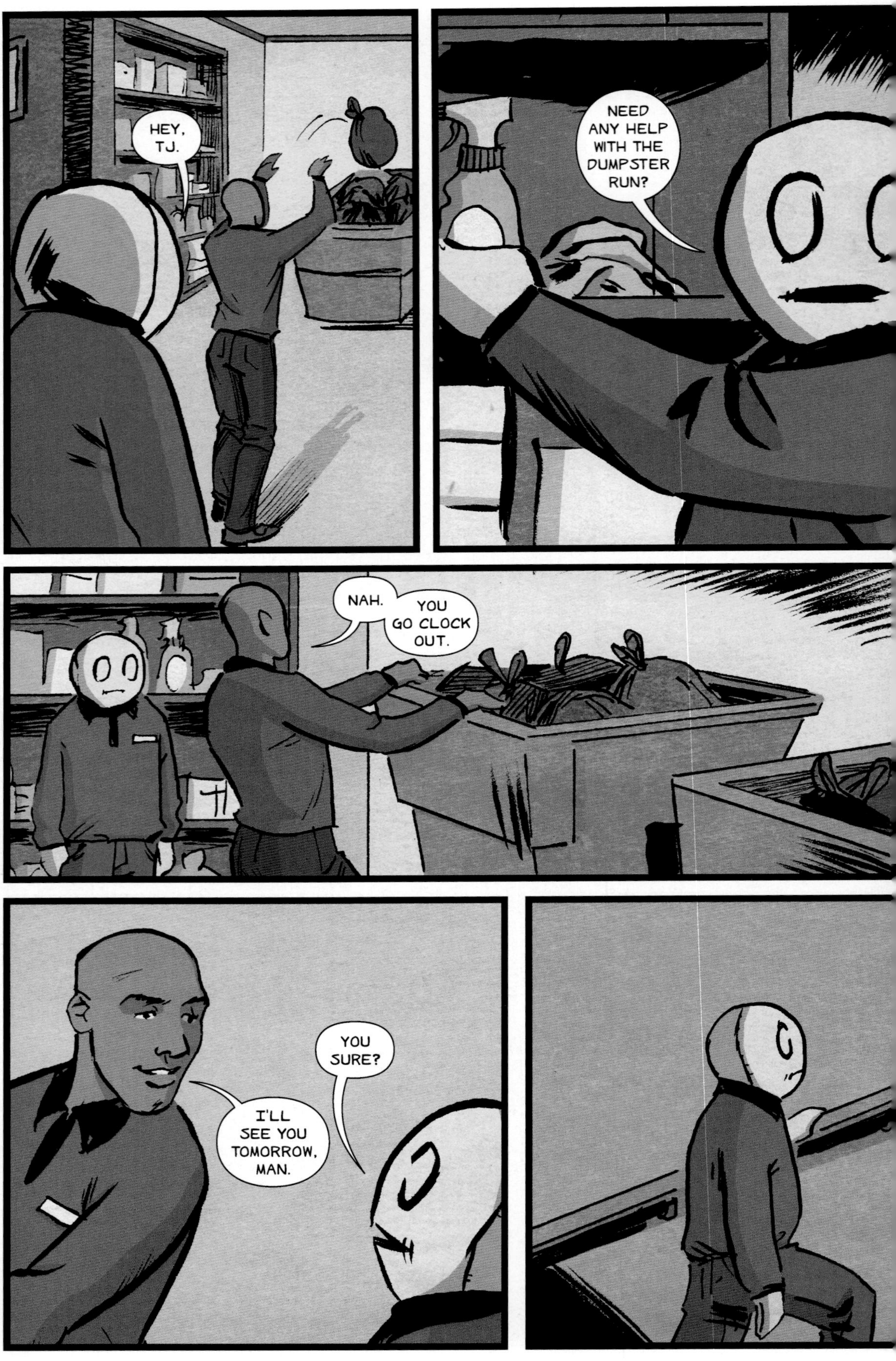
HEY, TJ.
NEED ANY HELP WITH THE DUMPSTER RUN?
NAH.
YOU GO CLOCK OUT.
YOU SURE?
I'LL SEE YOU TOMORROW, MAN.

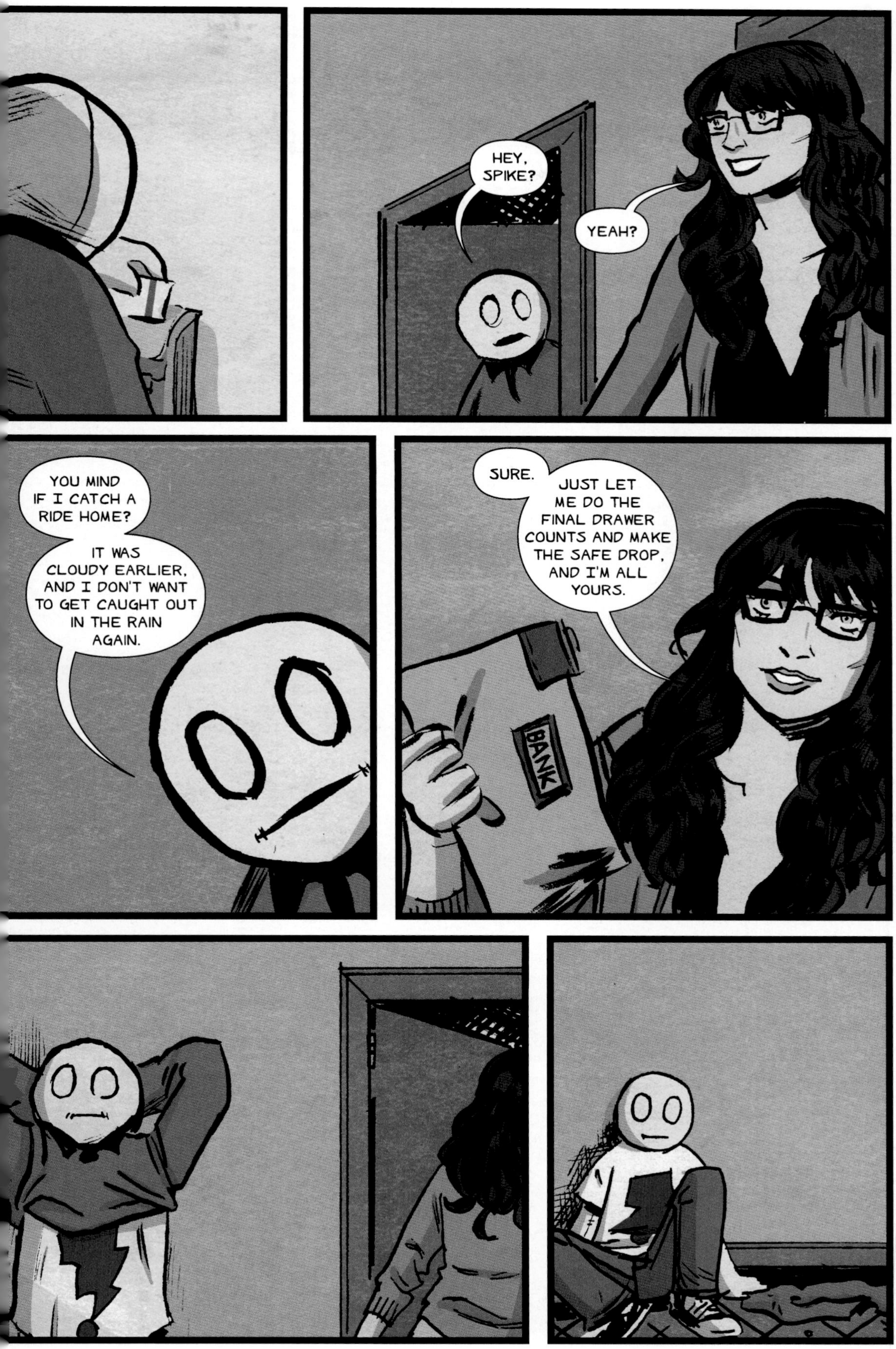
HEY, SPIKE?
YEAH?
YOU MIND IF I CATCH A RIDE HOME?
IT WAS CLOUDY EARLIER, AND I DON'T WANT TO GET CAUGHT OUT IN THE RAIN AGAIN.
SURE.
JUST LET ME DO THE FINAL DRAWER COUNTS AND MAKE THE SAFE DROP, AND I'M ALL YOURS.
BANK

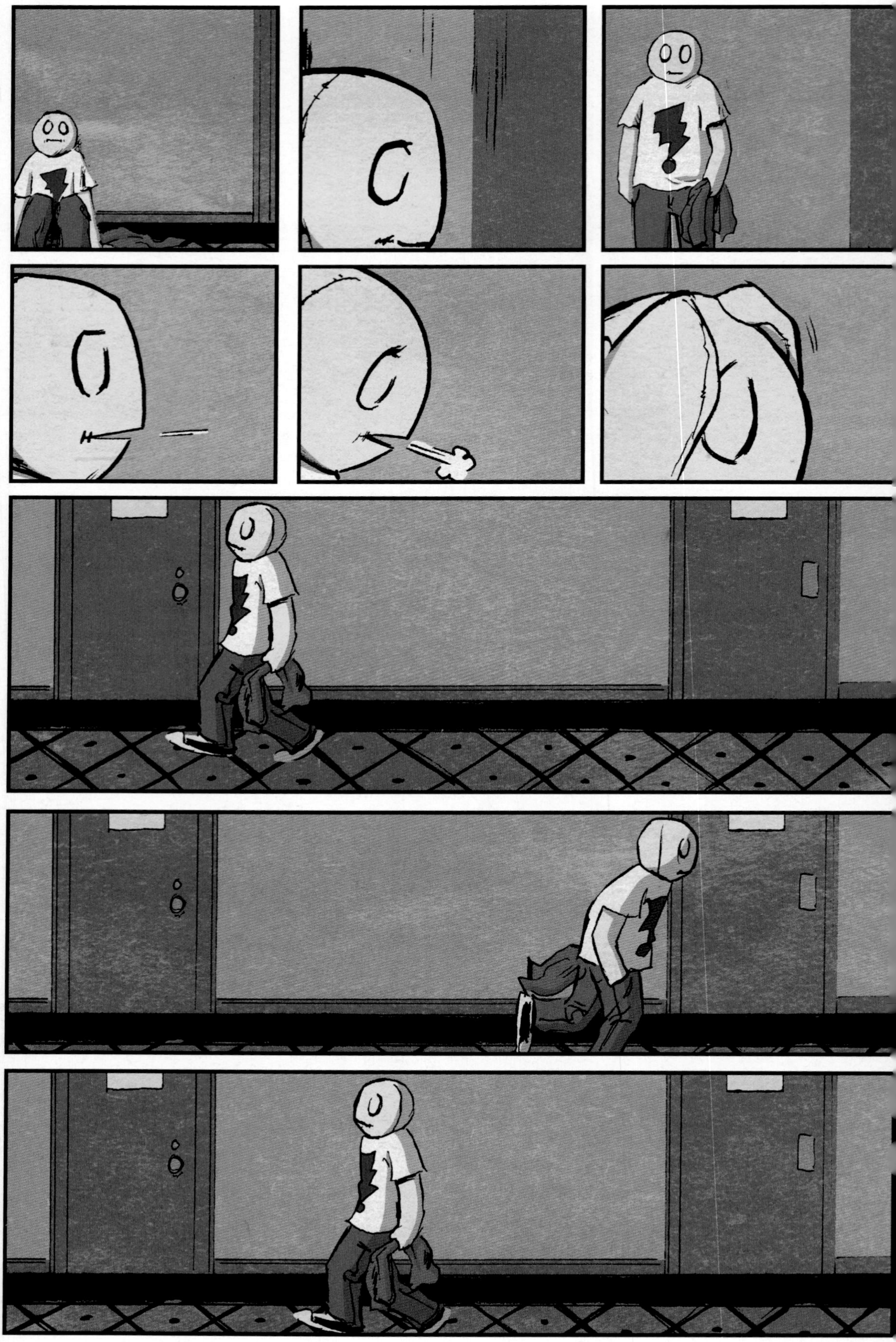

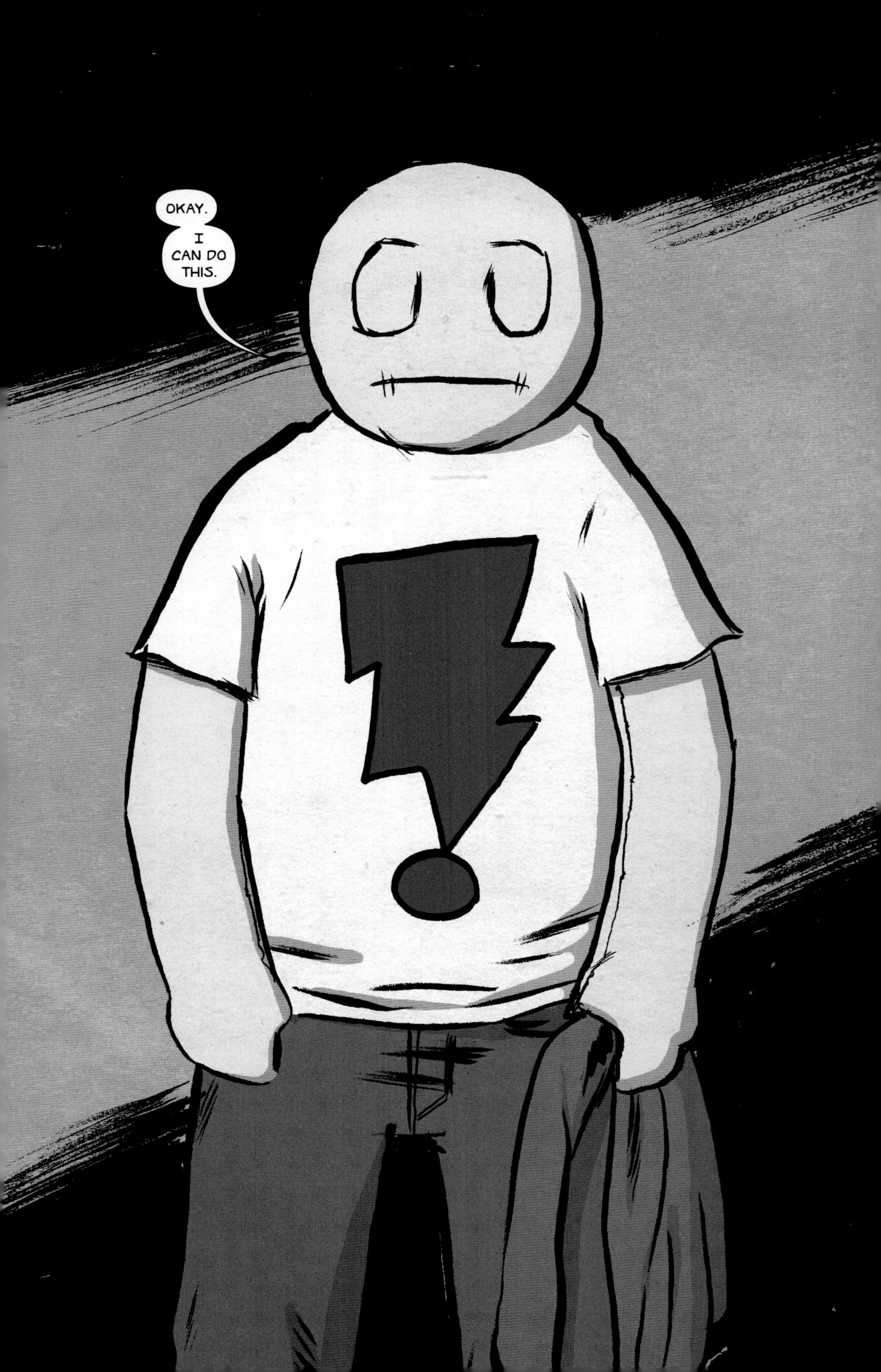
OKAY.
I CAN DO THIS.

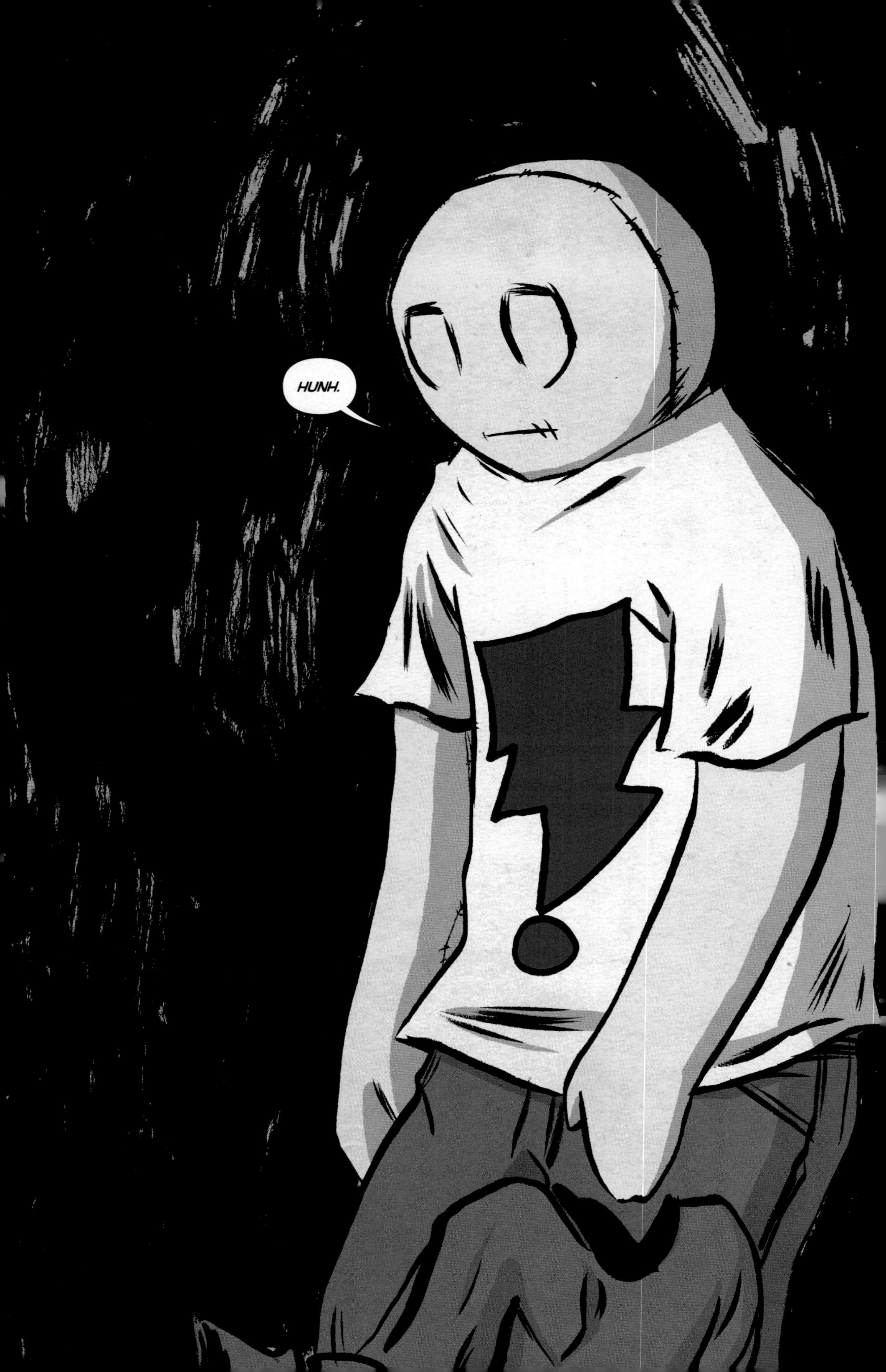
HUNH.

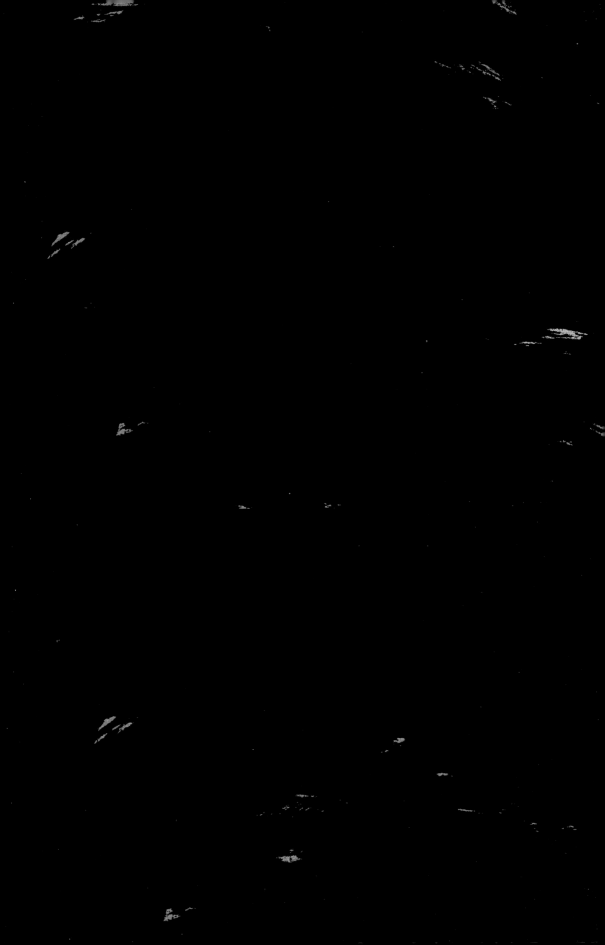

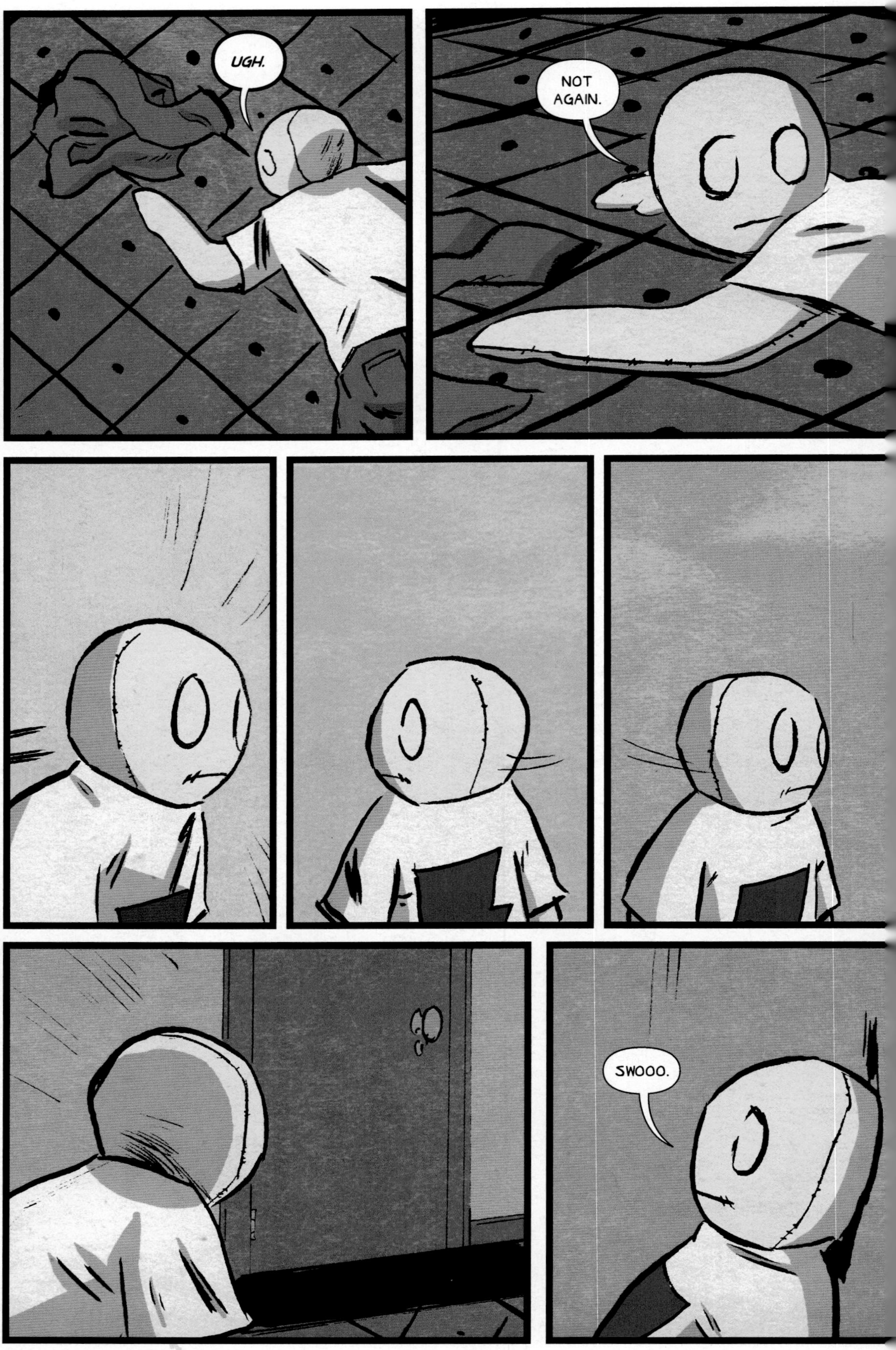
UGH.
NOT AGAIN.
SWOOO.

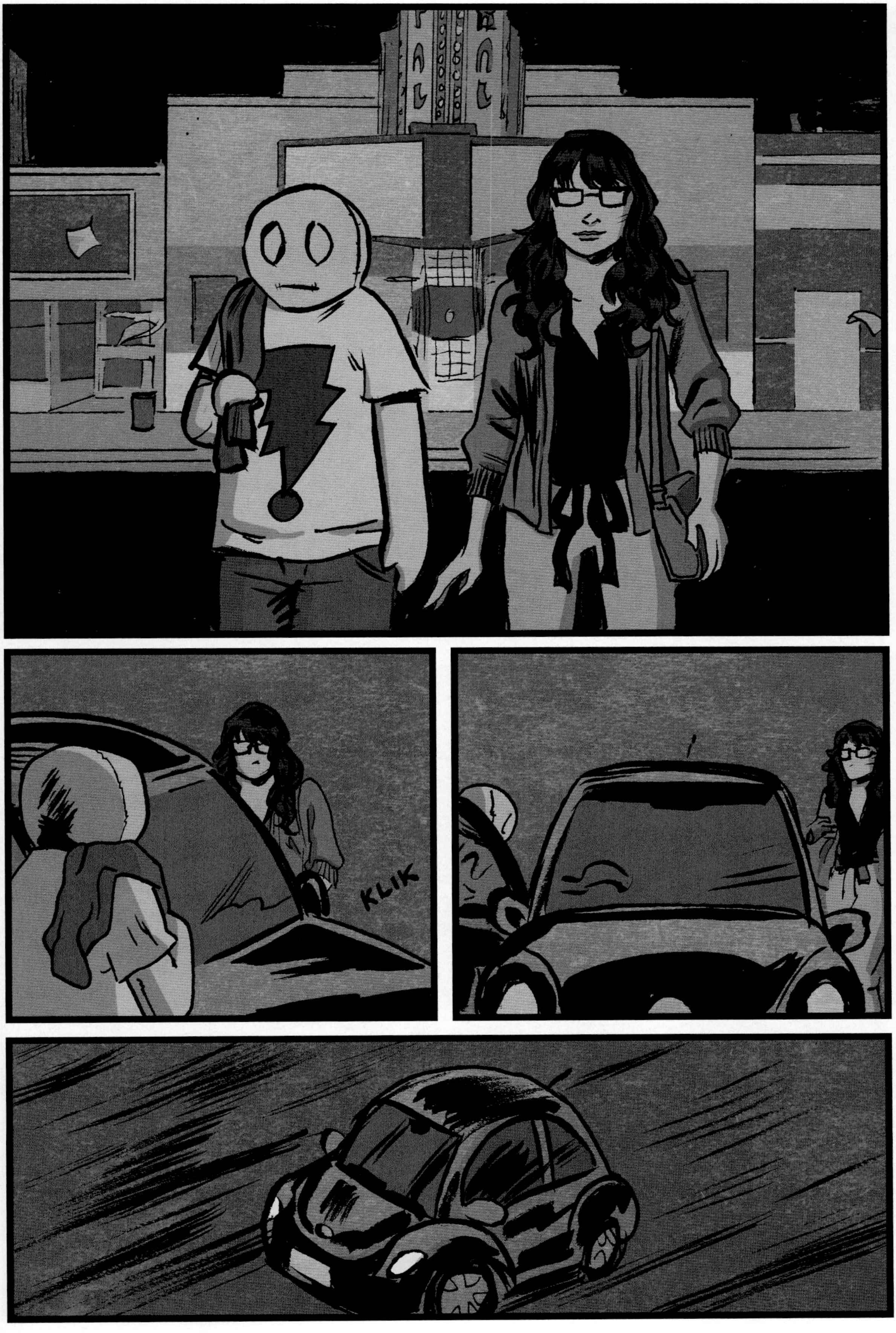
KLIK

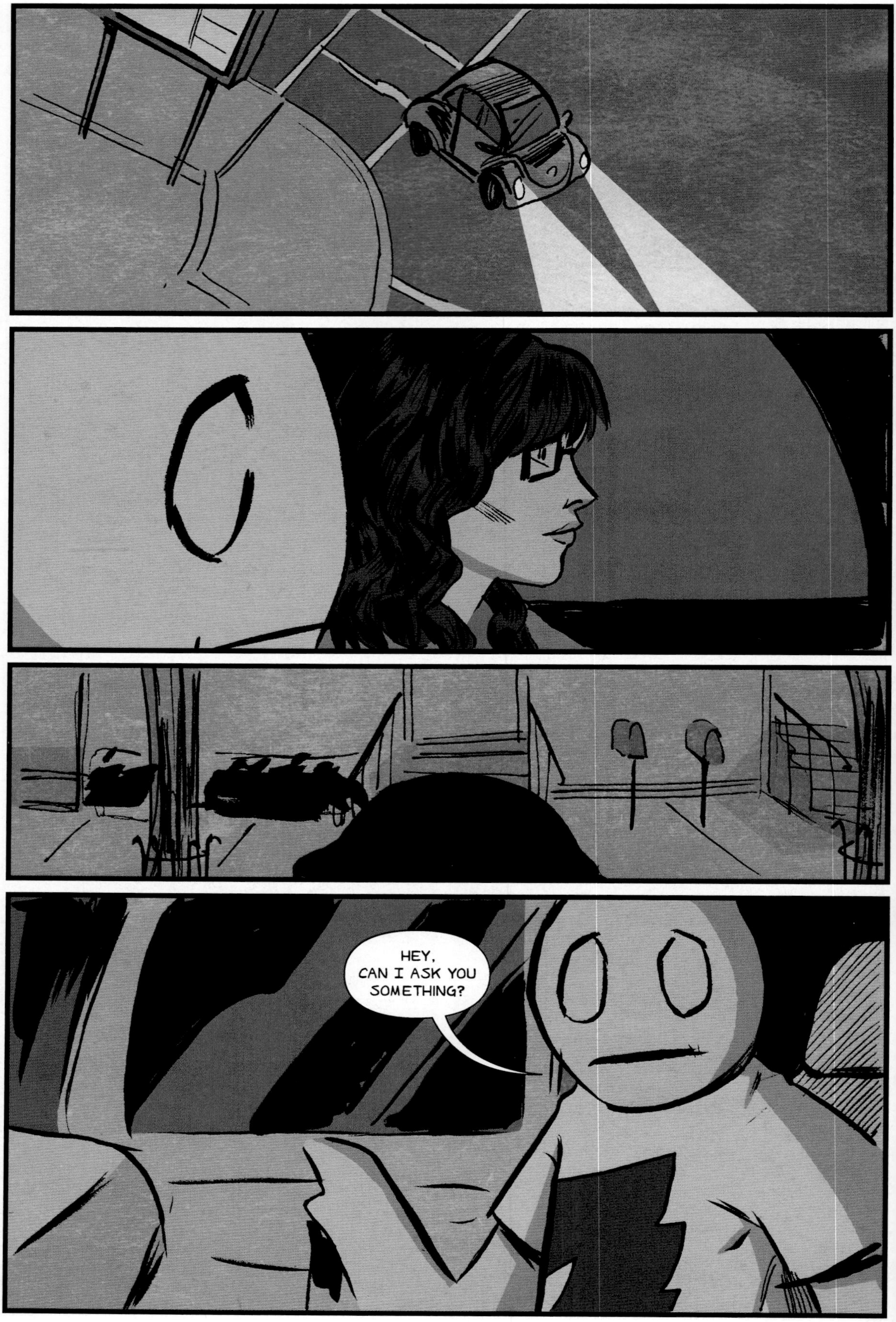
HEY,
CAN I ASK YOU
SOMETHING?

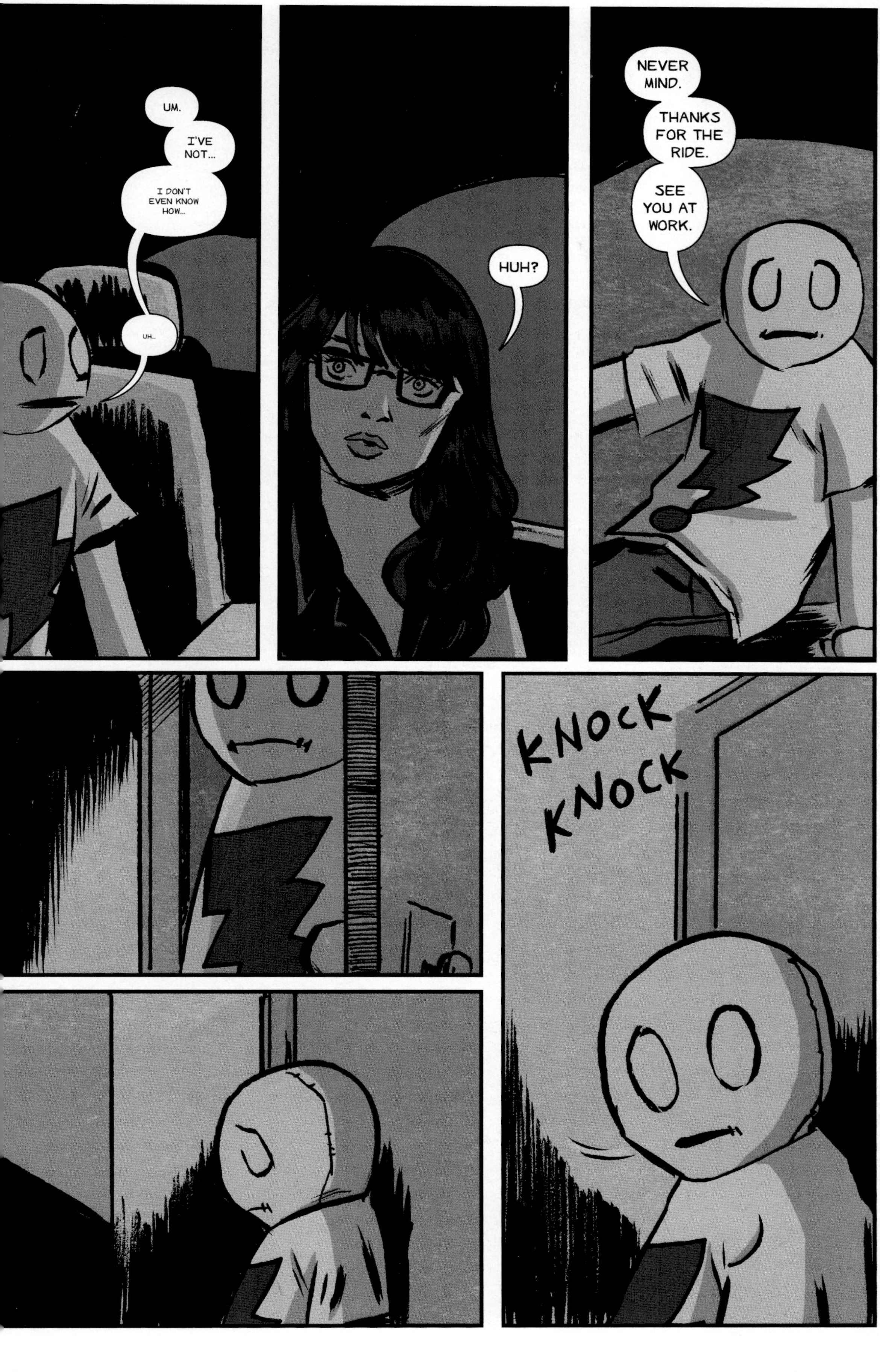
UM.
I'VE NOT...
I DON'T EVEN KNOW HOW...
UH...
HUH?
NEVER MIND.
THANKS FOR THE RIDE.
SEE YOU AT WORK.
KNOCK KNOCK

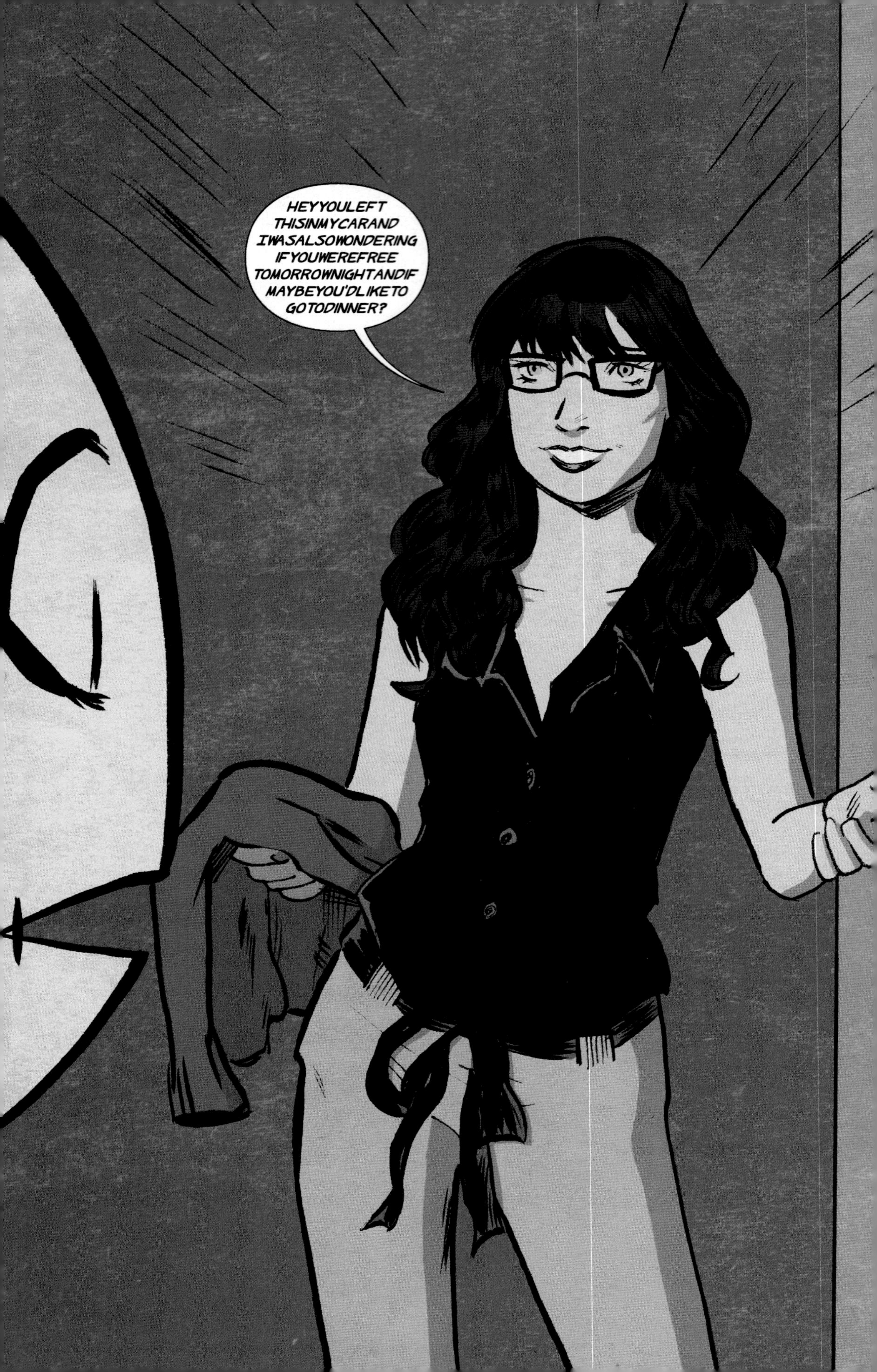
HEYYOULEFT THISINMYCARAND IWASALSOWONDERING IFYOUWEREFREE TOMORROWNIGHTANDIF MAYBEYOU'DLIKETO GOTODINNER?

"ALL THE SHINE"

SKETCHES, PIN-UPS AND SURPRISES

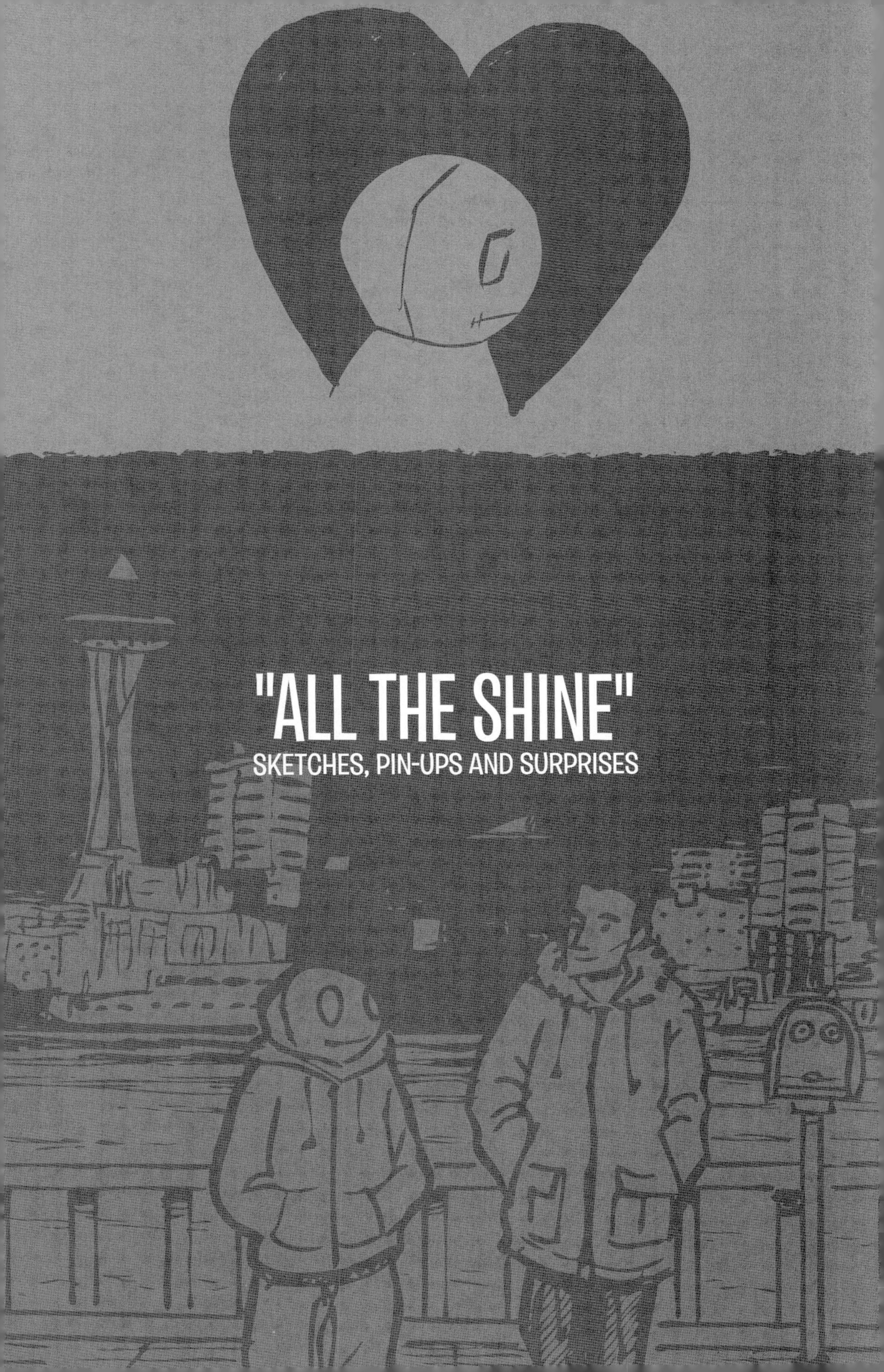

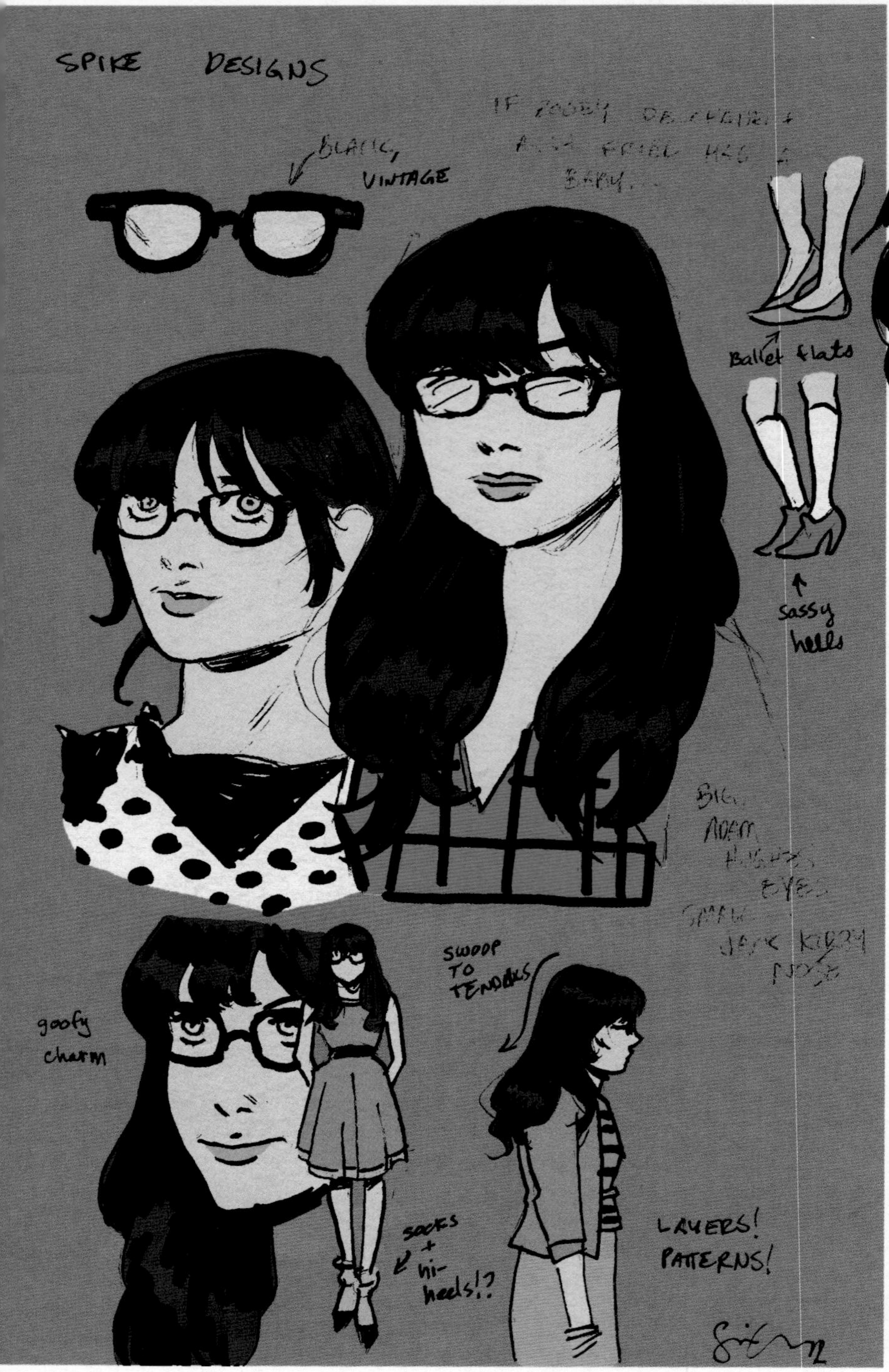
SPIKE DESIGNS
BLACK, VINTAGE
Ballet flats
sassy heels
BIG ADAM HUGHES EYES
SMALL JACK KIRBY NOSE
goofy charm
SWOOP TO TENDRILS
socks + hi-heels!?
LAYERS! PATTERNS!
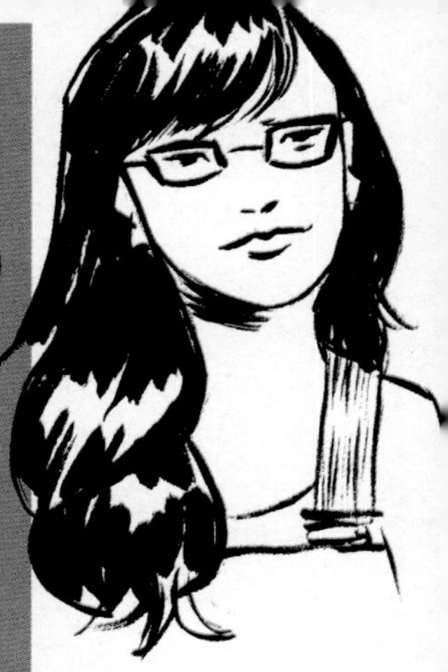
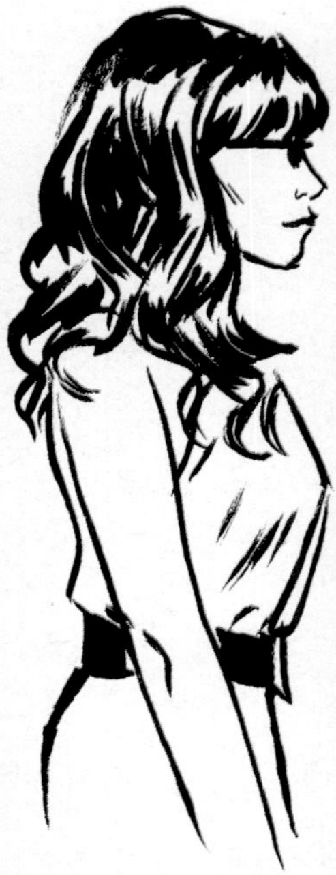
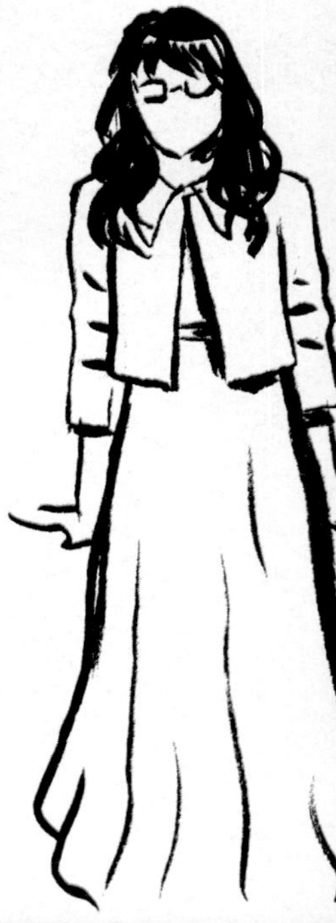
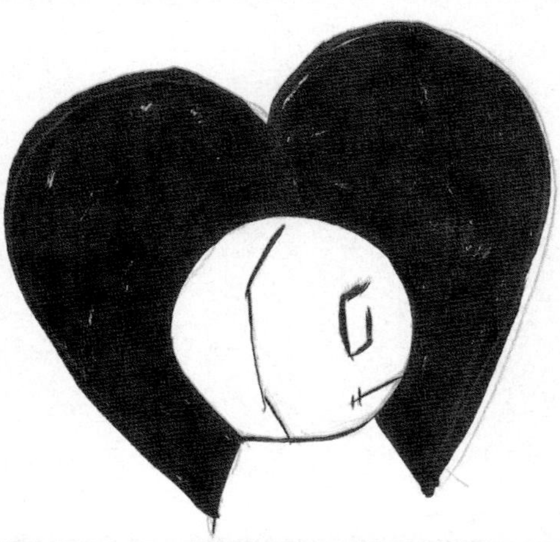

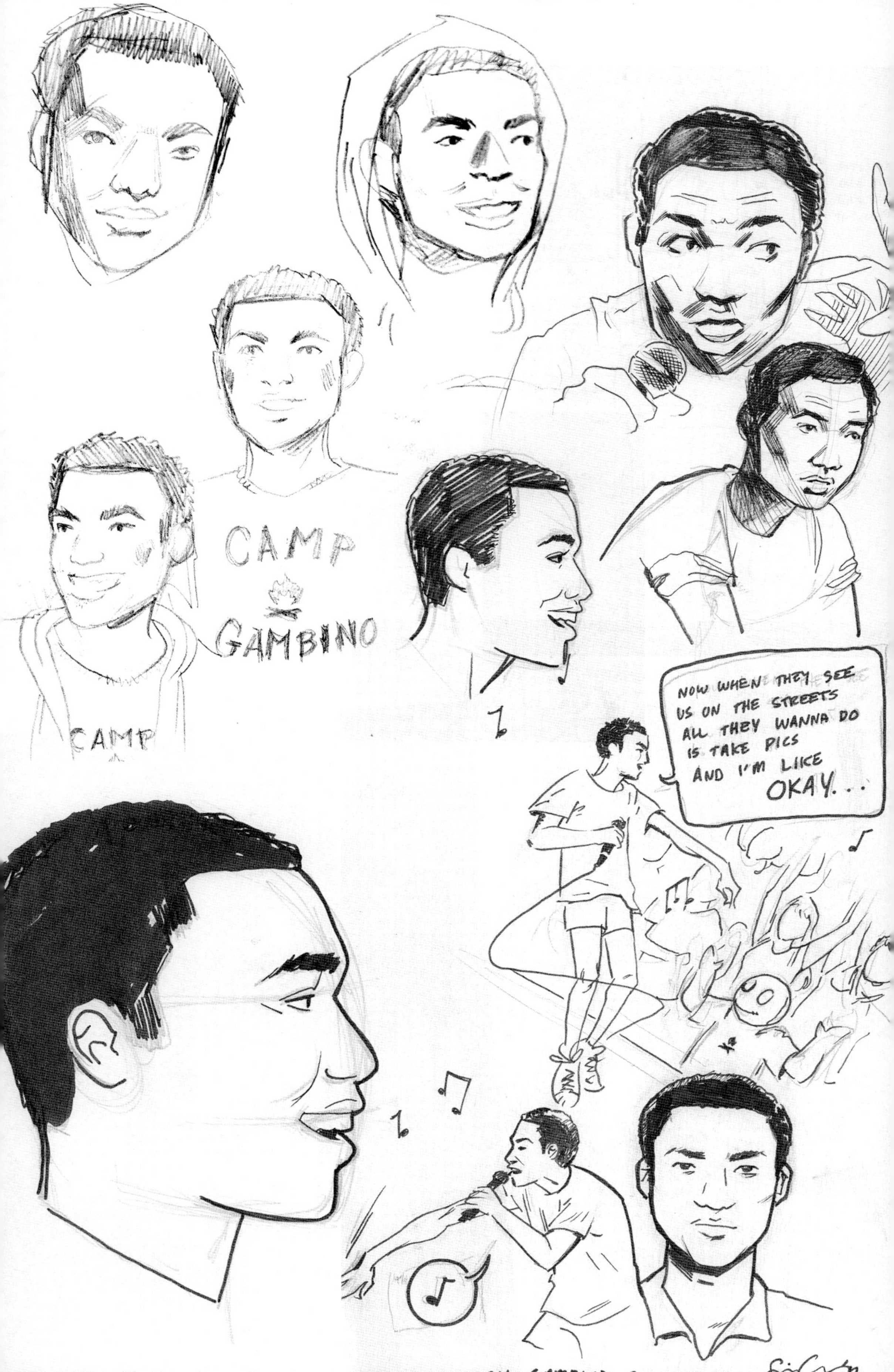
CAMP
GAMBINO
CAMP
NOW WHEN THEY SEE US ON THE STREETS ALL THEY WANNA DO IS TAKE PICS AND I'M LIKE OKAY...

CHILDISH GAMBINO SKETCHES

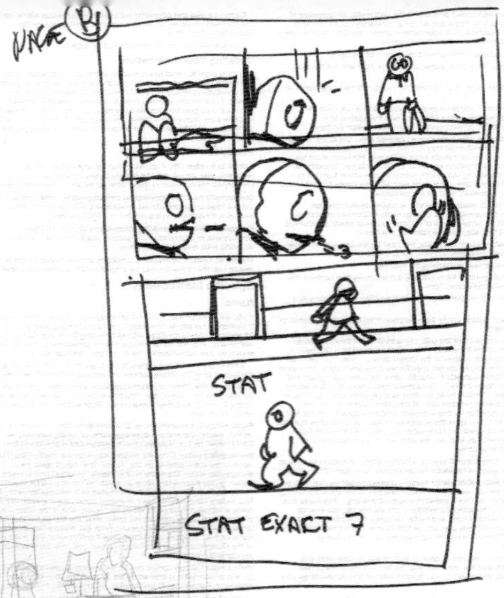
STAT
STAT EXACT 7

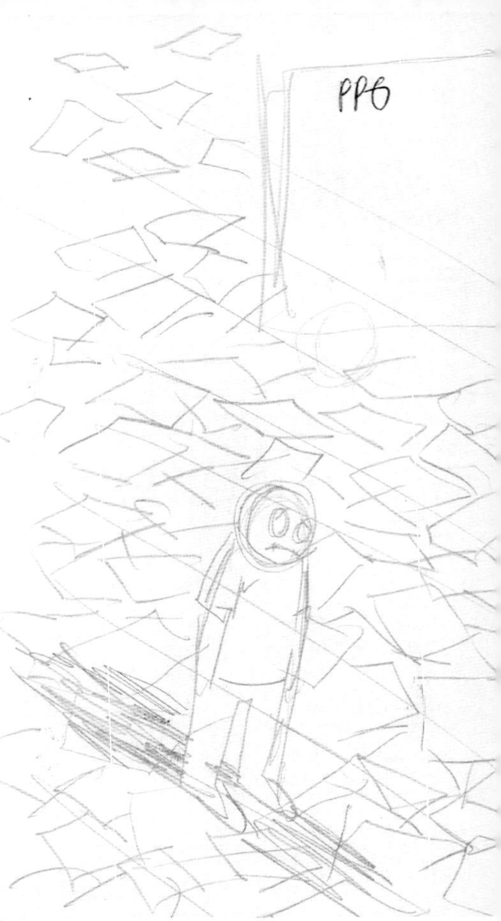
PPG

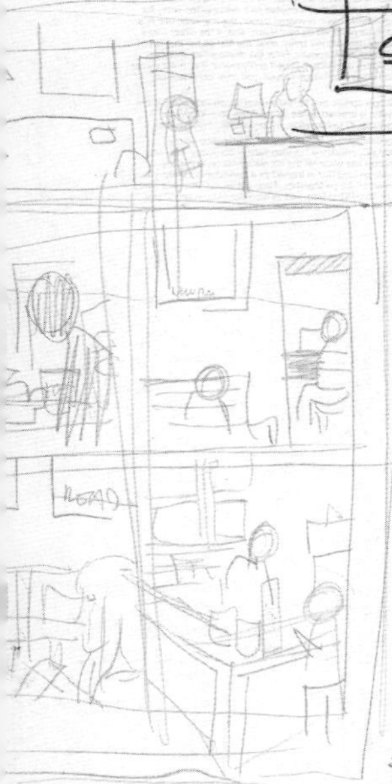

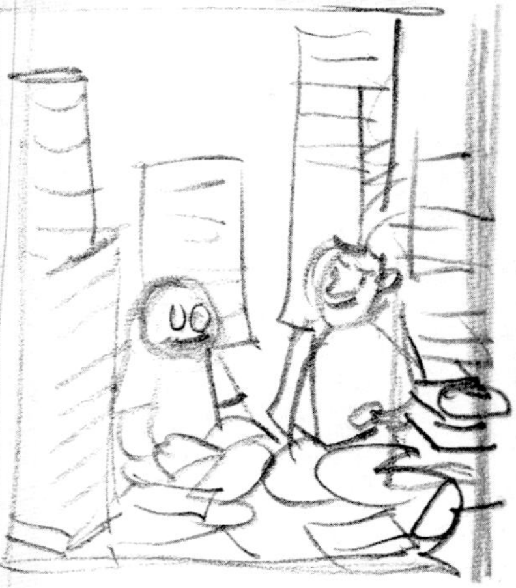

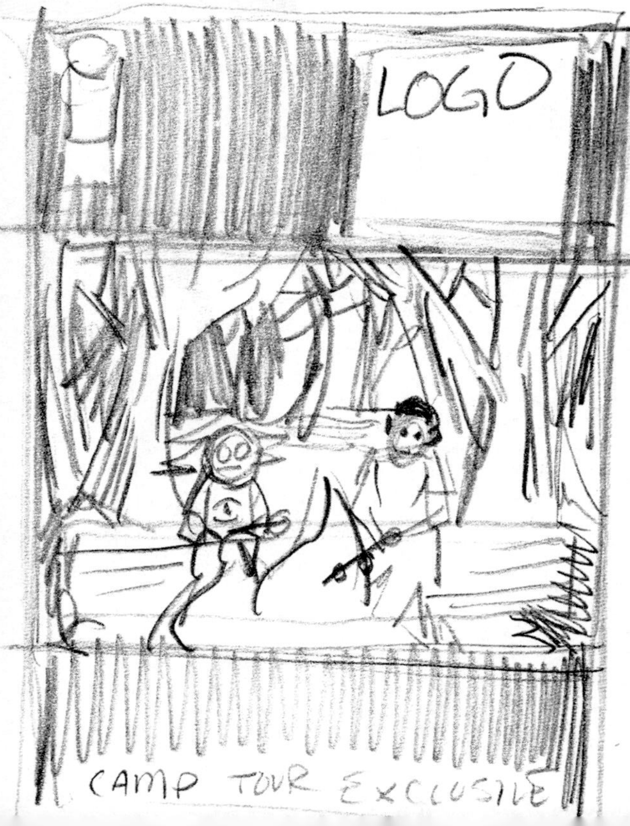
LOGO
CAMP TOUR EXCLUSIVE

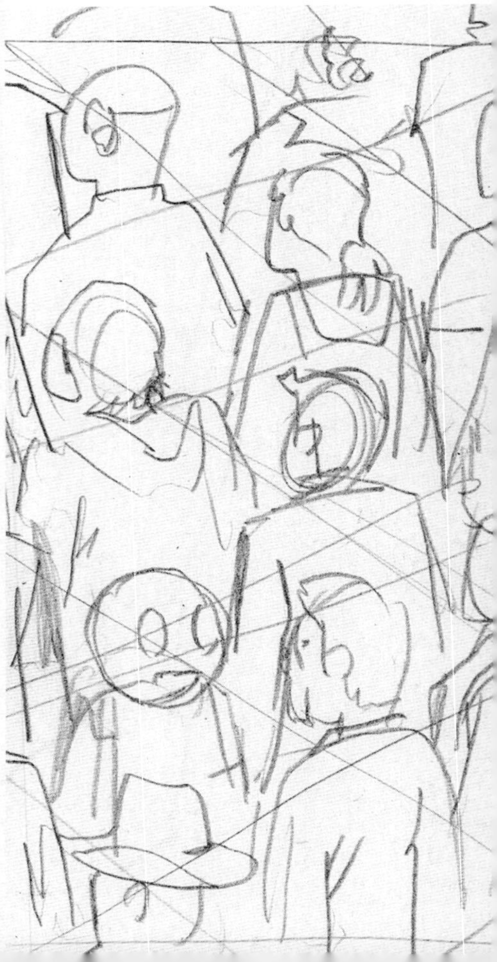

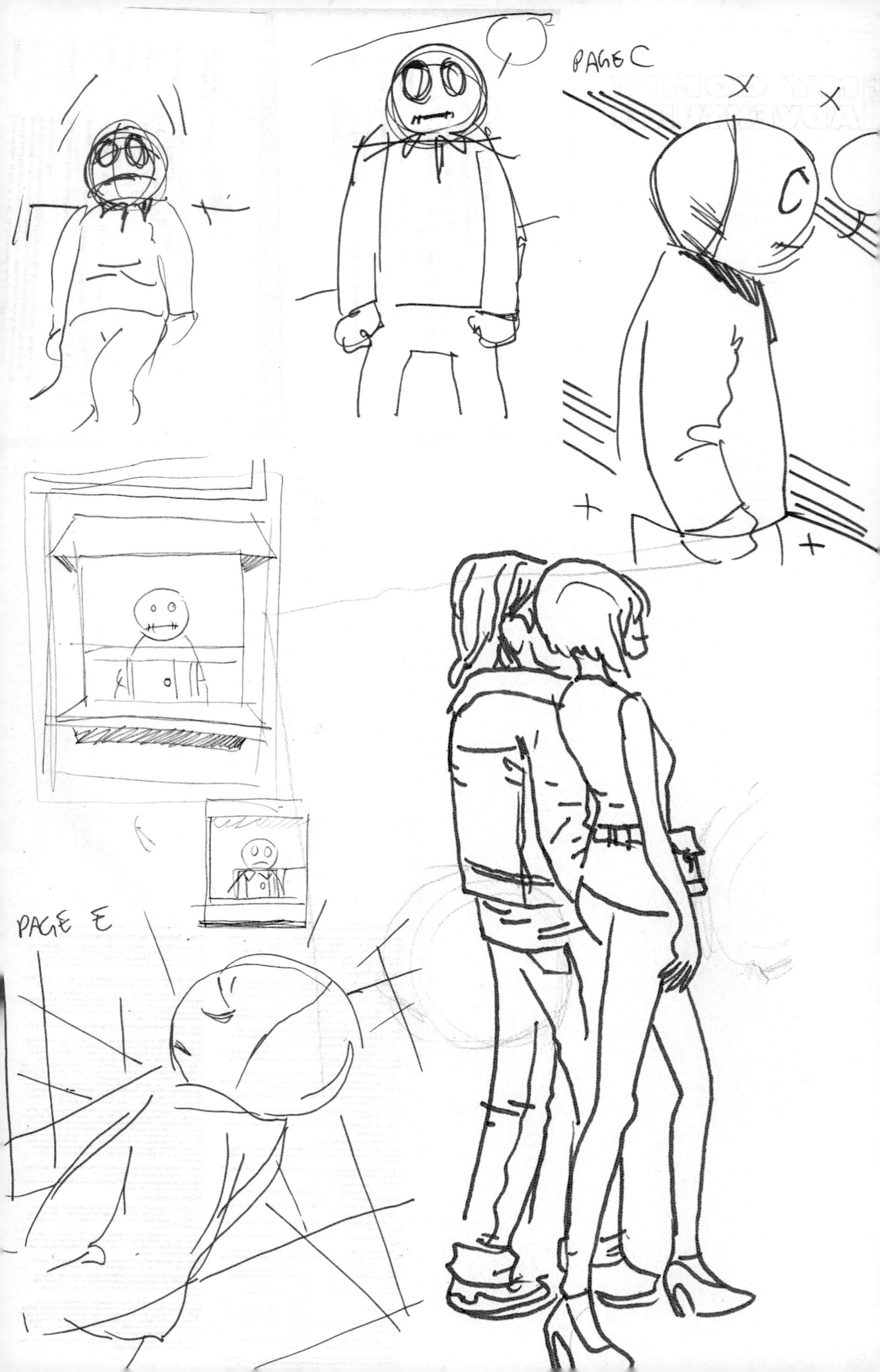
PAGE C
PAGE E

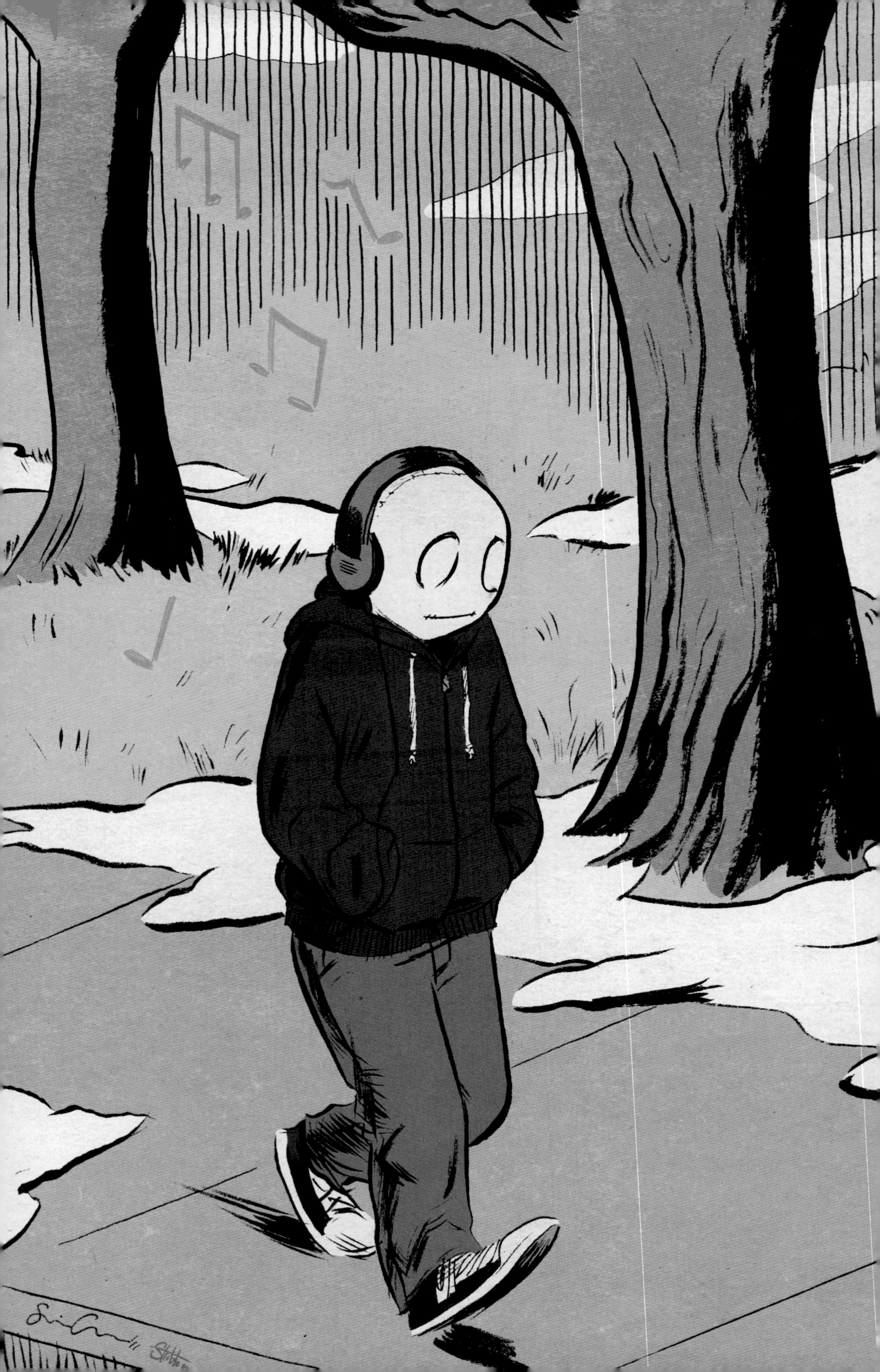

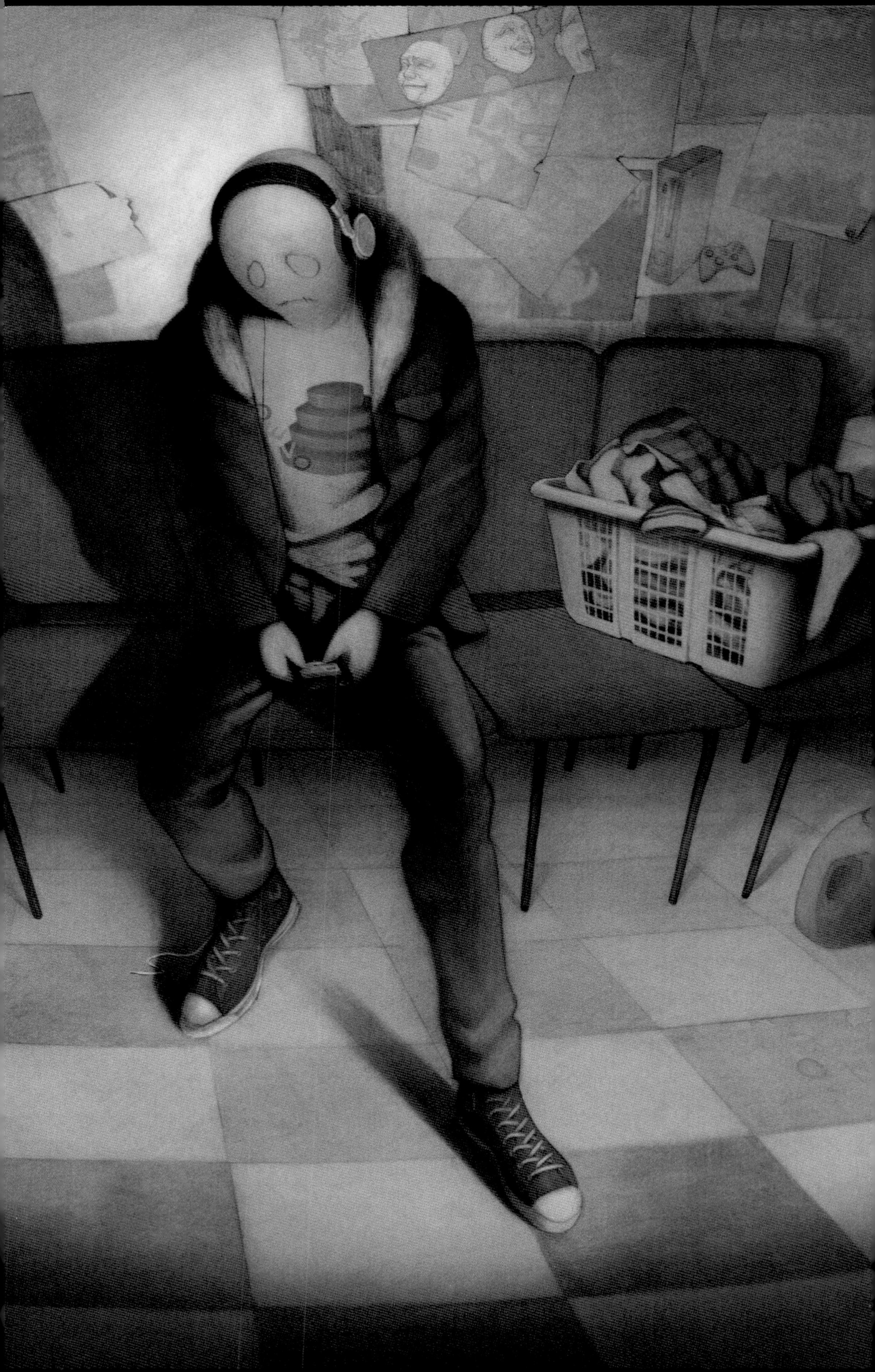

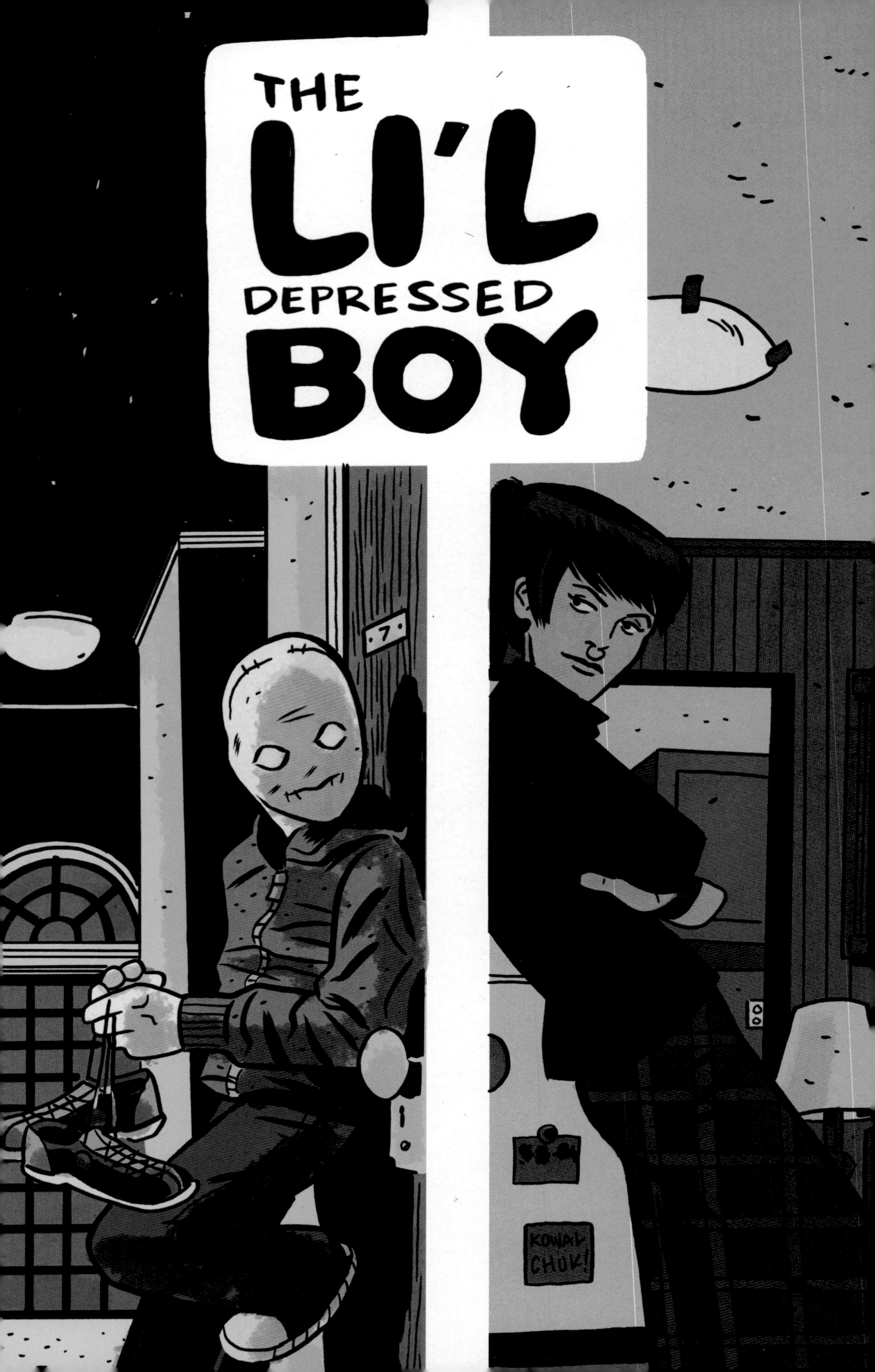
THE LI'L DEPRESSED BOY
7
KOWALCHUK!

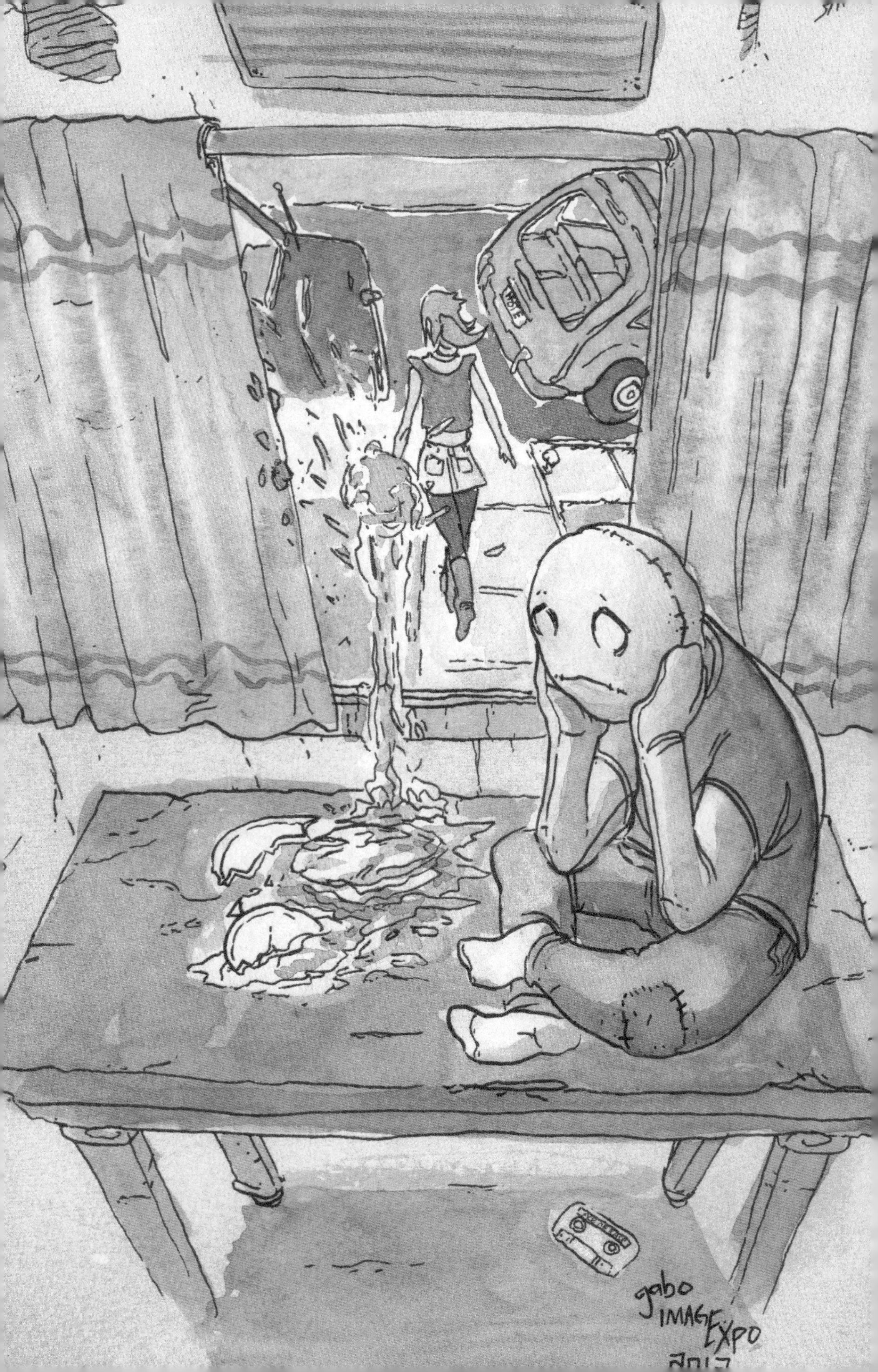
gabo
IMAGE EXPO

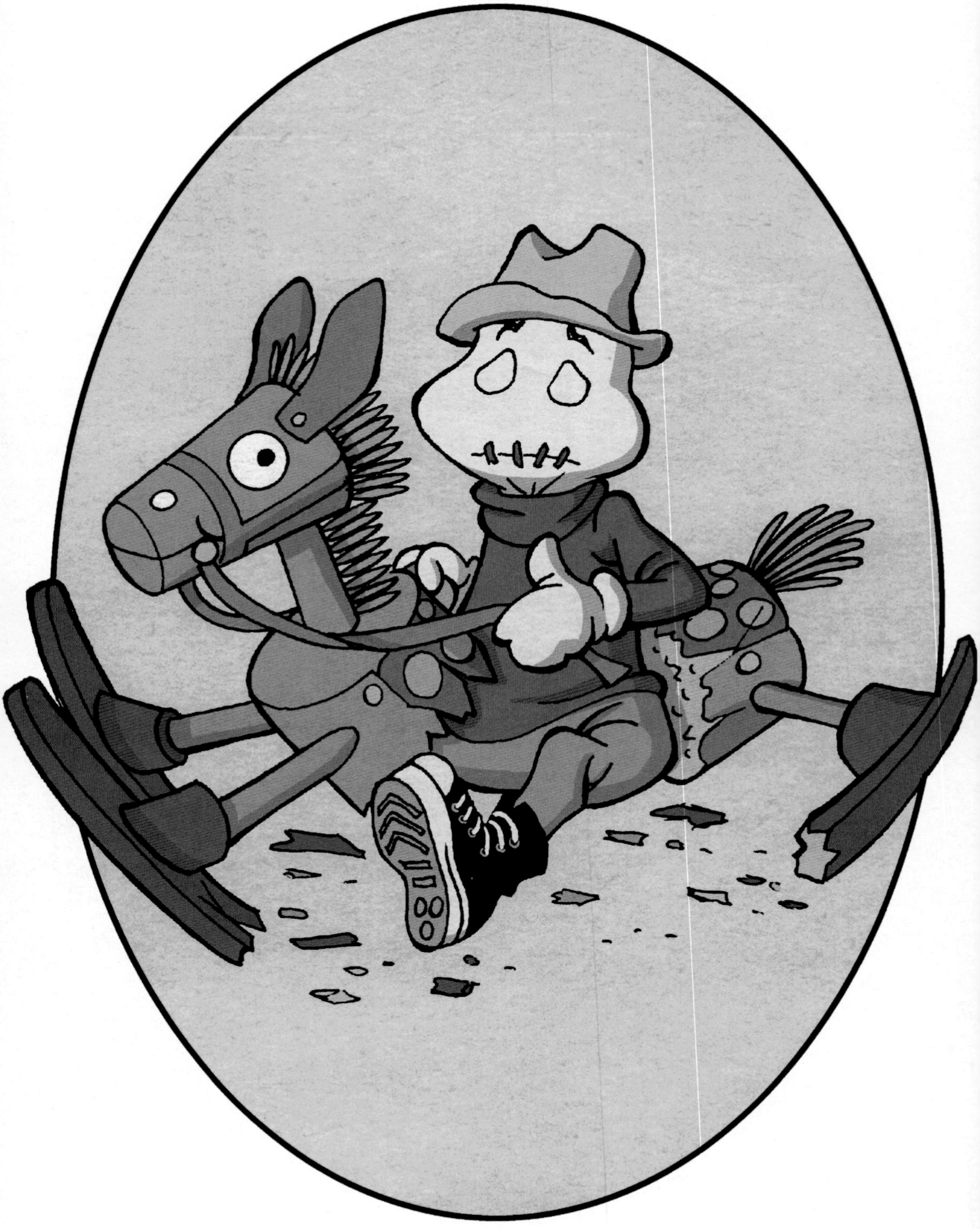

ernie colón - 2001

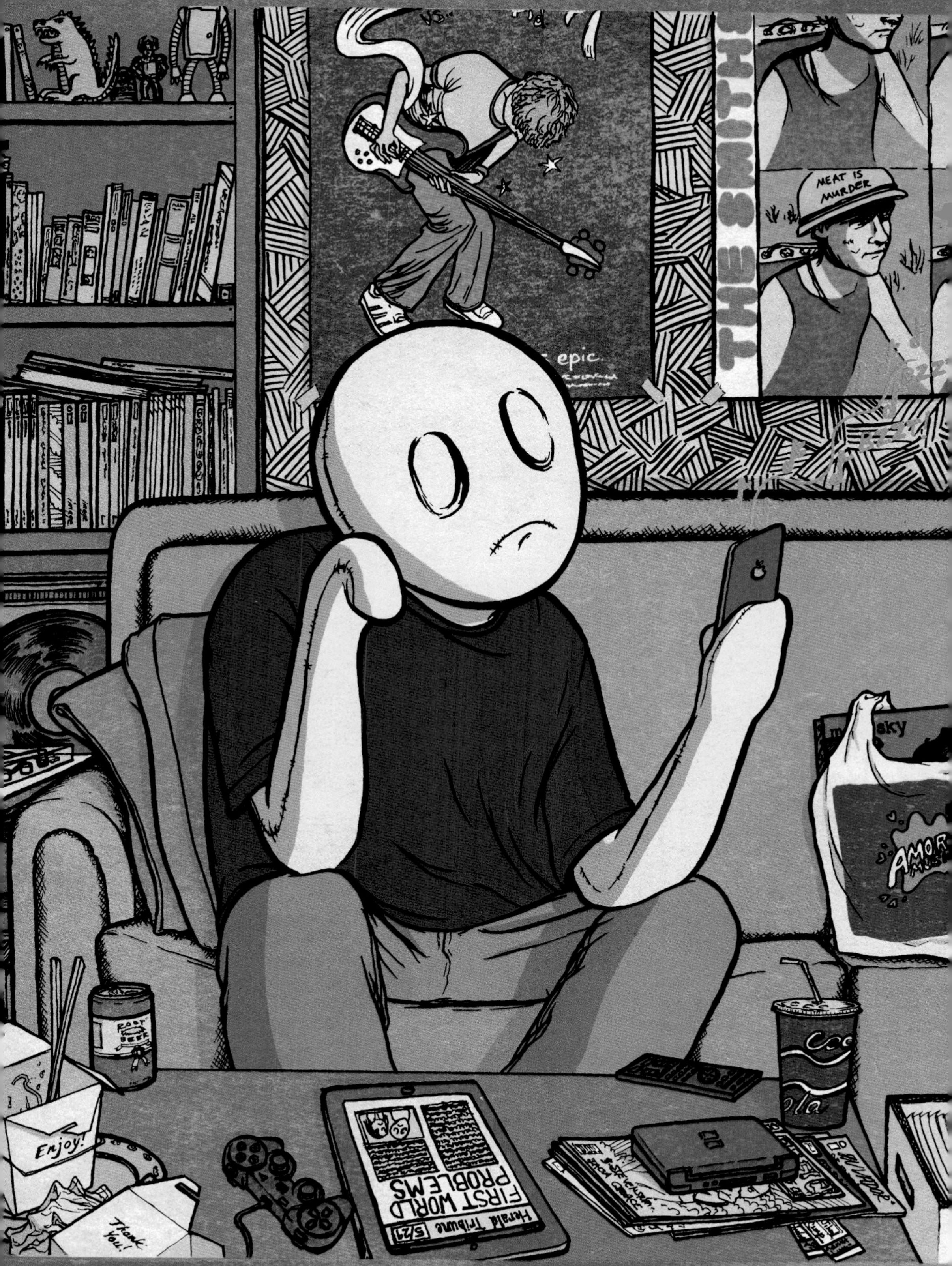
epic.
THE SMITHS
MEAT IS MURDER
ROOT BEER
Enjoy!
Thank you!
Herald Tribune 5/21
FIRST WORLD PROBLEMS

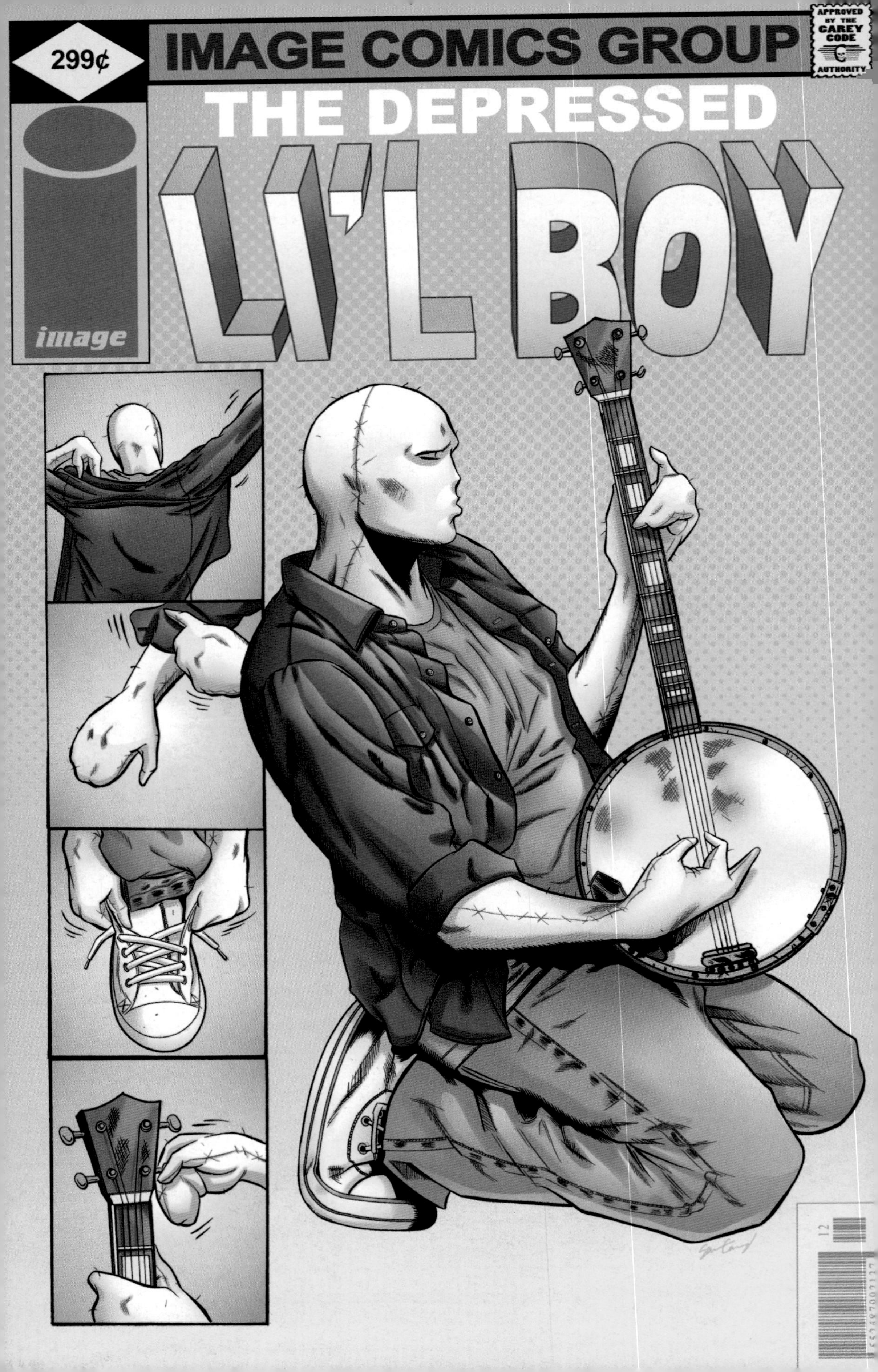

299¢
IMAGE COMICS GROUP
APPROVED BY THE CAREY CODE AUTHORITY
THE DEPRESSED
LI'L BOY
image

Pinups by:
Fiona Meng -- http://fionameng.com
Scott Kowalchuk -- http://scottkowalchuk.blogspot.com
Gabriel Bautista Jr. -- http://gobo.brofu.com
Ernie Colón -- http://en.wikipedia.org/wiki/ernie_colon
Sarah DeLaine -- http://twitter.com/sarahdelaine
Shane Carey -- http://theartofshanecarey.wordpress.com/

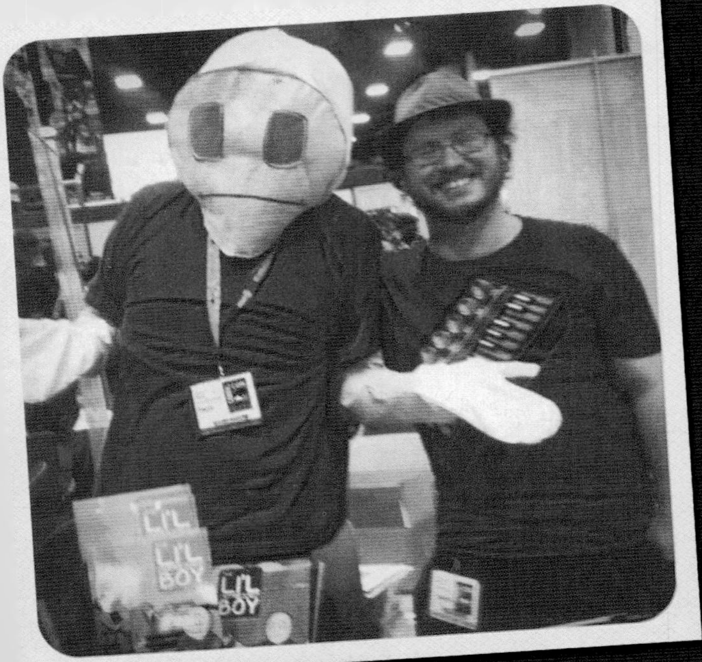

Photo by Jennifer de Guzman

S. STEVEN STRUBLE
MOVED TO AMARILLO, TX TO MAKE COMIC BOOKS. SURPRISINGLY, THIS PLAN ACTUALLY WORKED OUT. IN HIS SPARE TIME HE ALSO COLORS OTHER PEOPLE'S COMICS AND COMPETES ON THE POETRY SLAM CIRCUIT.

MORE AT
WWW.ILLITERATERAINBOW.COM

SINA GRACE
RAWS COMIC BOOKS (THE L DEPRESSED BOY), KIDS' BOOKS (AMONG THE HOSTS), AND BIG-PEOPLE OOKS (CEDRIC HOLLOWS N DIAL M FOR MAGIC) IN COFFEE SHOPS ALL OUND LOS ANGELES, CA. THE IMAGE COMICS APHIC NOVEL, *NOT MY AG*, IS THE FIRST HE'S VRITING & DRAWING.

MORE AT
WWW.SINAGRACE.COM

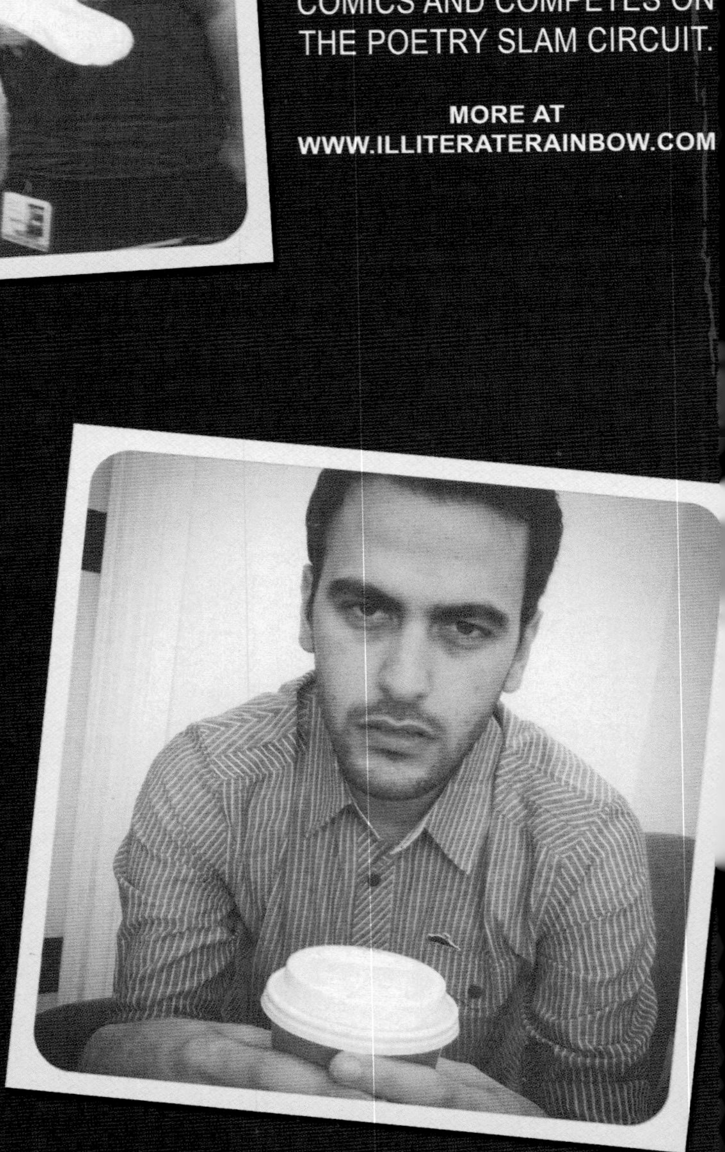

Photo by Shawn Kirkham